T0339761

WORK IS FOR THE PEOPLE

WORK IS FOR THE PEOPLE

A TREATISE ON THE -ISMS

Joseph W. Burrell

Algora Publishing
New York

© 2011 by Algora Publishing.
All Rights Reserved
www.algora.com

No portion of this book (beyond what is permitted by
Sections 107 or 108 of the United States Copyright Act of 1976)
may be reproduced by any process, stored in a retrieval system,
or transmitted in any form, or by any means, without the
express written permission of the publisher.

Library of Congress Cataloging-in-Publication Data —

Burrell, Joseph, 1930-
    Work is for the people: a treatise on the -isms / Joseph W. Burrell.
        p. cm.
    ISBN 978-0-87586-861-5 (soft cover: alk. paper) — ISBN 978-0-87586-862-2 (hard
cover: alk. paper) — ISBN 978-0-87586-863-9 (ebook) 1. Ideology—Political aspects. 2.
Ideology—Political aspects—United States. I. Title.
    JC348.B87 2011
    320.5—dc22

                            2011014295

Printed in the United States

All...share one trait, a common denominator — an aggressive, all-powerful, total irrationality. Anyone stricken with one of these plagues is beyond reason. In his head burns a sacred pyre that awaits only its sacrificial victims. Every attempt at calm conversation will fail....A mind touched by such a contagion is a closed mind, one-dimensional, monothematic, spinning round one subject only — its enemy.

—*Imperium*, Ryszard Kapuscinski, Polish journalist

"So, if you have a corporation, or for that matter, any business with top-down control that's run from the top, it's basically a totalitarian system, as close to totalitarianism as humans have been able to devise. Control is completely in the top. Orders go from top to bottom, down the hierarchy. If you're in the middle somewhere, if you're a manager, you take orders from above and hand them on below. At the very bottom, people are allowed to rent themselves to the system. It's called getting a job.

"And outsiders, their only connection to it is to consume. Hundreds of millions of dollars a year are spent trying to delude and deceive them into consumption. Anybody who's ever looked at a television knows that.

"Well, there's a system of hierarchy and authority. Is it legitimate? Should that totalitarian system be given the rights of a person? In fact, by now, rights far beyond those of a person? Well, those are quite serious questions."

—Noam Chomsky, interview by Nicholas Holt, *Asheville Global Report*, Apr. 20–26, 2006.

"It matters not one iota what political party is in power or what president holds the reins of office.... We are not politicians or public thinkers; we are the rich; we own America; we got it, God knows how, but we intend to keep it if we can by throwing all the tremendous weight of our support, our influence, our money, our political connections, our purchased senators, our hungry congressmen, our public-speaking demagogues into the scale against any legislature, any political platform, any presidential campaign that threatens the integrity of our estate."

—Frederick Townsend Martin, a wealthy American of the last century.

"What the world is, Krissie, is people owning things, and owning you."

—Eddy Diehl in *Little Bird of Heaven*, by Joyce Carol Oates

TABLE OF CONTENTS

INTRODUCTION   1

CHAPTER 1. ORIGIN OF CAPITALISM   7

CHAPTER 2. THE AMERICAN MODEL   13

CHAPTER 3. WORK IS FOR THE PEOPLE   17

CHAPTER 4. IS CAPITALISM DEMOCRATIC?   27

CHAPTER 5. NATURE OF CAPITALISM   33

CHAPTER 6. THE ACQUIRERS   37

CHAPTER 7. COMMUNISM   49

CHAPTER 8. THE REPUBLICAN PARTY'S FAKE ANTI-COMMUNISM   57

CHAPTER 9. CONSERVATISM, LIBERALISM, AND LIBERTARIANISM   71

CHAPTER 10. JEFFERSONIAN LIBERALISM   85

CHAPTER 11. REPUBLICANISM?   91

CHAPTER 12. REPUBLICAN FASCISM (CORPORATISM)   103

CHAPTER 13. CORPORATE TRIUMPHALISM   109

CHAPTER 14. CHRISTIANISM   117

CHAPTER 15. SECULARISM   131

CHAPTER 16. SOCIALISM   137

CHAPTER 17. DECONSTRUCTING REPUBLICANISM   147

Government Hate 149
Privatization and Deregulation 150
Consumer and Worker Rights 150
Church and State 151
Law and Regulation 153
Equality 154
Liberty 156
Relativism 157
Collectivism and Individualism 158
Centralization 159
Work is for the People 161
Absolutism 161
Tolerance 162
The Republican Attack Against Liberal America .. 163

CHAPTER 18. ZIONISM 165

Israel on the Attack 171

CHAPTER 19. IMPERIALISM: KILLING IRAQ 173

Ronald Reagan 179
H.W. Bush and Bill Clinton 182
Aug. 12, 1990 — Iraq invades Kuwait 185
George W. Bush and Dick Cheney: Iraq *Is not* a Threat .. 194
Iraq *Is* a Threat 195
The War 196
The Media 197
Analysis 200
The Media Again 201

CHAPTER 20. BARBARISM: TORTURE 215

INTRODUCTION

Most of the factual information in the following pages is a matter of public record. The opinions and conclusions are my own.

There are discussions in this book about eleven different isms. There is at least one chapter devoted to each of these isms except for atheism. Atheism does not have a chapter of its own because of its simplicity. Atheism is a disbelief in a god or a system of gods, nothing more. It has no dogmas and is entirely without content. I discuss three of the isms — conservatism, liberalism, and libertarianism — together in the same chapter because they are closely related and often contending political forces. Torture, war, and terrorism are not really isms in themselves but they certainly do occur because of one or more of the isms. Thus, I have a chapter on the Iraq war and one on torture.

Terrorism is an abstraction; it has no ideological meaning at all. Western governments define it as non-state violence carried out to achieve some political end. In fact, governments use it as an excuse to curtail the freedom of their own citizens and to attack others indiscriminately. It is an even emptier word than the word "communism." It is a propaganda word and it is currently at the center of the Republican Party's belief system. And, as it has so often done before, the Democratic Party is advancing the wars and aggressions of the Republican Party so it can avoid being described by Republican partisans as weak and treasonous.

I think that corporatism is identical to fascism. This is a matter of simple definition. Benito Mussolini established the first fascist party in 1919 and ruled Italy under it from 1922 until near the end of World War II when he was killed by his own people. When asked what fascism was, he said, "Fascism should more properly be called corporatism because it is the merger of state power and corporate power." Thus, I make a logical connection between corporatism and the Republican Party. As far as I know, no one else has made this claim or agrees with it. Nevertheless, it seems absolutely obvious to me that the Republican Party is fanatically devoted to corporatism and almost violently hostile to working people and their unions. To me at least, the Republican Party is the American Fascist Party.

When I use the term "conservative," I am including Republicans, libertarians, and neoconservatives in the mix. The term "conservative" is only slightly broader than the term "Republican." It also includes some Democrats, especially the DLC Democrats and the self-described "liberal hawks." Although some libertarians would blanch at being lumped together with conservatives, they are nevertheless dedicated members of the Republican Party and allies of the conservatives in their love of predatory capitalism; and all of them are deeply contemptuous of liberalism and the democratic government of the United States, indeed all democracy everywhere.

These different parts of conservatism share a common set of negative values, all of them anchored to an extreme hatred of democratic liberalism and peaceful moderation in world affairs. Furthermore, they are all social darwinist and eugenicist as well as aggressively militaristic and police statist. Each of them has an exceptionalist view of itself as standing against and towering over all others. They are not friendly to "strangers" nor do they respect the rights of different others. In time, their alliance will come apart and they will attack one another with the same fervor they now reserve for liberal democrats.

I think of capitalism and communism as overlapping and contending "religions." I am aware that the word "ideology" is commonly used to describe a belief in political or economic systems. The reason I sometimes refer to those systems as "religions" is because of the intensity of the faith and fanaticism of certain of their adherents. Thus, I see the warrior attitudes and the proselytizing behavior of the revolutionary communists and the "free-market" capitalists as religious. The attacking behaviors of both of those forces, especially in the Soviet Union and the United States, were very much based on a violent determination to "spread the faith" by demolishing every enemy, real or imagined. The "cold war" was indeed a very hot war. The two clashing forces were responsible for the deaths and woundings of millions of people, most of them more-or-less innocent bystanders. All of this was done to force dogmatic beliefs and practices on others just as were the missionary and jihadist campaigns of the christians and muslims.

The fanaticism of the "free-market" faith resulted in the establishment of a movement called "libertarianism." Its ideology or religion has been so intense that it has invaded and largely taken over the Republican Party and overwhelmed its claimed belief in an old time conservative faith. In 2010, the libertarian faith spawned a fake patriot movement that calls itself a "tea party." Its vague and confused mission is to destroy much of the democratic government of the United States in the interest of "limited government" and what its adherents claim will be greater freedom for everyone. However, the tea party movement was created and funded in great part by corporatists and is based on a desire to put all property and all services in the hands of the commercial interests so those interests can expand their control and profit beyond the unprecedented levels of excess they already enjoy. A second part of the tea party mission is to reduce taxes on the rich and, at the same time, to balance the government budget no matter how ruinous, self contradictory, or destructive the achievement of those goals are bound to be. These are the fanatical and irrational beliefs and goals of a religion, not just a practical, everyday ideology.

This book seeks to redefine and accurately describe these isms and related factions. I think the terms involved have been distorted and misused for a long time, especially since the rise of McCarthyism and the start of the cold war. And I think these distortions have corrupted American politics and undermined democratic liberalism everywhere in the western world and even in Eastern Europe.

A Grammatical Note

The capitalization in this book is not standard. Let me explain why. Christian grammarians and many authorities in the field of publishing require the capitalization of "pronouns referring to the Deity," but I find it impractical and pointless to capitalize the words "god" or "gods" simply because there are so many of them and because I don't believe those words mean anything consistent, coherent, or believable. I am not a believer myself, and I see very little sense in lending importance and exclusivity to the god and gods asserted by the many religions on this earth.

Indeed, christians themselves don't really believe in "the deity," that is, in just one god. To be a proper christian, you must believe in the sacredness of at least two gods, God the Father and Jesus the Son. In fact, most christians also believe in a third god, the Holy Ghost. Thus, most christians are trinitarians. Catholics also believe in the sacredness of the virgin Mary who, like the saints, can perform miracles, answer prayers, have virgin births, and ascend into the sky just as well as any of the other gods and goddesses.

Further, I believe that very few of today's so-called christians are christian at all. They show no respect for the words Jesus is reported to have spoken and do not follow his example even a little bit.

The jewish religion isn't nearly as complex in its god-system but the jewish god is so gaseous and vague that jews aren't even allowed to call his name much less define him. Thus, I can't tell whether or not jews are really monotheists, though they say they invented monotheism.

The muslims appear to be the only true monotheists in this lot, but they have many sects, each of which ascribes a different character, a different definition, and a different set of biases to their god. In some configurations, muslims are supposed to kill all christians and jews as well as many of their fellow muslims just as many christians and jews believe they are supposed to kill all of their closest competitors.

I do not capitalize the word "muslim" because it is a religious and not an ethnic or racial reference.

In any case, it's quite clear that the many sects of these various religions believe in a whole host of different gods and not at all in one or the same god.

There are, however, terms based on proper nouns, like Arabs from Arabia, and Americans from America; these I do capitalize, because I do believe in the map.

The ancient pagans were never this morally confused and few of them felt a need to kill those whose beliefs diverged from theirs. In truth, pagans as far as we know were more decent and tolerant with regard to religious belief than are many of today's self-proclaimed monotheists and christian grammarians. And so, in my view, the christians, the jews, and the muslims don't deserve their own preferential grammar.

As for the argument for capitalizing the words "Mohammedan," "Christian," and "Marxist," three isms presumably named after actual people, the terms are so often used inaccurately and in a polemical way to proselytize against and attack other competing ideologies that I think it more equitable not to capitalize these words, either. These isms are not really based on the actual beliefs and examples of the men around whom they are said to have been founded. Not very much at all is known about the first two. As for Marx, he is on record as disagreeing with the principles propounded by other contemporary "Marxists." Thus, I prefer not to capitalize these words or their derivatives.

It makes far better sense to capitalize none of them. Why bother? It requires so much effort and all of those capitals spoil the appearance of text on the page. The special respect such practices seek to claim is not deserved, in my opinion.

Now we come to specific "churches" and specific parties. Where necessary, not for religious but for practical reasons, I have no better idea than to use capitals. I use "Catholic" to designate a member of the Catholic Church; the word "catholic" means "whole, universal, all-inclusive, having broad sympathies or understanding, liberal, etc." Obviously, this definition cannot be used to describe Catholics. Similarly, a member of the Protestant Church ought not to be confused with a "protestant," which means "a person who protests." These days very few Protestants protest about anything in their particular religious sect or in their dogmatic belief system.

The word "Communist" no longer has any specific meaning beyond "member of the Communist Party." The McCarthyites (and many people even today) called just about everyone they disliked "Communists." The massive and indiscriminate use of the word "Communist" emptied it of just about all meaning. The same thinking applies to the terms socialist, capitalist, nazi, fascist, tory, conservative, liberal, democrat, or republican.

By the way, in this book I claim that both communism and capitalism are religions. They both embody fervent, even fanatical, belief systems and they both proselytize, often violently so. In practice, neither is even slightly democratic or tolerant of anything or anyone outside their dogmatic structures.

Now let's think for a moment about social "Darwinism." It is not Darwinist at all; rather, it is Lamarckian: the notion that acquired characteristics can be inherited. It was Herbert Spencer who propagated this idea. He invented the term "survival of the fittest" and applied it to social, economic, and political life. Therefore, I prefer to use the term "social darwinism." That may not be much of a corrective, but it is at least a mark of protest directed at the corruption of language.

Still, we must capitalize when invoking a specific party: the Socialist Party of France, for instance, or the Socialists who are its members.

My point in doing all of this is not only to refuse formal, written worship to certain systems of belief that I think are being forced on the world. I wanted to simplify my own writing and thought that my method was more coherent than that in the rule books. It is a battle too great to be won, but I remain faithful in making my slaps at orthodoxy.

As for other deviations from the orthodox, I do not punctuate as profusely as some writers do. I aim to spare the poor comma until it is needed to avoid confusion or to fence off trivial parenthetical information, or to indicate a pause to differentiate, continue, or qualify carry-over ideas and trains of thought. Our minds are cluttered enough without throwing in an unnecessary curve.

Chapter 1. Origin of Capitalism

Most people think they know exactly what capitalism is, where it came from, and how it works. In the Western world, especially in the United States, capitalism is represented as democratic or, at least, as a necessary condition of democracy. Accordingly, the facts about the definition, the origin, and the nature of capitalism have been vastly distorted as have the facts about socialism and communism, its presumed opposites.

I don't by any means accept the marxist idea that capitalism was a recent invention, one that replaced a worn-out feudalism and came into being because of the development of English and European agriculture in the sixteenth century and the soon-to-follow Industrial Revolution. I don't accept the prevailing definition of capitalism, either, or the common definition of socialism. I believe that capitalism is simply a system through which the few control the work of the many for their own narrow benefit; and I believe that socialism is economic democracy, that is, the voluntary cooperation of the many in the organization and performance of work and in the use of its benefits. In short, capitalism is about work and so is socialism.

No one knows precisely when or how in human history the few first took control of the work of the many but property certainly played an important part. Without much doubt, the property in question in early times was land and water, which became increasingly important with the rise of agriculture. No doubt there were numerous pecking orders in those times but as far as we know the nomadic tribalism that existed before agriculture became commonplace was essentially socialistic with people working together as equals and sharing the fruits of their labor. Then, the invention of agriculture and the need for control over land and water resulted in economic hierarchy and capitalism.

Karl Marx was mistaken in many ways but his central belief that capitalists are people who exploit the work of others to enrich and empower themselves was clearly true and irrefutable. That understanding did not originate with Marx, however. People have known that they were being used by their bosses and owners right from the time when capitalism began about ten or twelve thousand years ago with the invention of agriculture, the consequent narrow ownership of land and water, the hoarding of surplus food, and the end of nomadism.

Previous to that time, when people had lived by what they could hunt and gather, they had to follow their food supply and had no use for property in the large. With the invention of agriculture, concentrated populations increased so that there was not enough arable land for everyone in the community or enough water to make crops grow; at that point, those physically strong or numerous enough to seize and control land and water became the first owners and bosses. They forced those without resources to work for them and thus created a system of hired and coerced labor or even outright slavery.

Thus, the ownership of land and water and the control of food became a means by which some men could rule others. With the introduction of agriculture, food and drinking water became products of controlled labor rather than resources naturally available to all. From that time until the Industrial Revolution, capitalism was land-centered. Then it became centered on the products of industrial manufacture. For the first time, the acquisition of made products became important to great masses of people.

Thereafter, the industrial capitalists treated all of life's goods, processes, and services as commercial products. Everything was harnessed and controlled. Now, commercial interests are selling air, rocks, and dirt. They're even selling human blood, sperm, fetuses, body parts, and excrement. Everything is grist for the commercial mill.

As populations grew still more and the need for grown food increased, the owners of land, water, and food stores became increasingly rich and powerful. Those people who didn't own farmable land or have access to water became the first dependent class and, therefore, the first working class. Exploitation of the many by the few because of shortages of good land and water thus resulted in capitalism. In those geographical areas where there was, at first, enough land and water for everyone's agricultural use, there was no exploitation and oppression and no capitalism. Of course, capitalism has refined itself since then but it remains the means by which the few control the work of the many for their own enrichment and empowerment.

In pre-agricultural times, every person had a role to play, work to do. There was no unemployment or moneyed leisure in very early times. Unemployment and elitist leisure started with capitalism, when formal systems of work were first established, when the concept of one man working for another emerged. In tribal social arrangements, everyone played a role and everyone worked for the common good in a cooperative manner. Of course, those were not capitalist societies. They were cooperative rather than competitive, integrated rather than splintered, democratic rather than authoritarian. Capitalism grew out of the boss–worker relationship. Other expressions of the same kinds of controlling relationships are master–slave, king–subject, god–worshiper, father–son, husband–wife, etc.

In each of these configurations, there is a master and a subject. The master is strong and the subject is weak. The master orders and the subject obeys. The master takes and the subject gives. In the economic expression of this arrangement, a boss takes control of the work of one or more worker–subjects. The boss has all of the power; the workers have none. The entire point of capitalism is that the few control the work of the many for their own narrow benefit. Capitalism is not really about the ownership of property or the accumulation of capital although property and capital are a part of the system used by the few to control the work of the many.

When capitalist societies first began to develop, the only way for anyone to become rich was to have other people work for them. The more people you had working for you, the richer you could become. Obviously, you could not very well do all of the work by yourself. A man working only for himself was not physically or practically capable of doing anything in volume; therefore, he could not multiply his acquisition, manufacture, or profitable distribution of goods very far without inducing others to help him. Likewise, he could not provide very many services for profit through his own unaided effort. The purpose of capitalism for such a man was to get the many to work for him either through direct force or through some more indirect method. Thus, the first form of capitalism probably was slavery or, at least, servanthood.

An alternative or, more likely a simultaneous, source of origin for capitalism may have been the use of the labor of family members by a patriarch or, less likely, a matriarch. Patriarchy is the oldest form of supervision and control. To one degree or another, fathers controlled the work of their wives and children by force and threat of force. Thus, the first farming units may have been family farms and that may have been the beginning of capitalism. At any rate, capitalism certainly began with the first supervisory control of work by one or a few bosses of some kind.

At first, a group or a tribe of people could have had only a few slaves or servants because, in those times, it was not easy for the few to control the many. There was always the danger of revolt by direct physical force; obviously, the many were more powerful physically than the few and so the few could not very well rule the many against their will. But then came the invention of weapons and tools and the eventual organization of religious and economic dogma into forms that could be used to force the many into fearful obedience and slavery. Thus, groups and tribes began to use their advantage of newly discovered weapons to attack alien others and capture them. With their advantage in weapons, they could then enslave large numbers of people and keep them under control.

Within the limits of the existing knowledge of tools, the slaves could provide services and make things for their masters. Some of the slaves learned the secrets of the new weapons and tools and escaped to inform their own people. This began an arms race that was never to end. Whether you were a slave or a master depended, at first, on the strength of your numbers, then on your weaponry and tools, and, at last, on systems of religion, economics, and politics.

The developing capitalists learned how to use the technology of tools to increase domestic production just as they had learned to use weapons to their advantage. Weapons and tools were more-or-less the same thing, of course. The only difference in the one and the other was that one was a tool used to accomplish some domestic task and the other a tool used to attack and control others. They must have developed together. If only a very few knew how to make a particularly useful tool or weapon, then those few had enough power in their hands to exploit captives as well as their own tribesmen and to employ their slaves or servants more productively. Early on, property must have included the personal ownership of weapons and tools (clubs, rocks, knives, spears, and digging sticks) and, of course, later on, the formal ownership of land, water, and food stores.

It must be remembered that the mere ownership of property is not capitalism. To be a capitalist (according to my definition), you must use your property, or some alternate means, to bond others and use their work for your benefit. Even if you were one of a few who owned property or if you had a special knowledge or skill regarding the use of tools and weapons, you were not a capitalist unless you used that power to induce or compel the labor of others. If you merely exchanged it for something of equal value — tool for tool, for example — you were not a capitalist but merely a trader. If you were generous and shared your property, skill, or knowledge without any return, then you were not a capitalist but a philanthropist.

I think it makes better historical and practical sense to describe capitalism as the appropriation and control of work rather than the ownership of property or the accumulation of capital. Certainly, the elements in capitalism that oppress people the most relate to workers and their work, not just to the dead substances of property and money. The definition of capitalism as the control of work leads inevitably to the conclusion that capitalism is as old as the earliest agricultural settlements. Thus, the proper study of capitalism is anthropological, political, and social rather than just economic.

Chapter 2. The American Model

The United States is a totalitarian country. Ever since the Second World War and especially since the Reagan administration, this country has used a formulaic system of economic tyranny to dominate the world. This system consists of two primary tools: privatization and deregulation. The purpose of these tools is destruction of the social service systems put in place all over the world by more or less representative governments. Those social service systems (pioneered in the latter part of the nineteenth century by Bismarck) were the basis of the New Deal reforms promulgated by Franklin Roosevelt in the United States in the 1930s in response to the greatest capitalist failure of modern times, the Great Conservative Depression.

In other words, it was democratic governments that set out to restore the economies that were ruined by the abuses of private commercial power. Those restorations were successful and networks of public services were established throughout the world to the increasing rage of private owners and bosses. Thus, the privateers began to wage war against all public services and against the democratic governments that created and managed those services.

Democratic government is the target of all privatization and deregulation schemes. Private commercial owners all over the world consider democratic government their enemy and their competitor. They know that they can make huge profits if they can seize absolute control over all material resources, all service systems, and all human labor. They also know that their private ownership can be controlled to some extent by regulations designed to protect workers and consumers from the worst of their abuses and exploitations. Therefore, they are determined to grab control over absolutely everything in existence and they are determined to prevent their victims, workers and consumers, from using the regulatory power of democratic or other representative governments to protect themselves against the tyrannical power of the private owners and bosses.

Thus, there is an ongoing struggle between the predatory commercialists and democracy itself. Sadly, the commercialists are winning and they very much control all of the world's resources and services and most of its people. Even worse, new commodifications, including schemes to "protect" intellectual property, are being put in place every day. Their aim is totalitarian control over everything and everyone. A new world is being created, a world of maximum tyranny.

The International Monetary Fund, the World Bank, and all of the other global organizations, trade agreements, and consortiums that rule the world's economies are the implements of US and Western aggression. Every action that they take is designed to destroy democratic controls over resources and services and to open up every country to the predations and assaults of private power. When they offer, or pretend to offer, aid to destitute countries, that aid always comes with predatory strings attached. The country involved is always required to privatize and deregulate its economy, and it is always required to destroy any public services it has established for the benefit of its people, including even public and domestic provisions for food, water, electricity, and transportation. It is also required to offer up ownership of its resources and services to foreign corporations, usually American or Western European ones.

Inevitably, these aggressions are ruinous and great suffering is imposed on helpless citizens and their families. These bankers' tricks rarely (if ever) improve life for anyone other than the already rich. However, corporations benefit enormously and, when the opportunities for profits dwindle, as they always do in the end, those corporations bail out and leave their victims bereft and their countries devastated.

This system of economic tyranny (the American Model) is accepted just about everywhere today as the right and proper model for economic progress. It's impossible to believe that the predators don't know what they are doing to the world; and it's hard to imagine that such vicious greed can be their one and only motivation. I think that the ideology of social darwinism drives them even more than greed and ambition. The mantras of "free enterprise," "free markets," "entrepreneurial genius," "competitive drive," and "democratic capitalism" have been embraced as the foundations of a virtual religion for a long time now. Religious dogma is hard to shake. It is based on faith alone and has nothing to do with reality or with reason.

It will take an enormous economic conflagration or a revolution to detach the predators from their fanatical belief in the wonders of their commercial nirvana. Meanwhile, democracy is dying along with liberalism.

Chapter 3. Work is for the People

If a business can't charge its customers a fair price and pay its workers a living wage, then it has no right to exist. Work is for working people and consumers, the common people, not for owners and bosses. Making a profit is not the purpose of organized work. In the first place, the only legitimate reason for organizing work is to establish a shared community in which people can help one another live better and more securely. We can accomplish this by providing goods and services to one another in free and fair exchanges that don't exploit or abuse either the workers or the consumers.

This cannot mean a commerce unregulated by the democratic instruments of the community. It cannot mean dog-eat-dog competition and it cannot mean the triumph of the profit motive over the needs of ordinary people. Work must serve the requirements of the people first and the profits of the bosses last.

When you say, as a businessman, that you can't make a profit without paying your workers less than they need to support themselves and their families, you are saying that capitalism doesn't work. If the business being done by your company can only support the owners and bosses and not the workers, then that business is a failure and has no right to exist in any rational economic system. It's preposterous to say that the economic policies of a democratic country should guarantee the profits of the business owner at the expense of a living wage for those who do the work. If a country doesn't put the subsistence of the great majority — the workers and their families

— ahead of the profits of the owners, then that country has no right to call itself democratic. No owner or boss has a right to any luxury or high life that derives from the poverty and suffering of working people.

The rich are certainly not people of superior intelligence. Getting money is not a function of intelligence. Rather it is a function of ruthless drive, privilege, influence, greed, and position. Furthermore, privilege begets privilege and money generates more money. History shows quite clearly that many rich people are extremely stupid and many poor people very intelligent. The person who already has money only needs enough intelligence or good enough contacts to select competent money managers and advisers. Thereafter, he doesn't have to lift a finger or make a single decision to rake in the profits. A rich man can go broke, and some do, but it is not a common happening. Money protects money.

The money system is always arranged to benefit the haves at the expense of the have-nots. The instruments of wealth are exquisitely tailored to serve the interests of the wealthy alone. In the United States, an entire political party devotes itself completely to the care and protection of the rich and privileged; and the other party is also largely an instrument of the well off. For a short time, working people had a system of unions that offered them some protection, but those times have passed. Now, ordinary working people have very few representatives, either political or economic. The poor, the sick, the hungry, and homeless have no power and no voice. In fact, they are under constant assault from the Republican Party and the privileged class it represents. The wealthy own America and rule it.

The conservatives say you can't solve problems by "throwing money at them." The hell you can't. Give the bottom twenty percent of the population of this country a fair share of the wealth and just about every social problem we have would disappear. About the only serious problem that would still remain is the greed, corruption, and criminality of the upper class backed by the Republican Conservative Party.

The problem of crime would be reduced by half or more with economic fairness. The slums would disappear. Child abuse would dwindle. There would be no hunger and little malnutrition. Education would flourish. Intolerance and superstition would be greatly reduced. The corrupt christian churches would have to close their doors. Racism would recede. Sexism would be practiced only by christian fanatics and weak men worried about their manhood. The streets would be cleaner and much safer. Bad housing would cease to exist. The forests would grow, flowers would flourish, and clean streams would gush and tinkle.

There is no question that almost all of the major problems of this country have always come from economic inequality. It is the profit motive that has robbed us all of peace and justice. The brutal and grasping greed of a few million grabbers and gougers is responsible for the degradation of the many, and the Republican conservative party is the political force that has imposed this travesty of democracy on everyone else. That party has always been and remains the most thoroughly evil and tyrannical instrument ever to exist in America. Until the American people get rid of it once and for all, there can be no hope of justice and equality here or anywhere else.

Hitching human care of any kind to profits always results in violations of human rights and common decency. Privateers cannot operate institutions responsible for human care — hospitals, prisons, schools, etc. — more cheaply than nonprofit organizations without cheating workers and abusing their charges, i.e., their patients, inmates, and students. Anyone who claims a privateer can humanely operate an institution better and cheaper than a nonprofit entity is a liar or a fool or, more likely, both. Anyone capable of arithmetic knows that private enterprise must always be more costly than public enterprise unless there are massive abuses.

The fact is the privateers smear democratic government in order to corrupt the minds of citizens so that they will believe government is somehow automatically incompetent, corrupt, and wasteful; and then the privateers move in to take over and stuff their pockets with the people's money. All such antigovernment privateers are liars and crooks. Furthermore, they are traitors to democratic government and enemies of the people.

There is no one fouler than the conservative politicians and commercial rip-off artists who have been taking over the public institutions of this country in one corrupt scheme after another. What's going on here is an intensely avaricious bunko game, a swindle of the lowest order. The American people are being cheated at every turn and the Republican Party is the director of that criminal enterprise. People are getting cheated, hurt, and even killed by the Republican conservatives. The gougers, the graspers, the cheaters, the corrupters, and subverters are wiping out democracy in the United States. They are enemies of the Constitution and the flag. They are un-American.

Making money as a life's ambition? How degrading. How disgusting. It's one thing to want to escape poverty and deprivation and to be secure. It's quite another to turn your entire life into a quest for wealth. People who do this never get over it or beyond it. It spoils their lives. They don't know how to stop or when to stop. They define themselves eternally as greedy graspers, driven acquirers, ruthless exploiters, hustling salesmen, often as thieves and cheats. Nothing is more deeply immoral than a lust for wealth. It denies life. It corrupts life. It abuses and misuses life. It is finally and always an attack against others, a taking, a grabbing, a hoarding; an end in itself.

It is very strange that, for most, the purpose of getting money is not to enjoy it and to use it but just to have it, to own it, to be defined by it, and to be recognized as a person with money, that is, as an important person. If you get money enough, then you don't have to do anything creative or skillful or useful with your life. Owning money is enough. Owning money is the most praiseworthy thing of all things. If you have money, then you are, by definition, successful and noble and you are superior to the unsuccessful, the proven unfit. Your country loves you and, of course, you love yourself. You have in your bank account all of the proof you need of your worthiness, of your superiority.

But beware! For, if you lose your money, you lose your worth. So guard your riches against everyone. Trust no one. Put everything and everyone under surveillance. Suppress all revolutionary talk, all talk of justice, all hints about equality. Censor books. Cleanse away different others. Erect barriers against the foreign and the strange. Make your religion a dogmatic fortress, your country a security state, your home an isolated castle. Ban dissent and criticism. Triumph over all. And then die alone and hated.

The Industrial Revolution replaced chattel slavery with wage slavery. While workers were inside the factories, they were in slave status but they were on their own away from work. This was an improvement over full-time slavery, but not by much. Most people worked almost all the time, much more than slaves had, and they were so exhausted during off-duty hours that they could do very little beyond sleeping, eating, and preparing for work again. For several centuries, they worked every day from sunrise to sunset. They did not have free weekends, as now, but they did have Sundays off, thanks to the desire of religious leaders to keep some of the workers time available to them for more or less compulsory religious duties and rituals.

Industrialization arranged people in commercial patterns so that they could be used like machines to produce goods and services. Company towns, factories, coalmines, and the like were the result. In fact, traditional slavery was not as efficient, as profitable, or as practical as the slavery of industrial employment. In slave systems, masters were expected to care for their slaves, to keep them alive and well (after all, they were valuable property). Not under the industrial employment system, least of all when there is an ample supply of unemployed to draw on. Industrial employers are responsible for nothing except paying their workers and that as little as possible. Industrialization resulted in a decrease in responsibility and a much harder attitude toward the human pieces of the commercial machine. Although liberal reformers and unions have defeated much of the brutality, that same attitude continues today among employers.

It's better to live in a just country than in a rich and productive one. Fanatical busyness and drivenness are for people whose only interest is in getting rich, not for people who just want to live their lives normally without being coerced, hassled, and pushed by bosses to achieve business goals. Of course, some degree of productiveness is worthwhile. Good services and good products make life better and more comfortable, but when intense competition and bottomlineitis are raised to extreme levels, then there can be little happiness or comfort for anyone, including especially the success hounds.

Pursuing a goal too intensely results in stress and inefficiency. The massive accumulation of money and commercial property is unsatisfying and useless. To raise the collection of property and the pursuit of profit to the highest national priority works against the wellbeing, the safety, the health, and the happiness of working people. It also turns on itself and produces waste, artificiality, corruption, and violence in the strivers and graspers themselves.

The history of humankind has been a history of kings over subjects, of master's over slaves, of bosses over workers. Subject peoples have always resented and rebelled against their rulers. They have always demanded greater equality of reward and condition. Few of them have ever demanded absolute equality for everyone, however. What they have always wanted was fairness and decency. In short, they are social democrats. The proper definition of socialism is economic democracy, not economic equality. Of course, capitalism is fanatically hostile to any idea of even approximate equality and even more violently opposed to the idea that any economic decisions should be democratic.

As a general principle, economic equality of some degree is necessary just to maintain a civil, decent society. Great economic inequality always leads to abuse and tyranny. Ultimately, it leads to civil war or revolution. In the short run, it leads to crime, civil strife, and social instability. There is no excuse or sensible rationale for great privilege and great disparity in reward among the citizens of a country. There must be a proportional relationship between contributions and reward. If the efforts and the actual outputs of people are weighed sensibly and accurately, there cannot be a great disparity among them. Thus, the variation of rewards cannot be vastly different.

If you believe in a society in which work is organized and controlled for the common benefit of citizens and if you are also a decent person, then you must agree that work should first serve the needs of those who do the work. In such a society, the workers are also most of the consumers and it is those two interests that have to be served first. The social contract is between those who do the work and those masses of people who use the benefits of the work to live their lives. Property owners and bosses are an artificial and burdensome drag on that arrangement and, no matter what the conservatives say, they are not a necessary part of the equation. Working people and consumers can do without them very well, thank you. If owners and bosses are to be included in the economic mix, then their interests have to come after the interests of consumers and workers, that is, the great majority of citizens.

There is no moral or practical justification for a system that raises up a very few to the rich life by keeping the overwhelming majority down and by preventing them from working together for their mutual, maximum benefit. If owners and bosses continue to oppress consumers and working people, then a time will soon come when they will be removed so the rest of us can get along with our lives without their harsh supervision and their greedy and unjustified profit-taking.

The people who live inside an economy are all interdependent. Those who get rich do so at the sufferance and with the support of everyone else. The notion of a courageous capitalist genius standing alone against the mediocrity of the masses and raising himself up by the bootstraps, entirely unaided and without taking anything unjustly from others, is preposterous nonsense.

No one gets rich without exploiting others and, indeed, most so-called successful people not only know this very well but plan their careers so as to maximize their advantages over others. Economic success is part luck, part positioning and influence, and part drive. None of it has anything to do with merit, courage, or hard work. The effort to turn moneymakers into heroes is fraudulent and absurd. Unfortunately, due to the cuckoo conservative economic philosophy, millions of people actually venerate and even worship the rich. Ultimately, such antidemocratic claptrap is virulently fascist, anti-American, and anti-christian.

As a matter of morality, nothing is less admirable than making money. Living life in order to make money is a perversion of life. It is also a huge waste of time and effort. Money grabbing is fundamentally immoral and, in the end, it is always vicious, murderous, and self-defeating. Excepting only capitalist fanaticism, there has never been a philosophy that celebrates the act of getting and clutching as a virtuous way of life. The only modern philosophy more ludicrous than communism is capitalism. However fraudulent the claim was, communism at least pretended to be on the side of the workingman and sometimes was.

Waste has always been the engine of prosperity. Free spending for artificial purposes has always quickened the commercial enterprise and increased the amount of money being spent as well as the speed with which it moves through the economy. Looked at from an easy chair, it is not easy to distinguish between real need and waste. Obviously certain minimum levels of food, water, housing, clothing, and medical care are real needs. Most everything else is artificial to one degree or another.

Capitalism feeds on waste. It not only produces frivolous products and services, it creates the desire for them through massive advertising campaigns. Above all, it wants to sell, sell, sell. Marx said that capitalism would overproduce and create economic failure. In fact, it does do so, but first it creates inessential wants in citizens and raises itself up on a great flood of artificial goods and services. The capitalist machine produces profit and has kept expanding to this point only because of this vast waste, this frivolous and inauthentic consumption. Some of these goods and services become useful, or seem so, and seem to make life better or at least easier and more entertaining. However, the majority are not useful at all and do not improve the quality of life. In fact, they glut and complicate life and make it worse.

This consumption becomes an end in itself. This lust for things corrupts society but it is what the hustlers want at any cost to workers and consumers. Therefore, we all live and consume for the ultimate benefit of the capitalist machine and those who own it. We do not really have a free choice in the matter. The advertising campaign is massive and ubiquitous. It bombards us all day long every day. It is almost impossible to get away from it. It is bundled into our lives in intricate and total detail. Few people pass a single hour without being urged to buy something or do something commercial.

These ads are clever and effective. They use and poison human urges. They promise wonderful rewards and better lives; they promise sharper minds, leaner bodies, and purer spirits; they promise better sex, truer romance, greater thrills, improved skills and quicker responses. They promise everything and deliver very little, but people keep on hoping and believing. The ads are there every minute of every day to assure them and deceive them.

Without this waste, the US economy might be weaker than it is but life would certainly be more satisfying, more human, and more genuine. We don't need the great mound of goods we wallow in. This vast, superficial consumerism is destroying us and leading us deeper and deeper into a totalitarian commercialism that has as its central purpose our entire enslavement to the businessman's bottom line. We have become a very ugly country, the ugliest in human history. We are not democratic anymore. We are not free. We are not moral and we are not humane. Both as workers and as consumers, we are the slaves of commerce and profit.

Republican conservatives think that poor people, those they define as the "unsuccessful," envy and resent the rich, those they describe as the successful. What they want from the unsuccessful is resignation, that is, passive acceptance by the poor of their economic fate. Conservatives believe that the poor are exactly where they belong economically and that any interference by the government is unnatural. They believe that the laissez-faire economic system is derived from natural law and is supported by god and the constitution.

If poor people starve, it's because they won't work. If they are homeless, it's because they prefer the streets. If they sicken and die, it's because of their careless and immoral lifestyles. And anyway, they say, the federal government causes it all because its programs to feed the hungry cause hunger; its programs to house the homeless cause homelessness; its programs to heal the sick cause sickness. Its standards for safe food products poison the food supply and cause injury and death. Its work safety regulations cause accidents and deaths on the job. Gun controls cause people to die by gunfire. Speed limits on the roads cause auto accidents. Poisoned air and water are caused by environmentalist kooks, encouraged and supported by the government. And, of course, unions and the minimum wage cause unemployment. Government is the problem.

Chapter 4. Is Capitalism Democratic?

If you are rational, it isn't possible for you to represent capitalism as somehow democratic. Its very nature and structure are antidemocratic. Every capitalist organization is hierarchic and all power is at the top, in the hands of owners and bosses. Those who work in such an organization own nothing and control nothing. They do not vote on anything or participate in any way in the decision making that defines the work they do or the conditions under which they do it. They do not even own their own jobs but work at the absolute pleasure of the bosses. Outside of government regulations, they have no vested interests and no entitlements. They are entirely without economic power and have no economic rights of any kind.

Without some process of voting by the citizens of a country on political matters, the idea of political democracy is nonsense. Of course, in a democracy, citizens may vote directly on issues or they may vote for representatives who then decide issues by voting among themselves. No political system that denies citizens the right to vote in some such fashion can be described as democratic.

By the same token, there is no economic democracy if all economic issues are decided arbitrarily by property owners and business bosses. I do not know how that can be disputed. Yet, just about the only opinion ever heard in America is the opinion that capitalism and democracy are one and indivisible and that all of history's questions have been answered by the triumph of capitalism over socialism. I do not think that this corresponds to the facts in any way whatever.

It really ought to be clear that the eternal argument between workers and their bosses has always been about democracy. When has capitalism ever allowed workers or consumers to vote on anything? When has it ever allowed ordinary citizens to participate in any way in the control or direction of a business. When has the use or disposal of a piece of commercial property ever been a matter of democratic decision making? Capitalism cannot function through any system of democracy and remain capitalist. The minute it becomes democratic it becomes socialist.

No rational person can doubt that capitalism divides the economic world into two groups: those who own and rule and those who own little or nothing and are ruled. The whole history of capitalism is a history of working people having to kiss the asses of owners and bosses. How can anyone live in the world and not know that? How can anyone who has worked in such a system deny that it is authoritarian?

There is and there never can be any such thing as "democratic capitalism." Every corporation and company consists of rulers at the top and subordinates arranged in a descending pyramid of obedience and servanthood beneath them. The lower orders are under the thumb of the higher orders, and commands from above are absolutist and punitive. There is no democracy in any corporation and those who say there is are being irrational or dishonest. Plainly and simply, the corporatists, by definition, are fascists, not democrats. The literal definition of fascism is corporatism.

The argument that there is a necessary connection between capitalism and democracy is untrue. Capitalism is non-democratic, even anti-democratic; clearly, owners have total control of all property and even the workers themselves under capitalism. In the West as in the former Soviet Union, there is and there was no democratic vote on anything economic and no shared decision making. In such systems, workers have possession of nothing, control none of the property, and have nothing to say about working conditions or the nature and disposal of the product of their work. The worker can quit his job but all other jobs are also under the control of capitalists, whether Russian or American. That is certainly not economic democracy.

Though there is no conclusive proof of it, corporate capitalism may be the most productive economic system currently available to humans; but it is not a system of freedom. It cannot actually become democratic without becoming socialistic. Capitalism can only be absolute ownership and control by a few. Socialism is shared ownership and control by all workers, through democratic processes.

Its adherents claim that capitalism is an expression of man's true nature and that all other systems are artificial and illegitimate. They see capitalism as a natural system of freedom that ought to replace democratic and, indeed, all government. They think that democratic government is a system of bureaucratic tyranny restraining them unjustly. At the very least, they want government severely limited so that capitalism, entirely sufficient in itself, can govern men and women in detail, with or without their consent.

Well, capitalism is not the natural system. Physical force is the natural system. Should government allow the strongest to have whatever they can take? Is it illegitimate, unfair, or tyrannical of the government to interfere with the natural ability of a few to control everyone else through physical force? If not, should direct physical force be regulated but not economic force? Is physical force any crueler or any more tyrannical than economic force has been? Or any different?

The rich certainly do not deserve their money in any moral sense. They did not acquire it through their own unsupported, unaided effort. They acquired it only because of political, that is, societal constructions, patterns, and arrangements. Their success is a matter of privilege, not talent. They are not inherently superior to their fellow citizens. The force and quality of their efforts are not proportionate to the amounts by which their incomes exceed those of ordinary working people — commonly ten or a hundred or even a thousand times greater than the average.

Capitalism is authoritarian and stands in opposition to democratic government. It is an artificially arranged and imposed system. It is imposed, at home, by the police and, overseas, by the military. It is not natural. It is not democratic. And it is not sacred or moral or fair. Its beneficiaries are the rich. Its victims are the poor. And its chief propagandists are conservative politicians and journalists.

The system of capitalism is, in fact, an unelected system of government. It controls and dominates the working lives of employees but it also enormously influences and manipulates the personal lives of all citizens. Its power is far greater than the power of government. It owns virtually everything and governs nearly all of life's processes.

Capitalists want to limit government so that it does not impinge on *their* power. They believe that government itself must be severely limited but that there must be no limits of any kind on capitalism no matter what it chooses to do. Workers' unions must be suppressed and even prohibited because they interfere with business. Consumers must be prevented from organizing, assembling, and politicking because they just want to limit free markets. Environmentalists are anti–development kooks who slow the progress capitalists plan for us all.

When a businessman wants money to advance a political or ideological cause, he simply increases the price of his product or service or he cuts his workforce or decreases their pay. In other words, he "taxes" the workers and the customers. The customer has nothing to say about any of it, in fact doesn't even know what he is paying for. The businessman tells him that all the property and money belong to him and that he has an absolute right to do anything he wishes with them. This same businessman bitterly attacks the government for openly and democratically spending "his" taxes for programs he doesn't like and says that unions should be prevented from using the dues of workers for any political purpose whatever. He believes the government has a duty to suppress those who oppose him and disagree with him. When he talks of freedom, he means freedom for himself, not for anyone else.

Free enterprisers have a strange way of defining tyranny. To them it is any taxation whatever, especially of the rich, and any regulation of commercial interests. They believe that all liberties are inherent in property rights. To them, capitalism *is* freedom and everything else is tyranny. It doesn't matter to them if millions are hungry and homeless under capitalism just as long as the system is maintained, by military and police power if necessary.

Social engineering and planning for others is precisely what capitalism does with its power over the work of citizens. It is every bit as utopian and as controlling of the details of life as was communism. Capitalism is an ideology or religion and it imposes its interpretation of history and its laws on everyone else. Those who boss others in the interest of their own privilege and profit do so without any regard for the rights, the freedom, or the humanity of their servants and underlings. Capitalism is simply a system that imposes a very restricted way of life on the many so the few can get rich and control everyone and everything completely. In short, capitalism is totalitarian.

How can anyone doubt that a system of bosses is tyrannical and not at all voluntary? How can anyone doubt that owners, CEOs, and bosses are central planners and controllers every bit as much as were commissars? In the economic sphere, there is little difference between communism and capitalism. Western corporatism is smoother and more sophisticated than communism was and it allows more apparent political freedom. Nevertheless, it is utterly hostile to any open society and absolutely determined to use its economic power to prevent the free association of working people so they can advance their own interests. Capitalism is not a system of freedom and it does not allow any deviation from its grand plans for the total control and development of every piece of matter in existence through the compelled use of human labor.

Both the communists and the capitalists see government, especially democratic government, as the enemy. The communists say that a dictatorship of the proletariat will cause the state to wither away. The capitalist say that their privatization and deregulation of everything will allow them to drown the government in a bathtub. They both despise working people and consumers and think that they have a right to exploit and dominate them in the interest of their own power, profit, and privilege. In the economic sphere, there is no serious difference between communists and capitalists.

Even the feeble minded ought to be able to see that capitalism and economic democracy are opposite to one another, not identical and not complementary. The point isn't even arguable and yet it is falsely asserted all the time by the defenders of capitalism. To make their point, they invariably point to communism as an example of the failure of economic democracy as if anyone really believes that communism was democratic in its economic programs or in any other. The plain fact is that communism was just another form of capitalism; as noted earlier, some have called it state capitalism, a very apt term for it.

CHAPTER 5. NATURE OF CAPITALISM

Capitalism has one purpose and one purpose only: to aggregate money and property in the hands of a small class of privileged people at the top of society. The Republican Party serves capitalism. It consists of predatory parts called conservatism, neoconservatism, and libertarianism. Members of all of these parts believe in the punishing and killing power of a government towering over and directing a collection of working people and consumers forced by economic arrangements to serve the interests of "private" owners and bosses. Though they manage the economic world for their own profit only, these privateers are, in fact, a part of a fascist arrangement that should be seen as a private government in and of itself.

At the top, this government uses a vast network of police agencies and military forces to control ordinary citizens for the privateers' uses and abuses. They are held under police control while the privateers extract their labor and pick their pockets. The military is charged with overseas aggressions and conquests so that the privateers can seize whatever resources and raw materials they need and so that military and economic outposts can be established to extend the power of the privateers over the whole world. Capitalism, in this framework, is unalterably domineering and tyrannical. This is called the "American Model." Though its directors pretend to be democratic, they are, in fact, conquerors and despots acting always for the benefit of the privateers.

Republicans say that capitalism *is* democracy. They say that markets provide the only legitimate choices. They say that entrepreneurs are he-

roes and the champions of the people. They say that democratic government is evil and tyrannical, especially when it tries to regulate business or
guarantee civil rights or religious liberty for all. They say that labor unions
don't represent working people; bosses do. This is surely the craziest and
the most utopian stuff ever believed by anyone anywhere. And yet it is the
fundamental belief of millions of Americans, possibly a substantial majority
of the population.

The reason this incredible view now dominates America and indeed the
world is because the bosses utterly control all of the information and education systems. Very rarely are any contrary or critical views heard. Anyone
who criticizes capitalism or christianity is marginalized and isolated. If they
persist and gain any support, they are placed under attack and represented
as freaks, radicals, traitors, and pariahs. For most of the last century, they
were smeared, first as dangerous democratists, then as alien anarchists,
next as subversive communists, and now as foreign terrorists. In recent
years, they have all been routinely and irrationally condemned as the spawn
of big-government liberals, that is, as agents of the disgraceful democratic
government of the United States.

The most important weapons being used by the conservatives to destroy democratic government are privatization and deregulation. The idea
is to take everything public out of the hands of elected representatives of the
people so it can be placed in private hands, that is, in the hands of unelected
and unrepresentative commercial and religious bosses. Deregulation is an
attempt to prevent the people of this country from exerting any control
whatever over these private bosses. If everything is placed in the hands of
private owners and if no element of democratic government is allowed to
regulate any of it in the interest of the people, the result can only be a totalitarian system entirely under the control of the commercial and religious
bosses, in other words, under fascist control.

This monstrous perversion of democracy in America began with the
birth of the Republican Party and with its capture, just after the Civil War,
by the social darwinists and the eugenicists. Herbert Spencer, the Englishman who invented social darwinism, visited the United States just after the
war and was warmly embraced by the big business owners of that time,
especially by John D. Rockefeller, Andrew Mellon, and Andrew Carnegie.
His philosophy became their philosophy and they used it to justify their
enormous expansion of capitalist exploitation, especially of the prostrate
South and the undeveloped West. The eugenicist beliefs of another English-

man, Sir Francis Galton, connected naturally with social darwinism and the racist views of America's politicians, bosses, and religionists.

From then until the Great Conservative Depression, America was ruled by a one-party dictatorship. Nationally, the one party was the Republican Party. In the South, the one party was the Democratic Party but it collaborated with the national Republican Party and was pretty much its adjunct. The Republican Party was the party of the robber barons and all of the other big bosses in the country. Since then, it has always been the party of big business and the social darwinist party. Its privatization and deregulation of today simply return America to its servile status of yesterday, a status briefly interrupted by the New Deal to the continuing outrage of the Republicans.

When the consuming class began to grow and began to include working people, the profiteers needed a way to entice and deceive large numbers of ordinary people so they would buy a lot of things and services never available to them before. The tool of choice was advertising, a bag of tricks taken directly from street hustlers and traveling salesmen.

Those early entrepreneurs were shady characters who made a living by selling largely worthless medicines, toys, utensils, tools, and peepshow thrills to people in the streets. They brought entertainment, frills, gee gaws, pretties, color, and novelty to dull lives at cheap prices. Circus performers, musicians, gamblers, tricksters, and circuit-riding preachers were of the same ilk and practiced the same deceptions and manipulations. Advertising was a con game from the start. Its purpose was to exploit desire and create need by any means necessary. Profit was its be-all and end-all.

It took capitalism a very long time to change its ways enough to start including working people in its cycle of conspicuous consumption. It was the success of what Michael Harrington called "Fordism" that led capitalism to loosen its control over workers enough so that they could become large consumers. That meant paying them enough money as wages so they could buy the products and services of capitalism in volume. That resulted in an enormous boom in business and the need for capitalism to control workers and consumers in more subtle ways since they had now become something more than wage slaves and needed to be persuaded not only to do the work but to buy the capitalist output as well. The method of persuasion was advertising.

As communications technology advanced, capitalist owners seized control of it, with the help of a subservient government, and used it to deceive and manipulate the people. Newspapers, magazines, books, radio, and television were all controlled in the large by capitalist owners and their manager-servants. Advertising itself became a massive business and its entire purpose became one of totalitarian control over the minds and urges of citizens.

Entertainment, education, and even religion became mere commercial tools for use in this assault on the freedom of the people. From that time forward, few people in America ever again made an entirely free choice about anything at all. Everyone became servants and slaves of the system and all the processes of life fell under the domination of capitalist planning and manipulation. The result is a totalitarian society that supplies its servants with a mass of trivial goods as a means of controlling them and their work. It is a system that guarantees wealth for the few and poverty of the pocket, mind, and spirit for the many.

The real truth is that American capitalism is the most inefficient and wasteful economic system ever. That is its secret. That is why it works. If tomorrow it became truly efficient, the economy would shrink by a third. Then, there would be huge unemployment and a great depression.

Capitalism is a kind of clumsy, wasteful, inefficient perpetual motion machine. It never quite stops altogether but it often sputters and pauses or runs at breakneck speed and out of control. What keeps it going is the invention and proliferation of new and different products, most of them dead useless or at least frivolous. A large propaganda and entertainment network is required to sell these useless and frivolous products to the public. Of course, the public not only pays for the products but also pays for all the commercial propaganda and entertainment as well. In other words, they pay for the instruments of their own control and don't even know that that's what's happening to them.

There are actually millions of people in America who believe that everyone can get rich. Reagan was among them. Of course, it's absolutely impossible. Only a few can get rich and always at the expense of everyone else. The rich get their money either by inheriting it or by taking it from others. Some are just lucky but mostly its rapaciousness, greed, and deception that move the profiteers. They are schemers and graspers. Though it may help a little, you can't get rich by hard work alone or by talent or intelligence alone. And you can't get rich at all without taking every penny out of the labor and the consumption of your fellow citizens.

Chapter 6. The Acquirers

Conservatives love the market system. They believe it is sacred, that it proceeds by a kind of miraculous chemistry that makes everything come out perfectly. The market needs no regulating, no manipulating, and no correction of any kind, they say; they believe it is a sin and a crime to interfere with it in any way. Therefore, it is a crime to feed the hungry, house the homeless, cure the sick, or educate the ignorant through any government action or any action outside the market system. Democratic government must not be allowed to do anything except assist business through police action at home and military action abroad.

These marketers are even more utopian than Marx. Their beliefs about society are utterly fantastic. Everything is based on a blind faith in the magic market and, to them, the market is noble, godly, and patriotic by definition. Those who oppose it are evil and must be destroyed. It is self-defining and self-correcting and it always leads to the exact amounts and kinds of freedom and democracy that are proper for citizens. Of course, the marketers do not want freedom extended *too far* and they do not want any democracy in economic matters. And they definitely do not want any "new rights." They see freedom and democracy in the economic, religious, and social spheres as dangerous and threatening, and as inappropriate in a market economy.

All profit comes from workers and consumers, not from owners and bosses who contribute nothing to the take beyond organizing and funding the start-up and pocketing the profit. Only the already rich can "create" a business without borrowing other people's money (OPM). The borrower cannot get money without collateral. In other words, he must already have money or property or perhaps associates who are willing to trust him with a loan. Thus, going into business is an inside game. People without property or disposable income cannot easily start a business of any kind. Therefore, in a capitalist economy like ours, such people must work for an owner. There are few other possibilities. Of course, such closed economic arrangements result in a big divide and considerable hostility between owners and workers.

Only a limited number of people can get rich. Wealth is not "created" by entrepreneurs but by those who work and those who consume. Profiteers are exploiters, not creators. Rich people are on one side of the equal mark and workers and consumers on the other side of the equal mark. Unless regulated by governments, this adversarial division between owners and working people is bound to result in an ever-escalating inequality and an unhappy division of rights and rewards.

In this country over the last thirty years or so, the share of income going to the top 1 percent has greatly increased. During the "boom years" of the 1950s and 1960s, the top 1 percent got about 10 percent of national income. By 2007, that share had more than doubled; the 90 percent who made less than $110,000 a year earned only half of national income. The only other year of record with as much inequality was 1928, just before the Great Conservative Depression. Over 17 years, Wall Street pay increased by 112 percent from $190,000 in 1990 to more than $403,000 in 2007. Including Mayor Bloomberg, there were fifty-seven billionaires in New York City alone; they then increased their collective net worth by $19 billion between 2009 and 2010. During the same period, the number of New Yorkers using food pantries increased by 200,000. If it were a nation, New York City would have the fifteenth worst income concentration among 134 countries, ranking between Chile and Honduras.

Every study of income inequality I have seen shows massive growth in wealth at the top, especially since Ronald Reagan's tax cuts in the 1980s and George W. Bush's tax cuts in 2001 and 2003. In 2010, the top 1 percent of the population (3 million households) owned 35 percent of the nation's total wealth; by comparison, it was 29.5 percent in 1979. Still further, the top 20 percent got 49.4 percent of all income earned in 2010. Those below the federal poverty level got 3.4 percent. The ratio of 14.5 to 1 was the largest on record.

One would think that Republican efforts to drive down the incomes and the benefits of working people would result in balanced budgets, but look at the facts. Since 1963, there have been eight presidents finishing their terms. Five were Republicans (Nixon, Ford, Reagan, George H. W. Bush, and George W. Bush; they served 28 years). Three were Democrats (Johnson, Carter, and Clinton; they served for 17 years).

The total deficits of the Republicans was $3.8 trillion, an average of $135.8 billion a year. The total deficits of the Democrats was $592.7 billion, an average of $34.8 billion a year. The average annual deficits under the Republicans was almost four times that of the Democrats.

The worst annual deficits were those of Ronald Reagan and George W. Bush. Reagan's deficit was $167.3 billion, three times worse than that of Jimmy Carter. George W. Bush's deficits were the worst of them all: $254.7 billion, four and one half times worse than that of Jimmy Carter. If you ranked all of these eight presidents according to the amounts of their annual deficits, the four worst would be Republicans.

From 1964 to 1980, those in the top tax bracket made at least $200,000 a year and were heavily taxed at the rate of 70 percent. During those times, the rich were more heavily taxed than the poor and the middle class. Two Democrats and two Republicans served during that time. Then came Ronald Reagan and the tax code was twisted to benefit the rich at the expense of ordinary citizens.

Under Reagan, the top tax rate was reduced from 70 percent to 28 percent. The change put enormous amounts of money in the pockets of the rich. Reagan did not cut spending to make up for this huge drain on the treasury. His theory was that reducing the taxes of the rich would increase the intake and cut the deficit. In other words, he thought that adding to the deficit would reduce the deficit. That's how he created such astonishing annual deficits and added so much to the national debt. Now, in 2011, the Republicans are still making this absurd argument and they are hugely adding to the debt by giving billions in tax cuts for the rich.

Clinton was the most successful and the most fiscally responsible of them all. He raised Reagan's top rate from 28 percent to 39.6 percent, resulting in four years of annual budget surpluses. Clinton chose to lower the country's deficit. Reagan — celebrated by Republicans as the enemy of Big

Government — chose to increase government expenditures at more than twice the rate of Clinton. Now, The Republicans are using Reagan's record as a cover for their own dishonest manipulations.

There are conservatives who claim that Reagan drove the country into debt deliberately so he could cripple democratic government and destroy it. I myself doubt this because I don't believe Reagan was clever enough or competent enough to do such a thing. He was an extremely simple minded and ignorant man especially when it came to arithmetic or anything factual. However, if the conservatives are right, then he was the enemy of this country and a traitor in the bargain.

Even as the George W. Bush meltdown loomed, the top 1 percent of earners tripled their income in 2007; they earned as much as the bottom hundred and twenty million people. People who made two hundred thousand dollars a year paid taxes at the same rate as did those making two hundred million dollars a year. Reagan's supply-side dogma is still operative as is the Republican Party's perpetual belief in its trickle down theory.

The poverty rate was up to 12 percent (39 million) in 2008. Unemployment was around 10 percent not counting an almost equal number of under-employed. At least 14 percent had no health insurance and 15 percent were hungry. In 2008, median income dropped from $52,000 to $50,000, an unusually steep one-year drop. A Census Bureau survey in 2005 had found that one-fifth of Americans needed help from their families and friends to pay basic expenses.

Now in 2011, Republican Representative Paul Ryan of Wisconsin wants to make it worse. His budget proposal will tax those with incomes up to $100,000 at a rate of 10 percent and those with higher incomes at a rate of 25 percent. He would allow no deductions or exceptions except for the rich. He wants to exclude interest, capital gains, and dividends altogether. The richest 400 taxpayers in 2007 (worth $345 million) drew less than 7 percent of their income from salaries. Thus, Ryan would exempt 93 percent of their income while requiring their servants to pay the full tax. He apparently also wants to exclude the estate tax, another tax on unearned income. In fact, Republicans have long believed that unearned income should not be taxed at all. As Leona Helms, the rich real estate queen said, "Only poor people pay taxes."

Ryan demands repeal of the new health insurance law, leaving millions uninsured. He wants to eliminate Medicare and Medicaid and replace them with vouchers for private insurance companies. In private insurance companies, 32 percent of every dollar goes for profit and overhead; administrative costs for Medicare, Medicaid, and for all public social service programs are tiny compared to costs for private companies. Indeed, privatization of every one of the Republican's public targets will be enormously expensive because of high profits for the corporatist privateers.

Even Ryan's friendly critics say his budget plan would take 30 years to eliminate deficits and would require borrowing money that, over the next ten years, would increase the debt from $14.3 Trillion to $23 trillion. They complain because he does not include a plan to also rape the Social Security system.

No Republican ever wants to cut the budgets of the Pentagon, Homeland Security, or any police agency. Neither does Ryan. He also refuses to propose any new taxes but instead continues to support massive cuts for the rich by every means possible. Since 2000, the defense budget has increased by 80 percent, not counting the wars in Iraq and Afghanistan.

To contrast raids against the needy with handouts for the corporations, consider these facts. Although the official corporate tax rate in the U.S. is quite high at 35 percent, the rate actually paid dropped from 30 percent in the 1950s to about 6.6 percent today. In 2010, General Electric reported a profit of $14.2 billion worldwide, $5.1 billion in the U.S. Instead of paying taxes, they claimed a tax benefit of $3.2 billion. Instead of paying their share, they raided the treasury with the help of politicians. Since 2002, GE has eliminated a fifth of its workforce in the U.S.

It's not just GE. There are 500 corporations in the Standard and Poor index. Of those, 115 paid a total corporate tax rate of less than 20 percent over the last five years. Thirty-nine of these paid less than 10 percent. Over the past five years, Boeing paid 4.5 percent, Southwest Airlines 6.3 percent, Yahoo 7 percent, Prudential Financial 7.6 percent. Last year, the following paid no taxes at all: Exxon, Bank of America, Chevron, GE, and Boeing.

The Republican Party and the corporate interests want to reduce or eliminate labor costs. They mean to reduce those costs by destroying unions, substituting machines for employees, and by outsourcing jobs to those places that have the lowest wages and the least regulated and most dangerous work places they can find. The globalization policies of Reagan, Clinton, and the Bushes resulted in huge wealth at the top and an enormous disparity between the rich and the poor. In the New Deal days of 1932–

1968, this country used the taxing and regulating powers of the government to create an economy that benefited all classes. Reagan and the Bushes corrupted that economic arrangement and almost destroyed the middle class. To a great extent, their policies and practices were behind the Great Conservative Recession of 2007. This fact is driving the Republican's viciously irresponsible actions now.

The governors in at least half a dozen states are trying to destroy public unions and the rights of public employees by slashing salaries and benefits on the dishonest charge that it is the only way to balance state budgets. They say this even while they themselves are giving tax cuts of hundreds of millions of dollars to corporations; even the insane know you can't decrease a deficit by adding to it. All the while, they complain bitterly about the increasing national debt and the annual deficits while ignoring the plain fact that they and their party are responsible for nearly all of the debt. The 2010 deficit is $2.9 trillion. The national debt has risen to $14.1 trillion. In fact, about 80 percent of the national debt just before the Bush meltdown was created during the twelve years of the Reagan — H. W. Bush administrations with the full backing of the Republican Party. Major portions of that debt came from huge tax cuts for the rich and enormous and unnecessary increases in military budgets, all fully supported by Republican legislators. The deficits created by those two exceeded all of the deficits created by all previous presidents combined. We are talking about a species of economic hypocrisy rarely if ever equaled anywhere on earth.

Make no mistake: the Great Conservative Recession was created by the Republicans and the corporatists. However, the Democrats did not take the loss of jobs and homes by ordinary citizens all that seriously. Instead, they concentrated on saving banks and the financial interests from their own crimes and mistakes. As this is being written, there has been very little improvement in the lot of ordinary citizens. The following quote from an article by John Cassidy in the December 9, 2010, *New York Review of Books* is instructive.

> On Wall Street, the Great Recession didn't last very long. Having sustained losses of $42.6 billion in 2008, the securities industry generated $55 billion in profits in 2009, smashing the previous record, and it paid out $20.3 billion in bonuses. In the spring of 2010, the Wall Street geyser continued to spew money. Between January and March, the Citigroup's investment banking division made more than $2.5 billion in profits. Goldman Sachs's traders enjoyed their best quarter ever, generating an astonishing $7.4 billion in net revenues....

Washington...demonstrated that at least for one year, Keynes had been right: economies suffering from a speculative bust didn't have to be left to nature's cure or, more accurately, to the market's cure, which Andrew Mellon, Herbert Hoover's Treasury secretary, famously described as "liquidate, liquidate, liquidate."...

Only on Wall Street was the recovery palpable, however. In September 2010, 9.6 percent of the US workforce was still out of work, and that didn't include more than eleven million people who had stopped looking for jobs or who had been forced to accept part-time work.

The Obama administration didn't come out and say so, but enabling the banks to make big profits was one of its policy objectives.... [I]t had settled on a policy of allowing them to earn their way back to sound health....

*

Rich business people have a sweet deal in our country. The harder the worker works, the richer the profiteer gets. In good times, there may be a small trickle-down effect but the profit always goes into the hands of the profiteer first and he alone decides whether to keep it all or "give" some of it to the worker in the form of salary, benefits, or better working conditions. The worker has nothing to say about any of it.

The profiteer may also decide to buy more production machinery and fire more workers as a way to modernize or streamline the business or he may decide to move it somewhere else.

Ideally, the profiteer would like to automate everything and fire all of the workers. Workers have no way to stop automation or control it and they have no way to protect their jobs. They have no right to their jobs and no say in how the business is run. The rich man who owns and operates the business is a dictator and, while they are in his employ, he owns the workers and he can fire them any time he chooses to do so.

Thus, the profiteer is a kind of slaver. The only difference between his ownership and outright slavery is that that he does not permanently own the workers' actual bodies and does not own their minds and actions all of the time. The workers own their time away from work and they can quit their jobs. If they quit, however, then they will have to go to work for another profiteer since, under capitalism, there are few other possibilities. Of course, both consumers and working people have long been the victims of the profiteers.

Before the rise of mass industrial societies, there was a big cleavage between workers and the consumers of nonessential products and services. In those days, the profiteers (the rich people) were pretty much the only consumers of all but absolutely essential goods and services. Luxuries and comforts were not available to working people because the upper class did not want them to have privilege and refused to pay them enough to buy more than was necessary to stay alive and keep on working. The rich regarded consumption as one of their rightful privileges. In fact, this attitude was dominant in the US until "Fordism" began to broaden the consuming class as a way of increasing profits.

The idea of competition as the goal or driving force of capitalism is greatly exaggerated. Some enterprises do compete directly with others but that is not the central purpose or motive of those enterprises. Rather, their purpose is to make money. The idea of competition was artificially introduced in the late nineteenth century. It came from the concept of business as a darwinian struggle for the survival of the fittest. It was stimulated, after that, by dressing it up as patriotism and by comparing it with sports events and games.

The notion that everyone can get rich is just like the idea that everyone can win in sports. It never occurs to the sports fanatics that exactly half of the teams must always lose, that is, in every game, there must be a winner *and* a loser. Everyone can't be a winner all the time and yet this whole nation is driven by the nonsensical belief that they can and that those who lose are contemptible. Enormous amounts of money and effort are spent to make this or that team a winner and the sum result is exactly the same: half the teams win and the other half lose. The overall winning percentage must always be exactly the same. The apparent purpose of this absurd distortion of arithmetic is to drive athletes and their supporters to higher and higher levels of meaningless competition.

This squares with the acquirer's desire to extract more and more money from the economy by endlessly increasing productivity. No one must ever relax. The money machine must be stoked to higher and higher levels at any cost. Everything in existence must be harnessed, exploited, and used up. Growth and development are the highest of values, apparently the only values. Of course, the belief system that supports this monstrous perversion is absurd. This is no way for human beings to live. Living decently and in dignity is what matters, not growing everything to the maximum size possible.

Despite the pretense, most businesses do not really compete with one another. They merely advertise the wonders of their own products and services by associating them with someone or something well known and liked or by making extravagant and almost always untrue claims for those products and services. Only rarely do advertisements attack the competition directly. There is a fair amount of competition with brand x but this certainly cannot be described as direct or vigorous competition. More often than not clever advertisements literally create the "needs" and desires of customers. Competition is not involved at all.

Even when competition does play a role in a company's marketing, it is only among a small group of bosses, accountants, planners, and salesmen. Ordinary line workers could care less about competition. Consumers compare products to a certain extent but the process is certainly not rational and has little to do with competition. No doubt, business CEOs screw the competition when they can but this is just sabotage and back stabbing, not the kind of noble struggle envisioned by the promoters and defenders of competitive free enterprise.

Is it really true that capitalism is individualist and competitive rather than collective and cooperative (like communism, supposedly)? It is certainly individualist for the capitalist owner and, absent monopoly or economic conspiracy, it may be somewhat competitive. On the other hand, it cannot be individualist or competitive for the workers. In any enterprise, they must work together and especially so in modern assembly-line types of industries. Unlike workers, the owner can afford to be individualistic, even eccentric. After all, he isn't required to produce anything and he isn't supervised by anyone. In economic matters at least, the cult of individualism is restricted to the upper class.

You can't make much money without having someone else do the work for you and you can't make *any* money without customers, that is, without people willing to give you more for your products and services than you paid for them. The fact is, all of the parts of any economic system are interdependent; nobody can become rich without the help and cooperation of others. No one becomes rich through his own unaided effort.

Pretending that the acquirers are noble geniuses "creating wealth" for everyone or that they create wealth at all is nonsense. All wealth comes from the whole population. It comes from everyone, not from the lonely entrepreneur fighting some heroic battle against the evil forces of democratic government and against an ignorant population out to rob him of his deserved and exclusively earned property. Every man who owns anything got it from someone else and through the efforts of others. He did not get it alone and he has a public obligation to guarantee the wellbeing of those he climbed over in his headlong drive for wealth.

If the acquirer refuses his obligation, he is irresponsible and corrupt and he ought to be dealt with severely by those he used and abused for his own narrow, selfish ends. It is the purpose of governments to see that all citizens share fairly in the wealth that comes naturally from the association of citizens in their social and economic structures, whatever they may be. Those people who think they have a moral right to more than their fair share deserve to be ostracized, driven out, imprisoned, or, if violent, killed. People have to protect themselves from the money tyrants who steal from them and abuse them, and their instrument of protection is democratic government.

Why do you suppose entrepreneurs rage so bitterly and uncontrollably against the government of the United States? Well, it's because they see democratic government as the restrictor and the enemy of their power and profit. They don't care about the rights of working people or about fair play for consumers. Instead, they care about profit and their own success. People struggling to become rich know that all of their profits come out of the labor of workers and the pockets of consumers. They thus bitterly resent laws and regulations that protect the rights, the safety, the wages, and the employment security of workers and also resent any requirement that they not lie to or cheat consumers. What restricts the entrepreneur and might make him or her fail is democracy. What helps the entrepreneur is unrestricted capitalism, that is, the undemocratic exploitation of employees and customers.

There is always a direct conflict between the power of capitalist bosses and the rules of democratic government. Of course, the conservatives of the Republican Party have always tried to cancel out public — that is, democratic — power in the interest of private power. Thus, every conservative political act consists of an attack against democracy and an effort to make government serve the interests of capital against the rights and protections of working people and consumers.

Farmers markets are the best expression of democratic commerce in America. The people who sell the product are, for the most part, the people who grow it, transport it, display it, and deal directly and humanly with their customers. These farmers are workers as much and perhaps even more than they are business people. They have not separated themselves from the earth, from every day work, and from human contact as the soulless grasp-ers of commerce so often do. The things that are commendable about these small farmers are their independence, their directness and honesty, their modesty, their lack of greed, and their connection to what they sell and the people they sell it to. Most small farmers and many other small "busi-ness men" do not much resemble the usual commercial hucksters who rule American life and corrupt its politics.

These small marketers do their own work with the help of their families and perhaps a very few hired hands. They are bosses in only the most lim-ited sense and their personal involvement in the work and with the produc-tion of the food gives them dignity and humanity. Sad to say, many of them are political conservatives. It's hard to see why. The political conservatives are the enemy of everything they love and do with their lives. What they do is more socialist then capitalist. In fact, it isn't capitalist at all. The bottom-line definition of capitalism includes the exploitation of the work of others for one's own leisure and profit.

Those who work their own businesses belong with the liberals and the democrats (not necessarily with the Democrats). All too many of them have allowed themselves to be deceived about the so-called evils of big govern-ment and the nobility of all commerce, especially the big business versions thereof. Big business invariably undermines and often wipes out the small worker-seller. They have no greater enemy.

How can anyone believe that the privilege of owning land or a business contributes to the general condition of freedom? The right to own property is not identical with individual liberty nor does one flow from the other. Such ownership may well be desirable but it is not a matter of personal freedom. This confusion of rights leads to the abuse of liberty. Those who acquire large amounts of property become powerful and invariably use their power to attack the liberty and wellbeing of others. Everything that leads to great inequality will lead to tyranny and human abuse.

For a limited time, rich men can guarantee privilege for themselves at the expense of others but, in the long run, the many will overthrow the few. Unequal liberty is a contradiction in terms. It may seem that money can buy liberty but that is an illusion. Bought liberty for a few is merely privilege and, in the end, it always compromises itself.

Human history is stitched with systems of big men, priests, kings, and bosses. To one degree or another, they have all played the role of controller and oppressor. Economic bosses exercise the same power and enjoy the same privilege as the other tyrants. The industrial revolution in particular concentrated power in the hands of bosses and decreased the power of priests and kings. Then, the bosses began to act like priests and kings.

Bossism was and is the means through which distant owners control their workers. Being men of such fine sensibilities, they usually do not do their own bloody and dirty work, but hire others to do it for them. This authoritarian system is so firmly established now that few people can imagine another possibility. Anyone who has ever had a boss knows of the threat, abuse, arrogance, and tyranny of the system. Even the most benevolent boss is a tyrant who is forced by the culture of bossism to raise management whim above the worker's rights and welfare.

Bosses invariably act as if they own everything and have a right to do anything they choose to do with the world's resources and people. They often treat employees with contempt, harass them, and persecute them when they are not perfectly obedient and servile. What bosses always want is submission to their commands and no back talk of any kind. Bossism is tyranny by definition. The idea that bossism is somehow necessary to achieve economic goals is untrue. Bossism changes the emphasis from achieving goals to satisfying the emotional needs and demands of the boss. The boss is not the instrument of achievement and efficiency. Rather, he is the instrument of swollen ego, self-advancement, and personal greed. There has never been a boss who was not an asshole. A system in which a family's food, shelter, and health depend on pleasing a boss is totalitarian.

Chapter 7. Communism

Because my thesis is that communism wasn't communist, there is no need for me to discuss its origin and nature in any detail. However, a few generalizations might be helpful to those who doubt what I say.

First of all, it's necessary to draw a thick line between communism and socialism. They are not the same thing at all. I think that socialism is economic democracy, not economic equality. Communism was hung up on the idea of a more or less absolute economic equality for a long time. However, you can't have any extreme degree of economic equality unless it is imposed from above, presumably by the state. Karl Marx used the term "dictatorship of the proletariat" in his writings. What he meant is open to question. Michael Harrington thought he meant a democratic economy under the collective control of working people who would presumably decide workplace policies and practices by voting.

Lenin and Stalin thought that Marx meant an actual dictatorship, that is, one-man rule, a new kind of Czar, themselves. This became the theoretical model adopted by all of the so-called communist countries that came into being after the Russian revolution. They were all true dictatorships and they all pretended they were establishing egalitarian societies. They weren't.

According to Marx, his dictatorship, however it was defined, would force equality on everyone. After some years of this equality, a new socialist man would emerge and the state would wither away. A socialist paradise of equality and justice would follow.

Obviously, this cartoonish utopianism was nonsensical. I think that Karl Marx's description of capitalism was absolutely accurate but his predictions about its early demise were clearly wrong or at least premature. His utopian ideas were completely impossible and silly. States don't wither away and new men and women don't emerge because of economic policies. It's amazing to me that anyone ever took such ideas seriously.

Charges by Republicans that Barack Obama is a socialist have led a number of them to offer their definition of socialism. They say that socialism is "when the state owns the means of production." This is a distortion. What Marx meant was that the proletariat (working people), not the State, would own the means of production. In time, this "dictatorship of the proletariat" would wither the state.

Obviously, the state would not wither away if it owned the means of production. However, the state (government) might wither away somewhat if working people themselves owned the places where they worked and the product of their work. In other words, the factory workers would own the factory and they could appoint and remove the factory manager and the bosses by voting. Government would not be involved.

It's interesting that Ronald Reagan hated the democratic government of the United States, even when he was in charge of it. ("Government isn't the solution; it's the problem.") Indeed, all Republicans hate democratic government and want to privatize and defund it entirely, except for the military and police portions. When they speak of "limited government'" they mean everything public and national except the punitive and attacking power they know the corporations need in order to protect their property against rebellious workers and consumers. In other words, Reagan and the Republicans agree with Marx: They want to wither the state, or drown it in a bathtub. Should we call Reagan and the Republicans "communists?"

The bizarre Republican claim that Obama is a socialist is close to insane. Socialists don't give banks and Wall Street financiers trillions of dollars in bailout money and they don't pass health care legislation that requires thirty million citizens to buy insurance from private health care and drug corporations with no public option of any kind allowed.

The marxist idea made no more sense than the capitalist claim that absolutely everyone can get rich under a "free enterprise" system; like the communists, the capitalists believe that their system will also wither the state ("or drown it in a bath tub") and that noble businessmen will then be left in charge to establish a great utopia of capitalist happiness without end.

There is such a thing as communism but it isn't anything very precise or concrete. I think that communism has always been a utopian daydream, never even partially realized. Karl Marx claimed that tribal societies were communist, sharing work (hunting and gathering) and its product (food and water) and not owning any land. Wandering tribesmen had no use for land and water as permanent property. Although they had "pecking orders," they shared just about everything. Each tribe was a classless collective made up of closely cooperative and integrated familial units. There was no state or any outside authority. Tribal members were certainly egalitarian and dependent on one another for support and nurture. These communitarian ideals have been attractive to many people, especially christians.

Karl Marx thought that the practice of owning property came about when societies first began to produce a "surplus." I suppose so, but I think that capitalism itself should be described as the supervision of work. Because of Marx and the professional economists, far too much attention has been given to theories about the ownership of property and the accumulation of capital and also about state ownership of the means of production. I think that work is the central event in any economic system and in most lives and that, in and by themselves, property and capital are mere inert substances.

Marx thought that tribalism eventually became feudalism and that capitalism replaced feudalism. Today the marxists write books claiming that capitalism emerged from a tighter and more efficient organization of agriculture in England and Europe in the sixteenth and seventeenth centuries. Then, according to their scenario, the Industrial Revolution gave capitalism an enormous impetus during the eighteenth century. No doubt, this is true in a general way but I think the labels and interpretations are wrong.

Feudalism was simply an earlier phase of capitalism, not something fundamentally different from it. When kings began to rise up out of the feudal mix, they established the first stable ruling systems and the first nation states. Feudal enclaves were merely small and usually unstable little kingdoms and the strongest of the feudal lords massed them together and created states. I would call this the birth of nationalism and it was an important political development. However, that does not necessarily mean that capitalism was a successor to feudalism.

I am arguing that capitalism is appropriately understood as the supervision of work and that it started with the rise of agriculture more than ten thousand years ago. I am not foolish enough to try to slap down all of the many economists and anthropologists who accept the marxist view of history and the cultural and economic notions that arise from that view. Nevertheless, I think that my opinion is more logical and more useful as a way to understand what really matters to human beings. I am talking about work. The system of work matters more to the ordinary citizen than do complex economic theories about property and capital and the theoretical centralization of production in the state. There is more than one way to look at and interpret history and the evolution of political and economic systems. I offer an alternative view.

The lust of some men and women for power over others thus led to regionalisms and then nationalisms. Nation states emerged. The larger collectives began to gobble up the smaller ones and began to impose religious, social, political, and economic dogmas and beliefs on them by force of arms and brute pressures. The collective idea gained force and the communitarian and tribal arrangements became generalized and dispersed. Revolts of all kinds were common. Even today, national governments still struggle to hold together their peoples and territories. But there are frequent secessions and displacements. The world map is always changing. Some would like to see world government, one central power over all. Others would like to see massive scatterings and local independence right down to the level of the ancient tribes and villages. Some even want an individualism so radical that no man can govern any other or force others to collaborate unwillingly in any undertaking — a kind of caveman isolationism or hermiting away in single family units or even away from the family unit altogether in lonely pairings. Some even abandon organized society altogether but compromise enough to sit in the streets with their begging bowls while they contemplate their navels and dream of a painless, sexless nirvana beyond humanity and all joinings and pairings.

Is it any wonder that some huddle together in self-protective units, large and small, or that others seek escape and independence from the common herd? Given a deep human desire to supervise others, is it any wonder that entrepreneurs and other warriors set out to conquer and control everything they can grab, and everyone? This drive to conquer and use others is not universal, however. Most people only want to live their lives without oner-ous supervision or minute surveillance. But the entrepreneurs will not leave them be. Conquest is their game. Thus, the world is divided into two parts, the supervisors and the rest of us. The organizing principle of civilization seems to be supervision. To get things done, the supervisors say, we must have ardent and massive oversight. To get enough food, water, land, and other things of value, we must let them herd us all together and command us toward their purposes. Then, we will all have improved lives, they say, but they also say, they must take the largest proportion of the gain, and none of the loss, or they will lose their incentive and abandon us to our own individual devices. They think we will starve without them. We need them, they don't need us, they say. All too often we believe their propaganda.

There are volumes and volumes that go into minute detail about the def-initions of capitalism, communism, and christianism and about the many economic and philosophic theories concerning each. There are also numer-ous conflicting accounts about the nature of man and the state. I think that the invention or discovery of agriculture was an enormously important turning point in human development. In my mind, it ranks with the inven-tion of the wheel and the discovery of fire.

Systems for the acquisition and control of land and water and food were formalized at the time agriculture began and the narrow ownership of property resulted. Permanent settlements followed as did unequal relations between people, relations based on wealth, rank, and supervisory power. What mattered most was that some began to rise above and dominate oth-ers all in order to gain and hold position and property. Multilayered and hi-erarchic systems emerged. This was when servanthood and slavery became routine and when chiefs and eventually kings began to rule lesser men and women. Soon these rulers began to claim that they possessed royal blood and a permanent right to rule, a right that came from one or all of their gods. This was the first great advance for inequality based on the divine right of kings and aristocrats. All of this led to a two-class system based on the uses and abuses of human labor.

If tribalism is seen as communistic, then communism is older than capi-talism even according to my idea that capitalism arose with the birth of agriculture and the first organized supervision of workers. There have been numerous and widely varied communisms throughout human history. All of them can be related to the word "common" and all of them consisted of a drawing together of kindred populations into units with the same everyday needs and aims. Though there was always some hierarchy, these units were egalitarian. There were also strong elements of altruism in them. They were idealistic and often religious. When supervisory capitalism arose, it undermined these communitarian ideals. Because acquisitive impulses are very strong in humans, capitalism quickly gained ground. The common people and their needs and aims were subordinated to the greedier and narrower aims of rulers and bosses. Nation states conglomerated people under divine kings, their aristocracies, and their priests.

Because of their intense dedication to capitalism, most of today's christians are outraged whenever anyone points out that early christianity was heavily communistic and indeed remains communistic today in many of its concerns. Jesus disapproved of wealth and embraced the poor. He did not think that the path to salvation was open to the rich. He also thought that state and religious matters were separate concerns. He did not approve of war or aggression of any kind, including economic aggression. He drove the money-changers from the temple. Right from the start, the christians in the Roman world lived communal lives and often shared work and property. Paul's early churches were communitarian centers for believers. From then until now, christian communism has been present all over the world. There have been and there still are many such sects. In the 1960s, the United States was full of "Jesus Freaks," "flower children," "peaceniks," and young people who spoke of brotherhood, love, and common living. They also believed strongly in civil rights, human rights, and the rights of working people and they opposed cruelty and commercial abuse. In fact, most of them despised the commercial "rat race" and refused to be a part of it. And most of them were christians of some dimension.

I don't want to provide a history of christian communist sects here but anyone interested can find historical references that mention literally hundreds if not thousands of different movements and organizations dedicated in some way to communist principles. The reason today's standard christians are so outraged by the idea that christianity has always included communist elements is because they have been trained to hate communism and to regard it with an overwhelming and uninformed loathing. They have been taught that the Soviet Union and communist China were the true depositories of evil atheistic communist ideas. I say that those countries weren't communist but rather state capitalist. But then I also say that those who call themselves true christians usually aren't christian at all. And I say as well that the definitions used to describe the major isms of our time are inaccurate and often result in unnecessary conflict and endless war and aggression.

The modern versions of communism pretty much began with Karl Marx but what has followed his writings does not much match what he described. As I keep saying, I don't think that any of the so-called communist countries were communist, or marxist. As said earlier, AJP Taylor, the English historian, described the systems in use in the Soviet Union and China as state capitalist systems, not communist ones. If communism means that the workers own the means of production and share equally and fairly in the fruits of their labor, then Taylor was right. The "communist" countries were ruled by what was, in effect, an aristocracy consisting of a king and a royal court. There were no divine claims, of course, and no royal robes. Nevertheless, they were absolute rulers little different from what came before and they were not communists at all.

In a speech to the National Press Club on March 25, 1991, Lech Walesa said of Poland, "In our communist system, everything resembled one huge enterprise." Similarly, all of Russia was one gigantic business under the rule of a communist chief executive officer with a Board of Directors called the Politburo and a network of party functionaries who acted as company managers. On ABC's Nightline in June of 1991, Boris Yeltsin said of the Russian worker, "He doesn't own land. He doesn't own the factory, the enterprise, the shop or anything." It's absolutely clear that Russia was never communist in any sense, nor were any of the other so-called communist countries.

Historically, what really happened was that, initially, a democratic revolution displaced Czar Nicholas II, a divine king, and replaced him with Alexander Kerensky and a parliamentary government. Then, a small group of counterrevolutionary state capitalists (the Bolsheviks) deposed Kerensky and took over the country completely. A civil war followed. Workers had nothing to say about any of this. There was no workers' revolution and workers had absolutely no voice in how the new state was shaped or managed. They never even had the right to strike or express their grievances.

Thus, Russian communism took the means of production from the Czar, who owned everything, and put it in the hands of a narrow new class of privileged bosses, who owned everything. Lenin and Stalin were simply czars without the title or the royal blood. Absurdly, today's conservatives try to identify communism with the French Revolution and claim that every revolt against aristocracy and the divine rule of kings has been an attack against "freedom" and christianity.

And so, there was no "twilight struggle" between democratic capitalism and godless communism. In fact, there was no *democratic* capitalism and no communism. Both systems were capitalist and neither provided any economic rights at all for working people and ordinary citizens. Working people are the servants of a supervisory class wherever it is located and whatever it is called. Owners and bosses rule us all. For the most part, the property and the money belong to them. The media belongs to them as well and it expresses their views alone. The government belongs to them too. The police are there to suppress us and to protect their property against us. The military is there to help the owners and bosses capture foreign lands and resources and to attack and kill anyone who resists them, criticizes them too much, or interferes in any way with their property, their operations, or even their future plans. At times (increasingly so), our rulers attack others for no sane reason at all. Naturally, the working class has to provide the troops and the troops have to kill and die for the owners and bosses. They say they are defending us all but really they are just defending themselves and their property.

Chapter 8. The Republican Party's Fake Anti-Communism

By now, I suppose almost everyone agrees that, during the twentieth century, there was a "twilight struggle" between capitalism and communism for control of the world and that capitalism won. Gorbachev's reforms convinced conservative American politicians that socialism had been defeated. They saw it all as a victory for American militarism and a vindication of the policies of McCarthyism at home and interventionism abroad. They thought that Gorbachev's reforms were an unconditional surrender to capitalism and that, therefore, history had ended. They thought that communism was socialism, that it was dead, and that it would never be heard from again. I think they were wrong.

The error of confusing communism with socialism, welfarism, and even liberalism completely warped the American political system until every election became an argument about communism. For more than fifty years, the Republican conservative propaganda was that Democrats and liberals were traitors and pro-communists. According to them, New Deal, Fair Deal, and Great Society programs were all socialist schemes. The civil rights movement was a communist plot; Martin Luther King Jr. and Earl Warren were communist agents. Jimmy Carter's human rights policies were an attack against "our friends," that is, anti-communist military dictators everywhere. These Republican conservatives claimed that liberals deliberately weakened American values and subverted the US military in order to prepare the way for communist victory. The world was so polarized by this "anti-communist" fanaticism that there weren't even words or concepts in common use to describe a third alternative; and there still aren't.

These distortions led quite naturally to McCarthyism. McCarthyism was not just what Senator Joe McCarthy said and did. It was the attack philosophy of Republican conservatism, the political arm of corporate capitalism. This attack philosophy gained political control of America under Dwight Eisenhower and Richard Nixon and greatly multiplied it under Ronald Reagan. It is no accident that Nixon and Reagan became the greatest appeasers of the Russian and Chinese communist states. They had used communism against liberalism and the Democratic Party in order to gain power for themselves. Once they had power, it was no longer useful to carry on a war against communism. In control of America, they could diminish their cold war with Russia and China while concentrating their attack on liberalism and the Democratic Party.

State capitalism (that is, Soviet communism) was but one form of a broader system that should be called totalitarian capitalism. In the United States and elsewhere in the West, the most repressive forms of corporate capitalism are also a part of the totalitarian system. Thus, economically, there was little difference between the Western countries and the communist countries. Soviet state capitalism and Western corporate capitalism were brothers. In the Soviet-style system, there was no political democracy and no economic democracy. In the United States, there is a carefully limited political democracy but no economic democracy. Instead of economic democracy there is an antidemocratic system of predatory capitalism.

You really can't discuss communism in America without also discussing anti-communism. In the twentieth century, there was very little communism here but there was an enormous amount of anti-communism and the anti-communism was far more fanatical and far more subversive of democracy than was the communism itself. In fact, anti-communism really wasn't an attack against communism at all; rather, it was an attack against domestic foes — liberalism, unionism, civil rights, and the democratic government of the United States. Accusations of communism were simply the dirty brush used by conservatives to attack their own country and those citizens they disagreed with.

The notion that communism was an entirely new kind of "totalitarian" tyranny worse than the old "authoritarian" tyranny was absurd. Of course, this view was advanced and supported by those sympathetic to the old tyranny and fanatically determined to support it as a legitimate alternative to what they saw as the absolute evil of communism. Communism was an excuse used by the anti-communist authoritarians to establish and maintain tyrannies of their own. In Western countries, anti-communism became a weapon for the authoritarian conservatives to use dishonestly against liberals, socialists, modernists, progressives, humanists, evolutionists, jews, blacks, and any democrats.

Western capitalists were happy to identify communism with socialism. It not only gave them a useful enemy but also gave them an excuse to attack democratic socialism, in fact, all forms of economic democracy. Consequently, the conservatives saw politics in the twentieth century as a struggle between noble conservative capitalism and evil liberal socialism. This distortion has corrupted history and led to the weakening of democracy where it has been tried. Democracy cannot emerge anywhere as long as every principle of economic justice is misrepresented.

*

I don't think the hostility between the United States and the Soviet Union was a result of communism. If there had been no revolution in the Russian empire and no communism, there would still have been a cold war or perhaps a hot war. Wars are fought to acquire resources or to avoid having resources taken, no matter which –ism is used to motivate the populace to lay their lives on the line.

At the end of World War II, there were just two dominant countries left and they pretty much controlled the world. There had to be a rivalry; in fact, Alexis de Tocqueville foresaw such a rivalry years ago. Communism was all but irrelevant.

Communism was promoted as *the* great issue because it was a useful bogeyman, used to goad Westerners — especially Americans — to fear the working man and believe that the industrial masses were about to rise up, seize the production machinery, and depose the property owners and bosses. The working man was, of course, unhappy during the Great Conservative Depression. At some point, it looked to the capitalists as if Karl Marx had been right. Neither they nor anyone else could imagine that the masses would accept their miserable lot without revolt. Then, Franklin Roosevelt and the New Deal saved the capitalists from themselves.

Capitalists have always been leery of any ism that reminded workers they were being taken advantage of. What if the masses actually demanded a fair share, and took away their money and power? The Russian Revolution and the depression terrified them and made them into fanatical and indiscriminate anti-communists. They didn't just hate theoretical communism; they hated everything they could associate with it, everything that they thought might threaten their comfortable lives and destabilize the social, political, and economic order. Thus, they hated civil rights, human rights, and all of the rights of working people; they hated liberalism, progressivism, and democratic government; and, although Roosevelt was in the process of saving them, they hated him too. Naturally, this intense feeling translated into a deep and eternal hostility to the Soviet Union, the only communist country in the world at that time.

Communism certainly complicated the rivalry between the US and the USSR but did not cause it. There was increased class warfare during this time. However, it wasn't workers who started it; their resentment had been tempered by the New Deal reforms, the patriotism that was triggered by entry into World War II, and the return of relative prosperity that came with increased production related to the war, not to mention the benefits that came with winning the war. It was the capitalists and Republicans who went to war against working people and against every molecule of dissent and nonconformity in the country. They saw enemies everywhere and, by their definition, those enemies were all communists. Their definition included all liberals, all government employees, and most members of the Democratic Party.

As soon as the Second World War ended, they launched a massive attack against communism but the Soviet Union wasn't their main concern. They were worried about the loyalty of their fellow citizens. This climate created McCarthyism and the rise of a fanatical Republican Party that would spend the next sixty years raging against the democratic government of the United States. Even while they falsely attacked others for trying to overthrow the government by "force and violence," that is precisely what they were themselves doing. And, to this very day, the Republican Party remains a subversive, antidemocratic force.

The Soviet Union was never much of a threat to the United States. It was a nuisance and irritant, little more. It was never a rich or prosperous society. It never had a large middle class. It was never an industrial power. It did have military power, and could put together large armies. Even so, the

United States, all by itself, was always far more powerful than the Soviet Union and all of its allies put together.

Corrupt American and Western politicians made the Soviet Union seem a great threat. It served their purposes to have a great and powerful enemy. It put them in power; it kept them in power. That's what McCarthyism, Nixonism, Reaganism, and Bushism were all about. It's why the imperialist neo-conservative movement arose on the fringes of American and Western political life. Fanatical and irrational anti-communism was the force that drove all of these isms. Without them, American life would be entirely different and far better.

*

Communist China and the Soviet Union weren't expansionist. They did proselytize through their dogma just like other ideologies and religions — islam, christianity, capitalism, etc. But so what? Communism was always a weak religion. Its success came almost entirely from the abuses and stupidities of capitalism, not from any special appeal of its own. The only part of the communist ideology that was useful, true, and accurate was its criticism of capitalism and there was nothing new or special about that either. The victims of capitalism have always known it was abusive and exploitative and have always bitterly resented it. They still do and they always will. Throughout history, every tyrannical system has always been resented and resisted. And overthrown.

Every overseas effort to redistribute even a little of the property and wealth of the rich oligarchies was regularly assaulted by American forces, both overt and covert. In each case, the US pretended that purely local movements were part of an international communist conspiracy. The US charged those countries with subverting themselves even while it organized coups against them, assassinated their leaders, manipulated their internal politics, blocked their trade, subverted their currencies, shipped arms to subversive forces undermining them, and organized and directed terrorist groups in murderous attacks against their people. In these ways, the US eventually drove many small, terrified, weak countries into the arms of communism, then claimed it had been right all along when it had accused them of being communist satellites.

Conservative Republicans originated this fake anti-communism but the idea was supported by people who called themselves liberal Democrats. One way to look at it is that the Democrats really had little choice because the Republican conservatives were calling them traitors and subversives with every breath and were thus driving them headlong into the oppressive embrace of right-wing dictators. Another way to look at it is that the Democrats were gutless and cowardly, a charge that was certainly true then and is still true now.

The rightists could not or would not see that communism was just another rightist oligarchy. What really scared them was the communist propaganda about raising the workingman up from capitalist slavery and putting him in charge of society. The rightist needn't have worried: the communist propaganda was always a fraud. By the time they began to understand this, if they ever did, the communist "threat" had become a useful tool to them in their virulent campaign against every form of economic democracy.

The cold war was a gigantic con game that served the interests of both the communists and the anti-communists. Both blocks gained and maintained power through opposition to one another. Many millions of innocent and foolish people actually believed their cold war propaganda.

The Soviet Union never made any military attacks against any Western nation. Of course, it did send troops into Eastern European countries on its own borders, that is, the so-called satellites. Those interventions were all carried out to defend existing communist regimes. The purpose quite obviously was to assure a protective border around the USSR. The Soviet Union was merely defending the empire it had put together before, during, and just after the Second World War. As many of his own citizens as he slaughtered and as dictatorial as he was toward the countries on his borders, Stalin was not trying to conquer the world. He was just defending his existing lands and his existing power. Stalin believed in "Communism in one country." It was Trotsky, that darling of those who eventually became neoconservatives, who believed in aggressive world communist revolution. The disagreement caused Stalin to send his agents to Mexico where they murdered the exiled Trotsky.

Is there a sense in which the US and the USSR were trying to conquer the world? If so, it wasn't a matter of conquering territory. The Soviets made no attacks against anyone for that purpose. After WW II and except for a handful of advisors and technicians here and there, it sent no troops into or against any other country beyond its own array of perimeter satellites. The USSR had no need of additional property or resources and certainly didn't want to supervise any more troublesome ethnic populations. It already owned one-sixth of all the land on earth and that land was rich in resources. It also had a huge ethnic population speaking a greater number of different languages than in any other place.

The US record was much worse in that it sent troops almost everywhere and fought an endless series of wars against others, most notably Korea, Panama, Vietnam, Nicaragua, El Salvador, Guatemala, Grenada, Haiti, The Dominican Republic, Cuba, Iraq, Serbia, Afghanistan, etc. However, the US wasn't interested in acquiring territory any more than was the USSR. Both countries had more than enough territory and also had many intractable problems with their disparate and sometimes hostile ethnic citizens. The conquest of more territory would have meant large occupation armies and the suppression of resistant populations. For the most part, the Soviet Union was merely defending its borders although it did occasionally give supplies and money to so-called socialist countries. The US was more aggressive and its excuse was that it was fighting a defensive war against evil communism, a communism that wasn't attacking.

What the US was really interested in was markets and a world it could dominate commercially. Capitalism is an extremely aggressive, proselytizing force very much like christianity. By contrast, communism was never the militant aggressor the US and other Western nations said it was. Indeed, the West *was* terrified of communism but not because it was a conquering military horde. This fear came from the dread that working people might be inspired by communism and that at-home citizens might revolt against capitalism. It was an idle and false fear. Communism never represented working people, not in any of the so-called communist countries or anywhere else. It was just another kind of capitalism. True enough, it was heretical and it arranged its commercial structures in configurations different from those in the West. However, the communist countries did not put the workingman in charge or enlarge his power and freedom at all. The communists were just capitalist predators pretending to be socialist lambs.

It's certainly true that communist leaders like Stalin, Mao, Pol Pot, and a few others were mass murderers but mostly they killed their own people and most of those victims were communists themselves or, at least, people who accepted communism or lived compliantly under it. The communist dictators did not, in fact, kill outsiders or very often attack them and they certainly did not attack the West, least of all Western anti-communists.

The anti-communist propaganda of that time was very peculiar. It claimed the communist countries were engaged in a furious assault against the West and were trying to conquer the world for communism. Since it was obvious to any sane observer that the Soviet Union was not attacking any American territory on earth or any American citizens, the anti-communists needed a rationale of some kind to support their claim that America was under attack. Thus, they made up the ridiculous canard of "internal subversion."

According to this claim, the Soviet Union was trying to conquer America by subverting its population, that is, by stealing away the loyalty of its citizens. In other words, large numbers of Americans were becoming traitors and servants of the Soviet Union. Communism was a threat because of its irresistible appeal to Americans and other Westerners. The only way the anti-communists could fight back was by attacking disloyal Americans. However, they couldn't find enough communists to support their thesis. Therefore, they broadened their attack against the American population to include fellow travelers, com-symps, anti-anti-communists, fifth-amendment communists, pinkos, members of workers unions, those who supported civil rights, members of the Democratic Party, socialists, liberals, progressives, intellectuals (eggheads), feminists, pacifist christians, peaceniks, hippies, drug users, dentist who supported the use of fluoride, agnostics, atheists, quakers, unitarians, new ageists, witches, rock musicians, folk musicians, abstract artists, employees of the federal government, and indeed every American who was not a dedicated conservative.

In other words, according to the Republicans, the Soviet Union and China had a vast army of agents and spies inside the United States and all other Western nations and those wily traitors were working to overthrow Western governments by "force and violence." In fact, there were very, very few cases in which internal subversives used force and violence against their own countries' governments, any of their citizens, or any property at all. I know of no such violence in the United States ever but I might have missed something. In truth, there were millions of fanatical anti-communists in the United States and no more than a few hundred or perhaps a few thousand communists. (By contrast, in 1925, there were more than a million members of the KKK in America and literally tens of millions of sympathizers.) Furthermore, except for a handful of actual spies, most of these communists were passive and theoretical communists, people who never acted on their beliefs at all.

I can't remember any violence even by that handful of actual spies or any subversion either unless the theft of a few government secrets comes under that heading. Except for the Rosenbergs' theft of some minor details about the atom bomb, what they stole was so trivial that no one then and no one now can even remember it or describe it clearly. The triviality of the take doesn't lessen the guilt, of course, but the Soviet Union at that time was a valued ally, not an enemy. Throughout World War II, the US routinely shared information with its allies, and even when such sharing was not authorized, it was considered only an unwise indiscretion, not a crime. Much more unauthorized information was shared with England, with other Western countries, and later with Israel, Iraq, Saudi Arabia, and Pakistan than with the Soviet Union. Later, the Soviet Union became an enemy and many people were then fervently accused and their retroactive offenses were then hugely magnified long after the context had been obscured.

Of course, the McCarthyites and all conservative Republicans actually believed the United States was full of violent communist subversives but they had believed this ever since communism was first invented in the middle of the nineteenth century. It had always been a target of opportunity for them. Still, upon examination, it turned out that most of those they called subversives were Democratic opponents, liberals, those who supported civil rights for blacks and jews, and virtually all government employees. In addition, there were assorted librarians, charwomen, piano tuners, army dentists, movie actors and directors, song and dance men, scientists, abstract artists, and many writers. The list was almost endless. At times, it seemed that all Americans were subversives including even some of the people who were attacking communism.

Communists in the US and in Western Europe were not uniformly evil and tyrannical. In fact, most of them worked for civil rights and the rights of working people. Perhaps some of them were insincere but it is quite clear that most Americans who associated themselves with the communist movement did so because they believed in civil rights and were appalled by the viciousness and tyranny of the failed capitalism they saw around them. Communism in the West was never a monolith and it was not a subversive force trying to overthrow democracy. The so-called communist dupes, fellow travelers, pinkos, and the like who were so viciously persecuted by the

McCarthyites were very largely loyal and decent people out to democratize their country and increase the civil rights and the economic freedom of their fellow citizens. No doubt they were naive but they were also patriotic, idealistic, and innocent of any wrongdoing.

Internal communism was never of any importance in the United States. It never had any power and it did very little harm. It was not violent and it did not try to overthrow the government or subvert the American way of life. It was, in fact, rather pathetic. The only power and influence it ever had came from the vicious abuses of capitalism and the worst of those abuses, in this country, happened between the Civil War and the Great Conservative Depression during which time the owners and bosses took to assaulting and sometimes killing working people because they dared to ask for a tiny amount of decent and fair treatment. When working people tried to organize themselves into unions, the bosses took up arms against them and tried to intimidate, disempower, smear, and even kill them. Quite often, they were successful. They claimed always that they were attacking communists because they thought that anyone who believed that workers had rights was a communist.

The communists were often present in very small numbers during those confrontations but they neither caused the problems nor controlled the organizers and strikers. However cynical some of them may have been, they were mostly on the side of justice. In fact, most of them were sincere, decent people who foolishly joined a useless and rather silly ideology but they did not deserve to be insulted, assaulted, or killed. The owners used the presence of these few communists as an excuse for their violence against workers and their unions; and Republican politicians used the very existence of communism as a reason to spread hatred against the rights of working people and against all progressive ideas, including those in the constitution. Thus, the real fathers of violence in America were the anti-communists, not the communists.

And so I don't think that any American communist ever tried to overthrow the government of the United States by force and violence. I don't know of any violent act ever by a communist against the American government or any organized force dedicated to such violence. In fact, there is little evidence that any American communist ever even advocated violent overthrow except perhaps in some rhetorical flourish about a utopian workers' revolution at some vague point in the dim and unplanned future. However, there have been real acts of violence, threats of violence, and subversions against the government and us all by the conservatives.

For a long time, the South has been full of lynchings, bombings, riots, uprisings, and violent plots against government entities and officials. Across the country, the so-called militias have often resorted to gunfire and bombings and have issued loud threats of violence against the government and against specific officials in the government, including lately Bill Clinton and his family. Right wing radio talkers all but pleaded for violent acts against officials. Some of them even went so far as to provide instructions about just where to shoot Clinton and members of his administration and family. The racists wanted to hang Earl Warren and other members of the Supreme Court and regularly urged, and resorted to, violent resistance to integration, busing, voting by blacks, and affirmative action.

The christians have been bombing abortion clinics at the urging and with the support of Henry Hyde and many other Republicans; they have murdered doctors and medical personnel and, on occasion, federal and state officials. William Buckley screamed hysterically for the castration of Bill Clinton and Jesse Helms called for the military in North Carolina to attack and presumably assassinate him.

Ann Coulter, a loony right-wing Republican, also demanded Clinton's assassination and repeatedly called for the killing of American liberals and the slaughter of muslims. Timothy McVeigh, a homegrown terrorist aroused by the Republican and christian fundamentalist hatred of Bill Clinton and the democratic government of the United States, bombed the federal building in Kansas City and murdered 168 government employees and members of their families. Eric Rudolph, inspired by Republican and christian anti-abortion fanatics, bombed numerous public places and murdered innocent citizens in a rage against the reproductive freedom guaranteed by federal law and court rulings.

Watergate as well as the Iran and Contra scandals were, in fact, violent criminal conspiracies against democratic government by conservative government officials in league with subversive elements in the Republican Party and in its many un-American adjuncts. The impeachment of Bill Clinton was just the end piece of a series of lawless conservative plots, plots that included the most incredible personal vilification ever known in this country and also included subversive efforts to remove him from office, in any way and by any means necessary, no matter how violent or criminal.

The impeachment itself involved acts of coercion, blackmail, and bribery by Republican Tom De Lay as well as the dishonest use of false allegations in raw FBI files improperly supplied by Kenneth Starr and Louis J. Freeh as well as by Bear Bryant, Freeh's fanatical, Clinton-hating assistant. Then, in the presidential election of 2000, De Lay sent criminal thugs, led by Jesse Helms acolyte John Bolton, to Florida to assault poll workers and stop an honest and objective recount ordered by the Florida Supreme Court. This treasonous subversion likely rescued the Bush family fix as the ultraconservatives on the US Supreme Court wouldn't have dared to abort the election with Gore ahead in the count. This was an out-and-out coup, carried out by the Republican Party.

Only a year or so ago, an apparently-drunk Charleton Heston appeared on television before a mob of gun lovers where he grabbed a rifle and shook it above his head while screaming out his hatred for Democrats in office and urging the mob on as they shook their fists and raged uncontrollably against democratic government and anyone who dared to think of regulating their guns. Heston said that the so-called "right to bear arms" is precious because it would allow him and his gun chums to march on and overthrow the government if it dares to do anything that gun owners and other "patriots" don't like.

In just the same way, Attorney General John Ashcroft has also called for the overthrow of the government of the United States by force and violence and has promised to personally interpret and apply the second amendment of the Constitution in accord with the wishes of the extremist gun lovers and without any regard for the rule of law or any court decision whatever.

With his racist employment of the repressive "Patriot Act," Ashcroft has also established the elements of a police state in this country and has created a climate of fear and hate that is on display every day against journalists, entertainers, librarians, book readers, legal immigrants, and just anyone who criticizes or disagrees with George Bush in any way. I have never heard of any American communist behaving like this, ever threatening blatantly to overthrow the government, ever subverting the Constitution, ever stealing an election, ever shooting anyone, ever throwing any bomb.

If communism had been a race or a nationality, the conservatives would be guilty of a vast genocide, certainly the worst in American history. The enormous hatred of communists inspired in the American people by the McCarthyites would be disgusting to everyone if it had been directed against any other group of people. This hatred was required of American citizens as a proof of patriotic loyalty and even religious morality. It was an article of fanatical belief that every communist and everyone who could be associated with communism in any way, however strained and false, was absolutely evil and demonic. Anyone accused of any form of communism was auto-matically guilty. It was so evil a force in the minds of the anti-communists that just being accused was proof enough; after all, if your anti-communist hatred was intense enough, then no one could accuse *you* of being a com-munist, a dupe, or a sympathizer.

In short, it was a sin, a crime, and a treason not to hate communism with all of your being, enough to convince everyone of your deep desire to attack, decimate, spit upon, and kill anyone accused or suspected. Active and vio-lent hatred is what the anti-communists warriors demanded of everyone, hatred without reservation or equivocation, hatred without discrimination or proof of guilt, hatred based on the fervor of faith alone, murderous and merciless hatred, genocidal hatred.

And so it went for fifty years. The Republicans fed on communism with great hunger during that time and got tremendously fat politically off of their own propaganda. Millions of Americans believed most of what they said and, in addition to voting for their wonderful patriotism, gave them trillions of dollars to fight communism with. Anti-communism was a ter-rific business and it enriched many and made still more famous and morally upright. Even today, the American military is still hugely bloated at least partly because the conservative politicians and the generals are afraid that communism will resurrect itself, perhaps this time in the guise of world-terrorism or muslim fanaticism.

No, anti-communism isn't dead. In the 1992 presidential election, George H.W. Bush, James Baker, and their operatives called Bill Clinton a communist and tried to fake paperwork to make it seem that, like Oswald, he had traveled to Moscow and Prague to renounce his citizenship and join the Soviets. Then, conservative judges and prosecutors conspired to cover up the facts so as to protect the Bush family from punishment for its own crimes and treasons. As for all of those millions of internal subversives, they seem to have withered away or converted into something else. You can be sure the Republicans will revive them when they need them again in future elections or to justify still greater military spending.

So what if you can prove that, in the distant past, somebody was a com-munist? It doesn't mean anything. If you want to become an anti-commu-nist hero, you have to prove that such a person was an actual spy and a foreign agent, that he or she actually did something criminal and subversive. In the days of capitalist failure, people often called themselves communists or socialists or even signed up as actual members of the Communist Party for all kinds of reasons, some of them noble and patriotic. The Great Conservative Depression caused enormous suffering throughout the world. The capitalists were responsible for this suffering and deprivation and, when the economic catastrophe arrived, they hunkered down and intensified their abuse of the poor, the hungry, the homeless, and the jobless. As a direct result, many suffered great agony and some died. That is why large numbers of people became disgusted with capitalism and became socialists or even communists. It was not only understandable, it was inevitable and, under the circumstances, maybe even moral. It was not evil and it did not make those who joined up into traitors and enemies of the state.

All of this rebellion against capitalism frightened and outraged the owners and bosses and they swore they would hunt down and destroy every last communist on earth. Sad to say, they defined communism so as to include progressives, socialists, liberals, moderates, secularists, relativists, trade unionists, humanists, evolutionists, anarchists, democrats, ad infinitum. From that day to this one, the conservatives, especially those in the Republican Party, have been engaged in a vast campaign of accusation and retribution. Everyone who flirted with communism for even a second, everyone who spoke a single word in favor of working people or the poor, everyone who believed in and worked for civil rights, everyone who joined a union or opposed a war, everyone who believed in actual democracy was the enemy and had to be punished. The hate campaign continues even now, after the demise of actually existing communism. The fanaticism and viciousness of the Republicans is unequaled in American history and there is no question that anti-communism was, in fact, a fascist attack against democracy in the guise of patriotism and state security.

Now, these exact same things are happening all over again. George W. Bush is the new McCarthy and anti-terrorism is the new anti-communism; and, unfortunately for us all, the American people are once again supporting the demagoguery, hatred, and violence of the Republicans including brutal wars against innocent and defenseless civilians who have never threatened or attacked the United States in any way at all.

Chapter 9. Conservatism, Liberalism, and Libertarianism

The dictionary defines conservatism as opposition to change and defense of the existing order and its institutions. Words used to define it further include prudence, restraint, stability, dependability, safety, efficiency, et cetera. The order and the institutions these words were used to defend included the rule of divine kings and their aristocratic courts. A little more than two centuries ago, that aristocracy was threatened by the Enlightenment and then by the American and French revolutions. Those uprisings were directed against kings, aristocrats, and priests. The defenders of that old order were such people as Edmund Burke, Joseph de Maistre, Thomas Hobbes, and Thomas Malthus.

Then, the Industrial Revolution brought wealth to rising numbers of middle class business people. Their power soon began to eclipse the divine order. The new aristocracy of money did not end the old aristocratic order, however. Instead, it melded with the old order and embraced its values. A new conservative order was born. Over time, it began to gobble up the old order without revolting against it. This new order was neither liberal nor democratic. The old royal definitions no longer applied but the love of fixed authority, a stable and rigid order, and a safe haven for money and property still remained.

And so today the Republican Party is the leader of a worldwide conservative movement that began long ago with the rule of divine kings and royal aristocracies. It is reactionary. It seeks to return us all to the earlier days of fixed authority and dominant aristocracy. To do this, it has had to reshape its belief system.

Thanks to the American and French revolutions, divine kings, royal blood, and formal aristocracies are no longer acceptable. Succession to power can no longer be based on bloodlines and god's holy anointment. All the same, today's conservatives still claim that their god puts them in power and that Jesus is their inspiration and guide. This was in evidence in the administrations of William McKinley, Ronald Reagan, and George W. Bush. It's astonishing that they should claim Jesus as a model since they reject every one of his beliefs and sayings and embrace a system of belief that totally opposes everything Jesus represented.

The conservatives are still absolutists. They rage against equality, secularism, relativism (they mean tolerance), civil rights, human rights, democratic government, dissent, and, most of all, liberalism. They fiercely defend the rights of inheritance and attack any taxing of unearned income, that is, the income of those who don't work and live off of their property and wealth. They demand austerity and balanced budgets from government and, at the same time, oppose any government assistance for working people, the poor, the sick, the hungry, the homeless, and the old and worn. No matter what it costs, they seek overseas conquests in the interests of business success and missionary christianity. Accordingly, they fervently support all military and police power and bitterly condemn "peaceniks," pacifists, and welfarists as unpatriotic, weak, and subversive of the order and obedience they yearn for. In other words, they retain the beliefs of the old, divine aristocracies and they rage against the very same enemies. It's shocking that they should claim to be christians, the followers of Jesus.

These modern conservatives are social darwinists and eugenicists. With the fall of divine and royal power, they needed a new justification for their system of rule. They now rely on the hegemony of capitalism. The social darwinist and eugenicist movements provide the rationale. This thinking identifies capitalism as god's holy instrument; competitive success under its rule is proof of superiority. In their world, the fit survive and the unfit go under. According to conservatives, the successfully rich and eminent are fit to rule. Workers and the poor are not. The conservatives see biology and the hand of god in their own rise and rule.

They believe that their country and their religion are exceptional and that they themselves are fated to rule the world for god, country, and corporation. Any opposition to them is sinful and unpatriotic. They think that they have a divine right to power. This philosophy is embedded in the Republican Party and, though expressed in somewhat different frameworks, it infuses the conservative and libertarian movements too.

In the last few decades, the neoconservatives have joined the conservative meld. That movement began as a kind of confused Trotskyism informed by a corrupted form of dominionist zionism. The operating philosophy of this strange group comes from the writings of Leo Strauss, a former University of Chicago philosophy professor who said that "the rule of the wise must be absolute rule" and "true democracy is an act against nature and must be prevented at all costs." This describes the true mission of the neoconservative and zionist movements as well as the continuing mission of the old conservative order.

Many conservatives hearken back to the days of English, Roman, and Spartan imperialism and proudly call themselves imperialist and even colonialist. However, journalists and political intellectuals choose to ignore these pronouncements and describe the Iraq war, for example, as an attempt by Republicans, especially neoconservatives, to establish a system of democratic liberalism in Iraq and the Middle East.

Even "liberal Hawks" endorse this fantastic claim and criticize the Bush war against Iraq only because of its incompetence and its failure to achieve a victory and establish an orderly occupation there. They apparently cannot see that Republicans do not believe in or like democracy and never have. That they see Republicans as somehow liberal is astonishing. The quickest way to insult and anger a Republican or any conservative is to call him or her a liberal. And certainly no one in touch with American reality can believe that Republicans ever miss an opportunity to sneer at and attack the government, even when they are in charge of it. This government that they attack so consistently and with such contempt is the democratic government of the United States. Attacking democracy does not amount to supporting it nor does it square with aggressive war and an occupation maintained by armed might and corporate domination.

The conservative movement today is driven by a fear of democracy and a hatred for permissiveness. Permissiveness is the name given to freedom by its enemies. Today, the conservative movement is about opposing, attacking, repressing, and restraining ordinary people; it is about rising above them, holding them down, and knocking them back and away from the table. It is not about the prudence and restraint it claims for itself nor is it about small government or minding your own business or about family values or moral uprightness. At its heart, it is violent and assaultive; it is aggressive toward and distrustful of different others; it is suspicious and stingy; it is greedy and grasping and ungenerous. It is unmerciful and often cruel.

The conservative movement is anti-democratic and anti-humanistic. It opposes every civil right for the dispossessed and embraces every wealthy privilege for the few. It has no active program that does not promote private power, police force, and military conquest over despised enemies. It allies itself and this country with tyrants and death squads across the world just as long as those tyrants are or pretend to be against any ism that threatens oligarchy or promotes the welfare of the people. It isn't about conserving anything. It's about developing everything, using it up — for a profit. It's about establishing wealth and privilege and maintaining them on the backs of working people and consumers. Conservatives even curse the fresh and greening earth, the free-flowing waters, and the very bosom of the earth.

The libertarian movement is part of the conservative movement and the Republican Party is the political arm of both. It is a fairly recent phenomenon but its adherents claim its ideas stem from John Locke, John Stuart Mill, Thomas Hobbes, and Adam Smith. In the United States, however, it got its main impetus from Ayn Rand and the Chicago school of economics that imported the ideas of Ludwig von Mises and Fredrick von Hayek from the Austrian school of economics.

I include in this chapter an extensive description of the nature of libertarian belief because I think the libertarian movement has redefined the conservative movement and the Republican Party in recent years. Although the libertarian movement takes its claimed belief in civil liberties and its opposition to unlimited military and police power from liberalism, it departs from liberalism in its hatred of democratic government and its fervent belief in the sacredness of private property. This love of property manifests itself as a predatory capitalism unregulated in any way by the instruments of democratic governance. Without the influence of democratic liberalism around its fringes, libertarianism would be easy to identify with conservatism and even fascism.

I think that American liberalism itself descends from the philosophy of Thomas Jefferson, the American Declaration of Independence and the Bill of

Rights, from the French Declaration of the Rights of Man and the Citizen, The United Nations Universal Declaration of Human Rights, the Emancipation Proclamation, and from the Thirteenth, Fourteenth, Fifteenth, and Nineteenth amendments to the American Constitution

Liberal democrats believe in civil rights, human rights, and the rights of working people and consumers. They believe as well in the constructive use of government to serve the interests of the whole people, to advance their welfare, and to protect their rights and their property through the instruments of democracy. They believe that both the predatory greed of uncontrolled capitalism and the proselytizing salvationism of fundamentalist religion are the enemies of democracy and that they must be regulated to prevent them from destroying democratic government and devouring the rights of the people.

The whole history of democracy has been a fight against the power of kings, big men, dictators, priests, preachers, mullahs, and imperial economic exploiters of all kinds. What these tyrants want is money, property, and privilege for themselves and they want it all to flow into their hands in a never-ending stream so that they and their inheritors can always be rich and stay on top. Thus, they know that they must control the work and the consumption of the masses to protect and preserve their greedy system. This struggle between masters and servants is, in large part, about the use and supervision of work.

Religion is also an instrument of conservative control. Its purpose is to keep the people docile and obedient. The religious system parallels and supports the economic system and it seeks, and has, massive amounts of property and privilege. In fact, the religious system is even more rigidly hierarchical and at least as predatory as the money system though it professes to be about morals rather than about material gain. It seeks to supervise the private lives of the people and to tell them what they may and may not believe about the nature of the world and the story of its beginning and its ultimate ending. Thus, religion roots out a wide space for itself in the niches of the economic system and helps that system keep the people under control and servile.

Franklin Roosevelt said, "Necessitous men are not free men." This was an important statement of purpose for the New Deal, an announcement of the government's responsibility to ordinary citizens. Though conservatives and libertarians deny it fanatically, the very freedom of the people depends on the protection of government against the abuses of private power, especially the abuses of predatory commerce and salvationist religion.

The New Deal provided the fullest expression of democracy ever seen in the United States, or anywhere. It did this under very trying circumstances, circumstances imposed by the Great Conservative Depression and then by the war against a rising fascism defined by the melding together of state power and corporate power in Italy and Germany. In both of those countries, the christian and conservative authorities joined the fascist meld and supported it as a bulwark against the egalitarian and democratic polity aroused by the Enlightenment and the American and French revolutions.

In theory, libertarianism is based on individual liberty, and owning property is considered a necessary part of that liberty. Thus, each person is considered to be the absolute owner of his life and property. Despite their differences, libertarianism is allied with conservatism. Some libertarian theoreticians like Mises, Hayek, Friedman, and James Buchanan claimed that liberty is tied to economic efficiency and that, therefore, they can tolerate a limited democracy as long as it is used to promote the interests of commerce and marketism.

Libertarians say that there must be no infringement on the rights of business owners. They say that everyone must be left free to discriminate against others in all personal and business dealings. They say that everyone must be allowed to take risks even to the point of harm, injury, or death. They say there must be no ban on any medical treatment or any drug or other substance. They say there must be no ban on and no regulation of gun ownership no matter how many people are killed by gunfire. They say that government must not ban or require a license for any product or service and must not prevent or regulate any kind of commercial advertising whether false or true. Libertarians justify economic inequality and overt racism as outcomes of people's freedom to choose their own actions. They consider all government ownership and regulation a form of mass compulsion. For these reasons, libertarians oppose liberal democracy. Without much evidence, libertarians claim that Thomas Jefferson was a libertarian.

There is a fundamental contradiction in the libertarian philosophy. When people live together, they have to establish some level of order and predictability in their shared communities and in their personal lives and relationships. It's up to them to decide collectively just what rules and standards their shared community can and should have. The only way this can be decided with any degree of fairness and with any hope of stability is through a system of voting or some other means of mutual agreement. This is known as democratic government. Libertarians don't like democratic government. They call it "collectivism." At best, they consider it a necessary evil. At worst, they consider it automatically tyrannical and somehow socialist or even communistic. They greatly fear majoritarian tyranny and want a special niche for themselves at the top of the pyramid. They don't admit that aristocracy at the top means subservience below.

The American and French revolutions took up these concerns and the revolutionaries decided that a declaration of individual and personal rights was necessary. Thus, the Americans adopted a Bill of Rights to protect individuals against majoritarian tyranny in certain private and personal areas. Later, the French adopted a Declaration of the Rights of Man and the Citizen. They went even further than the Americans in affirming the rights of their citizens. Ever since, the whole world has been phasing out divine kings and the aristocracies that helped them control the common people forced for so long to live under their dominance.

Libertarians do not want to compromise with their neighbors or live under any community or state rules and standards. They believe that they should have the unlimited right to use their personal force and their property to exploit others. What they want for themselves is aristocracy, not democracy. They know that they can live the privileged lives of extreme individualism and what they call "liberty" only if they can find or create a system that allows them to rise above other people. Their chosen system is unregulated capitalism, also known as competitive "free enterprise."

Rand Paul, the fervent libertarian Senator from Kentucky, says he personally believes in civil rights but that commercial property is so inviolate and so sacred that no government has a right to tell a property owner, through civil rights enactments or anything else, what he can and cannot do with his property. He describes this unchecked use of property as "libertarian," that is, as freedom incarnate. Indeed, if commercial property is owned and used strictly in private and for no public purpose whatever, then such behavior might be somewhat rational, maybe even permissible though a product of discriminatory hatred. However, if any property has a public use and/or purpose, then its use becomes a community matter and not just a personal and individual matter. Intruding private property into public space or air and using it for public purposes makes it public just as the violence of police and military acts are public functions governable by democratically elected officials and not by private individuals serving their own personal interests alone. No foreign power would be allowed to push its property, its people, or its functions into public space inside our country while pretending it was exercising a private right of property not subject to anyone else's control or regulation. Alien bodies and interests do not have privileged protections under a democratic society or any other.

It really ought to be clear to anyone that the very purpose of democracy is to establish a public sphere under the control and management of the people through their elected representatives. In other words, democracy establishes a common ground (call it a "marketplace" of ideas and activities if you like) on which we can all stand and act as equals, as citizens with full rights and full access to public goods and activities. Democracy does not abolish or appropriate private property or seek to tyrannize private behavior but it does insist that the private stay within its own bounds and not intrude on the public domain just as it insists that other foreign or alien bodies observe its sovereignty. Nevertheless, democracy does have a stern duty to regulate the often-aggressive encroachments of private power, especially the encroachments of religion and commerce. If everything is privatized, as libertarians wish, and, if nothing private is ever regulated by democratic enactments, then there can be no democracy and no liberty. The idea of a dominant private force immune from any and all democratic controls is totalitarian. Thus, the libertarians are not libertarian at all; instead they are or want to be elitist rulers practicing an especially aggressive form of extreme individualism. Libertarianism is a system of aristocratic privilege for the few, not a handmaiden of freedom as it pretends.

To square the circle, libertarians claim that they are devoted to a vague "non-aggression principle." Presumably, this means that they will not allow themselves to exploit, injure or kill their neighbors. Obviously, this principle can only apply to direct aggression but not to the indirect aggressions that are an inevitable part of owner–worker and owner–consumer arrangements. Libertarians say that all such arrangements are entirely voluntary and never hurtful or demeaning. In any case, they say, competition results in the rise of the fit and the proper positioning of the unfit at the bottom of the pyramid. The rich deserve to be rich, they say. The poor deserve to be poor. No government has any right to "level" the reward system or even the playing field. Some are inherently superior to others, they say. This is natural selection, they say, a matter of biology. Competition is the way nature (or god) determines the right levels of existence for us all. Efforts by government to create any degree of "artificial" equality are tyrannical and unnatural.

Conservatives and libertarians share a common contempt for democratic government and an intense desire to privatize everything in existence so it can all be made profitable. In fact, they not only want everything privatized, they also want to do away with democratic regulation altogether. This two-pronged policy seeks to turn all public property into private property and then seeks to prevent the public from regulating any of it. This is a clever way of canceling democracy entirely and it is a formula for aristocratic totalitarianism. Of course, they do make exceptions for the military and police power they know they need to protect their property and to keep down the resentful masses. That's why Republicans turn every election into a patriotic guise in praise of "our boys over there." They also virulently attack their electoral opponents as "soft" on communism and terrorism, or they use some other "security" issue to demean them; indeed their attacks are so extreme that they invariably call their opponents "traitors."

Libertarians don't want to live in a community of cooperating citizens. When they are forced to do so, they refuse nearly all shared responsibilities. They don't see that they have any duty to others as a condition of citizenship. They want to be totally free to discriminate against others, to use their money and property with no strings attached and with no care about what their "liberty" is certain to do to others. They don't think that government should tax them at all or require anything of them, no matter how much their behavior impinges on the lives of other people. In other words, libertarians believe that their property is sacred and that the people in their communities or businesses and on or near their property have no right to regulate, restrain, tax, or punish them no matter what they do.

Like conservatives, libertarians oppose everything public including free milk for children, vaccinations, free mail delivery, speed limits, traffic laws, gun controls, public parks, national forests, public roads, canals and harbors, public education, libraries, racial integration, the minimum wage, usury laws, unions, food for the hungry, public shelters, free burial even for veterans, all public health and sanitation programs, public radio and television, Social Security, environmental laws and regulations, and on and on endlessly.

No one should mistake Thomas Jefferson for a libertarian. He thought that the rising Hamiltonian commercialism he saw around him was tyrannical. Unlike Jefferson, libertarians claim that property is sacred; their greatest icon is commercial property, not so much ordinary personal property. They like property in the large and want it to be used for gain and exploitation. Their stock terms for their version of liberty are "free enterprise" and "free markets." They idolize "competition" and regard it as the motor of commercialism and the corporatism they so dearly love. They extol businessmen as heroic creators of wealth and condemn working people as business fodder, forever rebellious, disobedient, and completely unfit for anything better than everyday toil. The loyalty of libertarians is reserved for businessmen, entrepreneurs, and republican politicians who want to privatize everything public and "free" it all from any democratic regulation whatever.

Conservatives and libertarians are very much alike but, unlike conservatives, libertarians do believe somewhat in civil liberties and oppose foreign wars and interventions most of the time (not during the cold war, however). They each hate democratic government and love private commercial power and they each hate liberalism and all public enterprise. They both want to privatize everything public (except the military and police forces) and they both want to wipe out all forms of regulation and oversight over business activities. Unlike conservatives, libertarians are not religious or theocratic. Indeed, many are atheists as was Ayn Rand, their goddess. Also unlike the conservatives, they are not in favor of using government power to oversee and dictate the sex and reproductive lives of citizens and usually disapprove of government spying and wiretapping (unless it is directed against alleged communists, terrorists, and sometimes liberals). On the other hand, conservatives sometimes approve of social services and welfare measures. Libertarians never do.

Libertarians are people who pretend to believe in liberty above all else. So, did anyone ever hear of a libertarian who was a member of the Democratic Party? Did anyone ever see a libertarian marching with Martin Luther King Jr. or supporting integration or affirmative action? Were there any libertarians in the streets opposing the unjustified American attacks on Vietnam or Iraq or even its attacks against Guatemala, Nicaragua, El Salvador, Cuba, Grenada, or Panama? Do any libertarians agree with Michael Moore, Cindy Sheehan, Ralph Nader, Noam Chomsky, or Howard Zinn about anything at all?

Are libertarians secularist in any sense whatever? Many libertarians claim to be Ayn Rand atheists, but do any of them ever join liberals and democrats in efforts to protect children against forced school prayer or to protect government property and public discourse against the strictures and assaults of fanatical christians out to force their religion and their rituals on everyone else? Do any of them belong to Americans United for Separation of Church and State?

What liberty do libertarians support then? Well, they support the "liberty" of rich people with large amounts of property. In fact, they regard private property as sacred and worship predatory capitalism, which they regard as the one and only true depository of liberty. They think that the wealthy have a right to rule working people and consumers, because the successful and prominent have made it on their own, or through "just" inheritances of unearned income untaxed by any "death tax;" and they think that this makes them superior to the unfit middle and lower classes. Libertarians are social darwinists and reverse marxists. They have no use at all for civil rights, human rights, or the rights of working people. They are fervently antidemocratic because democracy is the great leveler and the great regulator of private power. Anyway, they say, government is always incompetent and always wrong because it is insufficiently obedient to the property owners.

Even their lost beloved, Ronald Reagan, did not go far enough in his assaults on the evil democratic government of the United States and in his efforts to cancel out such abominations as civil rights, human rights, environmentalism, regulation, and all government interference with the privileges of the wealthy property owners. Although his lust for a vast privatization of everything except military and police power accompanied by the rise of a dominant christian religion was noble, it did not go far enough and needed an even more fanatical Republican, George W. Bush, to complete the job and save America from the liberals and the communist/terrorists.

Of course, a few of the libertarians were slightly disturbed by the Reagan/Bush support for unbridled religion but they were always loyal and never said so out loud and in public. After all, they knew, or thought they knew, that their religion of unregulated capitalism was more powerful than that of the mumbling evangelicals. Better yet, many of the evangelicals have been converted and now describe themselves as "free-enterprise christians."

Ludwig von Mises, Friedrich August von Hayek, and Milton "von" Friedman were responsible for the preposterous claim that socialism is a system of centralized economic planning that leads inevitably to tyranny. In fact, like it or not, socialism is the ultimate decentralization, a means by which the worker, singly or in voluntary association with other workers, exercises control over his own work and the product of that work. It is capitalism that centralizes all authority, all planning, and all profit in the hands of a central owner (often a single owner) who exploits the work of others for his own profit and privilege. Centralized planning and control are the very essence of capitalism but the conservative and libertarian ideologues pretend that capitalism is, somehow, a system of rugged individualism that is the true expression of democracy.

One definition of tyranny is the arbitrary control of the many by one or a small number of authoritative figures. A factory owner or other business owner is such a figure. Has anyone ever heard of a factory owner being elected by the workers in the factory or even by the general population? Has anyone ever heard of a factory owner conducting a referendum on his policies and business practices or on anything at all? If language means anything, then quite obviously it is the owner in whom all the authority and power is centralized and it is the owner who is the tyrant, not workers controlling their own work and acting in voluntary association with other workers in their own interests. Socialism is obviously democratic by definition and capitalism is obviously anti-democratic. It is impossible for any rational person to draw any other conclusion.

The smartest of the conservative and libertarian lot don't quite say that capitalism *is* democracy because they know it's an absurd claim. Instead, they say, "capitalism is a necessary condition for democracy." In other words, the only way to have political democracy is by having economic tyranny. They pretend they don't understand that the absolute dominance of corporate or lesser bosses over all working people and all consumers restricts political democracy and corrupts it. Instead, they claim to believe that democratically elected government is tyrannical when it regulates, restricts, or taxes business owners in the interests of workers, consumers, the poor, the unemployed, and the down and out.

To be very generous, the two vons — Mises and Hayek — and Milton Friedman were certainly oddballs. That they were incredibly irrational and dead wrong is obvious. To be less generous, they were totalitarian capitalists, that is to say, fascists.

You will never hear a conservative or a so-called libertarian criticize private power. The only power they hate is the power of the federal government. However, it is not the coercive power of the feds that they hate. Rather, they hate the power of the government to regulate and diminish the coercive abuses of their private force. Conservatives and libertarians love private power, that is to say, the economic and religious power of their clients, the corporatists and, for the conservatives, the christian zealots as well. The government power that they hate is the democratic power that seeks to limit and regulate local and private tyranny.

They argue that the constitution protects the people against the power of democratic government but not against the tyranny of private power. They have always made such arguments. They have always believed that the democratic government of the United States has no power over the actions of business and religious interests. In other words, they believe that business and religious groups have a perfect right to oppress the people in any way they choose and that the government has no right to intervene.

Of course, this is a preposterous argument. To argue that laws and prohibitions are tyrannical when applied by democratic government but wonderful, free, and noble when applied by local authorities and private organizations is insane. It is only a way of devolving tyranny. They argue that even the Bill of Rights doesn't protect individual citizens from abuse of their rights unless the federal government is the abuser. Such a view not only devalues but utterly destroys the rights specified in the Bill of Rights and everywhere else in the constitution.

Can there be any doubt that what conservatives and libertarians really want is the total destruction of democratic government and the establishment of an absolute tyranny over the people by local authorities and by private economic and religious powers? Can there be any doubt that they hate democracy with a venomous force never equaled by any foreign enemy?

Chapter 10. Jeffersonian Liberalism

The libertarians and the conservatives both claim to be Jeffersonian. They endlessly tell us that the best form of government is one that governs least, a principle that they violate with every breath they draw. It's true that they oppose the helping and healing power of government; but they love its military and police power. The conservative program is always the same; it consists of imperial wars abroad as well as repression and censorship at home. In theory though rarely in practice, libertarians disagree with their conservative brothers about the need for war and repression.

Jefferson did not condemn government per se or oppose the constructive use of government to protect the freedom of the people and to improve their lot, as the libertarians and conservatives claim he did. What he did oppose was military, police, religious, and commercial tyranny and he condemned them equally, whether they came from government or private sources. He wanted no standing armies; he wanted severe limits on military and police power; he opposed the tyranny of organized religion and, most of all, he feared the potential tyranny of banks and industry. Jefferson was no laissez faire capitalist and he was no conservative or libertarian. In fact, Jefferson was the first American liberal and the descent of present-day liberalism from him is literal and direct.

The conservative movement has always stood against Jeffersonian liberalism. Alexander Hamilton, John Adams, and Theodore Roosevelt all execrated Jefferson for his liberalism. In colonial times, the conservatives were Tories, sometimes disguised as Federalists. Many of them opposed the American Revolution and, when the war had been won, they favored a constitutional monarchy, that is, a strong Hamiltonian central government with a king or a king-like figure at its head. Hamilton was a powerful tool for the banks and the commercial interests and, with Washington's icy tolerance, he set out to capture the American Revolution for this upper class. To a great extent, he succeeded.

Alexander Hamilton believed "the American economy required supervision and strategic management at the national level, and that concentrated wealth was a blessing rather than a curse." (Joseph J. Ellis, article, *The New Yorker*, October 29, 2001). Every Republican agrees absolutely with the second part of that statement. Of course, the extreme libertarians and conservatives (the anti-regulators and privateers) object to any government at all and want to "strangle government" or "drown it in a bath tub" or see it "wither away" entirely leaving only our commercial and religious masters to govern us all in detail.

I think that Thomas Jefferson was the real father of this country, not George Washington. George Washington provided no ideas and no eloquent words to guide his countrymen or inspire them. The Declaration of Independence was the first great statement of the American idea, the idea that citizens were free and equal and had a right to govern themselves. In writing the Declaration, Jefferson said he was trying to "say things that had never been said before" and called the Declaration "an expression of the American mind." Although he did not participate directly in the creation of the Bill of Rights, being in France at the time, the Bill of Rights was nevertheless another expression of the Jeffersonian idea. More than any other man, Jefferson embodied the spirit of modern democracy.

There were two great factions in America in those early days. Washington, Hamilton, and Adams were the Federalists, the conservatives of their time (but much more liberal than today's conservatives). They wanted a king-like governor and did not trust democracy; but they did not dare to stand against it openly because the Jeffersonian idea was in the wind and the great majority of citizens wanted democracy, not just independence. The Federalists also wanted a commerce and industry strong enough to dominate and rule over the nation in concert with a government subservient to commerce. It was Hamilton, backed by Washington and Adams, who fashioned the new commercial empire that would conquer the continent and finally, in our time, the whole world.

The Jeffersonians did not like the overweening power of banks and businessmen and did not want the fate of the people in their hands. In his last years, Jefferson saw the rising of a Hamiltonian state that he called, "a single and splendid government of an aristocracy, founded on banking institutions and moneyed corporations." Indeed, Jefferson wanted an amendment to the U.S. Constitution that would prevent commercial companies from becoming monopolies, stop them from dominating specific industries, and keep them from becoming so big they could control government. He said that such a market system would cause citizens to "eat one another" and also said "Banking establishments are more dangerous than standing armies." Jefferson believed in economic equality and participatory democracy with "every citizen an acting member of government."

One wonders how fools like Reagan, Helms, and Gingrich, who claimed Jefferson as their own, could possibly explain his loathing for the dominant commerce and corporatism that is worshipped today by the Republican conservatives and libertarians or his utter contempt for the organized christianity that those three conservatives tried with all of their might to impose on the people of America.

Astonishingly, libertarians and conservatives today claim that, like them, Jefferson hated democratic government and wanted to suppress it in favor of the private power of commerce and religion. In fact, what Jefferson hated above all else was the tyranny of private power; and his knowledge of the world then told him that commerce and religion were everywhere a part of the king's government and in the hands of his royal court. Jefferson wasn't objecting to the future power of a democratic government in the United States. He didn't know what such a democratic government would be like because there was nothing like it in the world then.

Of course, Jefferson was suspicious of central governments generally because he feared that they might form alliances with bankers, businessmen, preachers, and priests to the detriment of the people as indeed they have. Thus, he talked often of the rights and freedoms of the people and urged frequent revolutions against tyranny of every kind. To hear conservatives tell it, Jefferson would be on their side and against civil rights, human rights, and the rights of working people if he were alive today. Well, Jefferson was a great supporter of the French Revolution, a revolution that advanced these values and opposed autocratic power in all of its conservative and reactionary forms.

Conservatives and libertarians think they are endorsing Jefferson when they quote him as saying, "That government governs best that governs least." Though Jefferson probably didn't know much, if anything, about such isms, his statement can be taken as anarchistic or socialistic. Anarchism is no government at all and socialism is the ultimate decentralization, one that gives the working man and woman control over his and her own work and life without having to obey any orders from owners, bosses, and government bureaucrats.

Conservatives themselves believe in a collection of business and religious centralizations and they want all of the real power in private hands; but they want the collaboration of a weak and obedient government in the enforcement of their commercial policies and religious dogmas. It is surely obvious that every company and church is ruled by a central authority of some kind. In any case, conservatives only oppose central authority when it is democratic and thus not under their control.

The libertarians and conservatives claim that the Virginians, led by Jefferson, believed that proper economic policy was simply getting out of the way. I don't think that Jefferson saw it that way at all. He wanted to suppress the overweening power of banks, industry, and religion. He didn't want despotic private power any more than he wanted despotic government power. Shocked by the poverty he saw in France, he said, "Legislators cannot invent too many devices to subdivide property. We cannot let this happen in America." He also said, "Another means of silently lessening the inequality of property is to exempt all from taxation below a certain point, and to tax the higher portions of property in geometrical progression as they rise."

James Madison, a Jeffersonian to the core, said he supported "laws which, without violating the rights of property, reduce extreme wealth to a state of mediocrity, and raise extreme indigence toward a state of comfort." In the same spirit, Benjamin Franklin submitted a provision for inclusion in the Pennsylvania constitution which said: "that an enormous Proportion of Property vested in a few individuals is dangerous to the Rights, and destructive of the Common Happiness, of Mankind; and therefore every free state hath a Right by its Laws to discourage the Possession of such property." This provision was voted down by the wealthy property owners.

Though he didn't say it right out and it wasn't so clear at the time, I think it is inherent in Jefferson's philosophy that you cannot have individual liberty unless you have a reasonably strong democratic authority ready and able to protect that liberty against the attacks of local and private power, especially commercial and religious power. Thus, I don't agree — as the conservatives insist — that Franklin Roosevelt's New Deal was anti-Jeffersonian and anti-democratic. The New Deal was for the rights of the people and hostile to the abusive power of Big Business and the banks.

Furthermore, the people and the business interests of that time knew this very well. There's no way to tell but I think Jefferson would have been a New Dealer if he had lived during or after the Great Conservative Depression of 1929. Roosevelt himself believed this and considered Jefferson the great hero of the Democratic Party.

Libertarians and conservatives see the Declaration of Independence as being an attack against all "governmental power." On the contrary, it was a direct attack against the King's power, not an attack against any democratic government whatever. The libertarians and conservatives are being tricky and dishonest when they claim the revolutionary Thomas Jefferson as their philosophical father. Alexander Hamilton, the father of money, was their boy. It's true that, contrary to their pretended opposition to big government, Hamilton wanted big government but he wanted it entirely on the side of commerce and industry and not at all on the side of working people and consumers. Somewhere recently, I saw an account of how, in the 1920s and 1930s, the bankers in New York City hung Hamilton's picture on the wall at the Chamber of Commerce because he was "the one Founding Father who thought and cared a lot about money." Hamilton was the conservative authoritarian, Jefferson the liberal democrat.

The proof of Jefferson's greatness is in the words of the Declaration of Independence and in his Voltarian respect for truth, reason, and justice in politics, religion, and human endeavor. Tom Jefferson and Tom Paine were the true radicals of their time in America. Both greatly admired the French Revolution and both supported it strongly, Jefferson in the drawing rooms of Paris just before the revolution and Paine in the streets and eventually in a jail cell. They each had romantic ideas about revolution and thought it a necessary tool in the fight against oligarchy and royal rule.

They each believed in "The People" as a mystical force standing behind the principles of democracy and above their own rulers. Jefferson and Paine were the great revolutionaries and subversives of their times, the champions of self-governance by the masses. The fight against tyrannical and hereditary rule has continued everywhere in the world to this very day and it all started with the Jeffersonians. One of the great breaking points in human history was the American Revolution and the spirit of that revolution and the later French Revolution was Jeffersonian.

It seems to me that libertarian and conservative demands for weak democracy and strong private power are a distortion of the "true meaning of the American Revolution." The founding fathers did not fear and hate the central power of *democratic government*. They weren't attacking democracy; they were establishing a democratic government for us all. There was, at that time, no democratic government anywhere for them to fear or point to as a bad example as the conservatives of today point their dirty fingers at the democratic idea itself.

What the founders feared and hated was the central power of the English king and all kings. In their time, every government on earth was under the power of a king of some kind and virtually every king was in total control of political, commercial, and religious life. The king's power was monolithic and oppressive. That was what the founding fathers were against.

CHAPTER 11. REPUBLICANISM?

Thomas Jefferson founded the Democratic–Republican Party; later, the word "Republican" was dropped because it was redundant. Jefferson was an Enlightenment democrat and he was the father of American liberalism. The Jeffersonians opposed Alexander Hamilton's intense commercialism and his efforts to further the dominance of rich property owners in league with the government. Under John Adams, the Federalists passed alien and sedition laws and jailed a number of Jeffersonians under the provisions of those laws. Jefferson decided to run against President John Adams because he saw an aristocracy of money and privilege being put in place by the Federalist followers of Adams and Hamilton. The election of 1800 was the first time in history that all free white men were allowed to vote. In office, Jefferson was unable to halt Hamilton's commercial juggernaut but the alien and sedition acts were expired.

The Republican Party was organized in July of 1854 in Jackson, Michigan. A man named Joseph Medill suggested the name "Republican Party." The new party was abolitionist and hostile to Southern slavery. Its first candidate for the presidency was John C. Freemont; he lost the election of 1856 to James Buchanan.

In *The New York Review* of November 25, 2010, the historian James M. McPherson writing about *The Fiery Trial: Abraham Lincoln and American Slavery* by Eric Foner says that, in 1854, Abraham Lincoln protested the Stephen A. Douglas' Kansas–Nebraska Act that opened certain of the "territories carved out of the Louisiana Purchase" to slavery. Lincoln called this a "covert real zeal for the spread of slavery [that] I cannot but hate because of the monstrous injustice of slavery itself." McPherson observes that Douglas' action "sparked the formation of the 'new anti-Nebraska' Republican Party, which would nominate Lincoln for president six years later." When Lincoln ran against Douglas for the senate in 1858, he said, "I have always hated slavery I think as much as any Abolitionist." He also said, "If slavery is not wrong, nothing is wrong. I cannot remember when I did not so think and feel." McPherson observes that Lincoln was antislavery but not an abolitionist. He says that, like Jefferson, an antislavery slave owner, he "expected slavery eventually to die out in America."

Abraham Lincoln was the first member of the Republican Party to serve as president. He believed in the dominance of national government over state and local government and he came to believe in the abolition of slavery and in full citizenship for all Americans. He revered the Declaration of Independence and believed in Jefferson's "Jacobin" liberalism, including a belief in the superiority of labor over capital. He was not at all a believer in the principles that now dominate the Republican Party. He was, in fact, a liberal democrat as was the Theodore Roosevelt of the 1912 progressive presidential campaign.

Thus, initially, upon its founding shortly before the Civil War, the Republican Party contained within it strong abolitionist elements. After the war and after Lincoln's death, the Republican Party moved steadily to the right and became increasingly racist and far more conservative than it ever had been before. Rutherford B. Hayes was the first Republican to employ a "Southern Strategy." In a deal with Southern politicians, Hayes agreed to end Reconstruction and withdraw the remaining Northern troops in exchange for the Southern votes that made him president in 1876. This put the South entirely in the hands of white racists. Their party, the Southern Democratic Party, was based on white supremacy and a repressive system of Jim Crow segregation.

Segregation was simply a new kind of informal slavery maintained by regional threat and coercion rather than by any constitutional principle or any legitimate national law. In fact, segregation was clearly unconstitutional but the friendly Northern Republican Party and its judicial appointees supported segregation and refused to implement the "freedom amendments" which were passed by the "radical" Republican legislature in Washington and ratified just after the war. Thus, this country was ruled for nearly three quarters of a century by Republican presidents with the support of Southern congressional Democrats who quickly came to dominate the legislative system through a seniority rule that put Southerners in charge of nearly all congressional committees. During this time, there were only two Democratic presidents and both (Grover Cleveland and Woodrow Wilson) were conservatives who deviated very little from the principles of the Republican Party.

During this period, the Northern Democratic Party had little national power. It did have some regional and urban power heavily based on old Jeffersonian and abolitionist sentiments and on the influx and support of immigrants. A small handful of Republicans in the North continued to believe in the liberal Republican values of Abraham Lincoln and the prewar abolitionists. As the Republican Party was moving away from its civil rights and abolitionist principles, the Northern Democrats were embracing them.

Today's Republicans have adopted a John Birch Society claim that there are important differences between "democratism" and "republicanism" and that the Republican party embodies the original values of this country while the Democratic Party has become communistic or socialistic and has corrupted America's true values. In fact, there are no differences between the two terms. They mean the same thing but today's Republicans needed to invent a difference to justify their own deviation from the "Republican Democratic" principles of early America.

Both terms mean government by the people either directly or indirectly through elected representatives. These terms also mean majority rule but the American founders built in guarantees for minority and individual rights in certain personal and private areas of life by including a Bill of Rights. After the Civil War, newly minted amendments extended those rights to people of color and, later on, to women. Since then, the franchise has been growing and both social and economic rights have been expanding to the outrage of members of the Republican Party.

Another way of describing that original democratic republicanism includes the idea that the people rule as against rule by a single class, select group, or autocrat or by the rule of a commercial oligarchy. It may also be described as a doctrine of natural rights under which the elected rulers and the people are bound one to the other by a contract and by reciprocal obligations.

This real republicanism is far from the Republicanism of the Republican Party of today, indeed its near opposite. The Republicans' virulent contempt for democratic government ("government is the problem.") is contempt for real republicanism or democratism; after all, democratic *government* is the only democracy there is. The Republican Party of today is conservative, not republican, and its ideology aligns almost perfectly with the old royal European aristocracy and its fascist spawn; in other words, it is not even truly conservative.

Private commercial and religious powers cannot be democratic by their very natures. Both such private powers are rigidly hierarchic and each consists of rulers at the top and subordinates arranged in a descending pyramid of obedience and servanthood beneath them. The lower orders are under the thumb of the higher orders and commands from above are invariably absolutist and punitive. It should be noted that commercial and religious rulers are not elected and do not get their power from the people they seek to rule.

The Republican Party is the corporatist party and more and more it is becoming the theocratic party. It is no exaggeration to say that Republicans love private power and hate public power. Structurally, even today's democratic organizations look somewhat like the old kingly and aristocratic hierarchies; but in various ways, today's democratic arrangements include regulatory limits on the power at or near the top. Republicans despise these regulatory limiters and rage against "new rights," the "extension of rights," and liberal permissiveness. Indeed, they rage against everything public and demand that it all be privatized and deregulated in the interests of profit and dogma.

When I speak of the Republican Party, I am not just talking about the official membership of that Party. I am talking about an ancient conservative force led today by the Republican Party. Since shortly after the Republican Party's founding a century and a half ago and except for the period of the New Deal (from 1932 to 1968), this country has been under the control of that party's ideology. Thus, I finger the Republican Party as the leader and the engine of a worldwide conservative movement of disparate parts. Today it has no effective opposition anywhere on earth.

Over the last three centuries at least, the conservative movement has defined itself with some precision and it has produced a fairly definite group of spokespersons to spread its propaganda. These spokespersons have variously expressed their contempt for Western liberalism, for the central ideals of the Enlightenment and the American and French revolutions, and for the democratic government of the United States. They are still defending the divine rights of kings although they now attach those divine rights to theocratic and commercial institutions rather than specifically to a divine personage. In other words, they still believe in the same old aristocracy and in all of the values it held dear and forced on the lower orders through the imposition of rigid religious, ideological, and economic dogma. Thus, as of old, the conservative movement is reactionary, elitist, and tyrannical and it is still attacking the democratic revolution that overthrew the kings, the priests, and their followers. It is liberalism that led that democratic revolution and still defends it today against the onslaught of the authoritarian conservatives.

The struggle now is pretty much the same as it was three centuries ago. It is still a struggle between ordinary people — workers and consumers — and the bosses who rule over the economic, political, and religious spheres. It is still a struggle between democracy and tyranny and the words of the Republicans and the old conservatives make it abundantly clear just how much they despise democratic government and embrace absolutist private power.

It's interesting that the Republican Party has completely repudiated the policies and the philosophies of the only two great presidents it has ever produced: Theodore Roosevelt and Abraham Lincoln. The reason for this is the rise of McCarthyism, Nixonism, Reaganism, Gingrichism, and Bushism.

Just lately, there have been sneering attacks against Theodore Roosevelt by conservative and libertarian pundits and politicians because they realized with a shock that he believed in regulating the abuses of capitalism. Unlike them, he didn't believe that corporations could be trusted to respect the rights of consumers and working people; indeed, many described him as the "anti-trust" president. The Republican conservatives of his time, the Taft conservatives, detested Roosevelt. He ran against them in 1912 as a progressive and his campaign kept Taft from beating Wilson. Wilson was also a regulator but a tamer one than Roosevelt. Teddy Roosevelt's speeches in 1912 were a virtual blue print for the New Deal twenty years later. Of course, it was Teddy's nephew, Franklin, who finally put his progressive ideas about capitalism into effect against the outraged opposition of the Republican conservatives who claimed it was all a communist plot.

Teddy Roosevelt was only part liberal. He was a colonialist and an imperialist, a racist, a warmonger, an arrogant rich man, and a strong believer in tooth and fang individualism. These views are completely compatible with the predatory conservative view of today, of course. However, his distrust of capitalism and his belief in the regulatory power of government and in environmentalism made him the enemy of today's conservative and libertarian fanatics. For example, a number of them are demanding that Teddy Roosevelt's face be blasted off of the side of Mount Rushmore so it can be replaced with the face of their great hero, Ronald Wilson Reagan. Like them, Ronnie wanted everything possible privatized and deregulated. Like them, he was a fascist.

Abe Lincoln came to power as a negotiator and compromiser. He would not interfere with the Southern slavers if they would stay in the union and not insist on overwhelming the western territories with the institution of slavery. The Southern hotheads refused to compromise and doomed slavery for good. For all practical purposes, Southern fanaticism made Lincoln an abolitionist. The Civil War thus became a war against slavery. After the Emancipation Proclamation, the North could not have allowed the continuation of slavery. But then, after the war and with Lincoln safely dead, the Republican conservative politicians compromised with Southern conservative Democrats to allow the practical restoration of slavery in the form of segregation and Jim Crow separatism. Thus, it was the Republicans who were responsible for the continued repression of blacks in the South and the rise of the Ku Klux Klan.

The modern-day Southern Strategy of Goldwater, Nixon, and Reagan was simply a repeat of the post-Civil War accommodation of Rutherford B. Hayes and the Republican conservatives with Southern racists. It was then and it is now an attack against the progressive elements that used to exist in the Republican Party but now exists only in the Democratic Party. It's taken them a century and a half, since Abraham Lincoln's time, but now the Republican Party has at last defeated and destroyed the last vestiges of democratic progressivism in its ranks. There are now no progressive elements at all in the Republican Party. It is now fascist and totalitarian from end to end. Reagan and Gingrich were the latest symbols of the New Fascism. Worse is yet to come.

Republicans claim that they want a government forbidden from all except the most limited functions by which they mean that substantial military and police power are legitimate functions of the state but nothing else is. They never oppose increases of any kind in military and police power. The essence of liberalism and, at times, libertarianism is opposition to unlimited military and police power. When the founding fathers spoke of limited government, mostly they were referring to limits on military and police power.

Unlike the founders, the Republicans of today oppose all social and welfare services, especially for the poor. They do believe that government should favor and assist commercial and religious power against individual citizens. They demand government censorship; forced religious worship, especially for children; and rigid control of dissent and protest. They believe that business leaders and government should work together to suppress workers unions. In fact, they believe that workers and consumers have no rights; instead, all economic authority belongs to business and the state. They believe that education as well as the sex and reproductive lives of citizens should be controlled by the state and the christian religions. Liberals oppose all of these conservative controls over citizens. Libertarians claim that they also oppose them but, in fact, they ally themselves with conservatives every time some live issue of individual freedom is at stake.

Conservative Republicans and libertarians alike hate all government and believe that all of its actions are tyrannical by definition, no matter how beneficial to human freedom and welfare they may be. Liberals believe that government can be either for good or bad and they believe that government should guarantee freedom, justice, and equality for citizens through government action. Some liberals, perhaps most, also believe in government welfare programs to help the hungry, homeless, and sick. Republicans oppose all such welfare programs absolutely. What they really want is a totalitarian capitalist system with imperial money-kings and infallible bishops in tight control of a kingdom of business lords and worker vassals.

Almost without exception, the people at the top of military and police organizations (generals and police chiefs) are conservative and Republican. The police exist to protect the property of owners against the common people and to prevent any challenge from dissatisfied citizens to the existing power structure. Of course, America is the most policed nation on earth and has been so for a long time. That is because it is necessary to carefully police the instability that always results from economic inequality. Military power is simply the extension of police power to the rest of the world; it is necessary to protect and expand foreign markets.

The christian religion is the established religion in America as far as the Republicans are concerned. Though they give lip service to religious tolerance, they frequently slip and tell us what they really believe which is that no religion is legitimate or American unless it is christian and that no muslim, jew, atheist, or agnostic has any right to run for public office, hold a job, or express any unchristian belief or feeling.

From the Civil War to the Great Conservative Depression, America was ruled by a one-party dictatorship. The Republican Party ran the country in league with the commercial bosses everywhere except in the South where a collaborating conservative Democratic Party ran a dictatorship for the planters and the textile, tobacco, and coal bosses.

There was no democracy in America during that period and the people all lived cowed, obedient lives. Those who cooperated with the political and economic bosses fared reasonably well as long as they lived their narrow lives without complaint. Those who complained or rebelled were harassed, persecuted, jailed, assaulted, and sometimes killed. They were labeled first as trouble-making democrats, next as anarchists, then as communists, now as terrorists.

The Republicans resort to a whole series of Manichean arguments to justify their social darwinist ideology. They pit the private power of free enterprise against the public power of democratic government. They use the absolutist moralism of fundamentalist and dominionist religions against the relativism (they mean "tolerance") of democratic secularism. They praise competition as the engine of capitalism and condemn cooperative economic arrangements as communistic and socialist. They sneer at equality and praise themselves as heroic individualists fighting against the irresponsibility of the democratic mob. They attack "trial lawyers" for daring to represent ordinary people against the abuses and exploitations of corporations, banks, and insurance companies; and yet they themselves employ hordes of corporation lawyers to assist them in their vast manipulations of working people and consumers. They pass numerous product disparagement laws and then use them to attack anyone who truthfully examines and exposes the abuses and deceptions of their commercial clients.The Republicans say the unemployed are lazy and no account. They whine about the helping behavior of the "nanny state." They attack "welfare queens" (invariably black ones) and claim that they ride around in cadillacs, eat caviar, and drink champaign all bought with food stamps. They point to hungry children with distended stomachs and say they are "fat." They claim that business owners and bosses are the friends and benefactors of workers and that union bosses threaten, coerce, and abuse them. They attack the rights of the people and demand responsibility and accountability from them. They attack the government for taxing the unearned income of the rich while sneering at "equality" and fair play.

The Republicans believe fervently in punitive solutions to all problems. They embrace aggressive war as a way of forcing their version of democracy and "the American way" on others and bizarrely claim that war is the only true path to peace. Overseas, they launch indiscriminate attacks against the innocent and resort to abuse, torture, and persecution in their efforts to subdue and occupy any land they think they can exploit for a profit. At home, in response to legally conducted demonstrations against foreign wars and domestic abuses, they fill the streets with armed police officers and express their contempt for the protections of the Bill of Rights and all human rights organizations. They attack "liberal judges" for protecting the rights of those they so often falsely smear as communists, criminals, terrorists, or for other undefined offenses. They tell us that immigrants, those on welfare, and those who sleep in the streets are offensive to them and deserve harassment and contempt. They demand punitive action against disobedient children, peace demonstrators, homosexuals, striking workers, immigrants, atheists, and people who look funny, speak the wrong language, or dress in the wrong clothes.

In elections, Republicans use McCarthyite smears to vilify and demean their opponents. They suppress those voters least likely to vote for them and frequently tamper with the voting machinery. They disqualify large numbers of minority voters by manipulating, misinforming, and threatening them. For decades, the Republicans have routinely accused their Democratic opponents of being anarchists, communists, socialists, terrorists, weaklings, cowards, draft dodgers, traitors, rapists, thieves, drug fiends, sex maniacs, etc. During presidential campaigns, they have entered into conspiracies with foreign leaders and their agents in order to secretly manipulate issues of war and peace so that events could be arranged to assist their campaigns and damage the policies of their own government. In short, their rule has included torture, warrantless surveillance, imprisonment without charge, disappearances and renditions, arbitrary arrest, overflowing prisons, privately contracted paramilitaries, and millions of citizens without health care.

In the past, the working people of this country were enormously abused by the Republican Party and its wealthy clientele but a small number of them did share a few crumbs from the economic tables of their betters. That was when the "trickle-down" theory was first employed by the bosses and politicians and that was when balanced budgets in government, and only in government, became a reason for opposing all uses of government and national resources for the betterment of the whole population rather than just for the support of the economic oligarchy that ruled America then and now again today.

The first duty of any truly democratic government is to working people and consumers, not to owners and bosses. Except when elections and public discourse are corrupted as is the case now (in the early 2000s), government is responsible to the great mass of people who put it in power. If it does not serve the needs and wants of those citizens, it is not democratic. People live in communities and they have community obligations that the majority has a right to insist on. But this cannot mean a majoritarian tyranny imposed on minorities and individuals in matters that are personal and intrinsic. That is why we have a Bill of Rights. A majority does not have the right to invade the private and personal lives of fellow citizens or the right to coerce their political, religious, and individual beliefs or to censor their expressions. Thus, communities and governments have an obligation to respect the private consciences and beliefs of individuals and minorities. Such personal and private integrity must be respected no matter how unique or divergent it is. The founders of this country believed in democracy without majoritarian tyranny and they fashioned a government designed to prevent such abuse.

Nevertheless, in the life of any organized society, there will eventually be a drift toward tyranny and it will be impelled by efforts to merge the powers of commerce and/or religion with the power of government. When commerce and government come together in a big way, the result is corporate fascism. When religion and government merge, the result is theocratic fascism. Only firmly democratic and secular governments can withstand the assaults by fundamentalist religion and unregulated commerce against the rights of the people.

Religion and commerce must be separate from government, and those two powers must be regulated by the government in the interest of the freedom of the people. Individual citizens must be left free to make their own private choices and government must guarantee this freedom especially against the aggressions and suppressions of religion and commerce. This does not mean tyrannical dominance over religion and commerce by government but it does mean that religion and commerce have to be made to respect individual freedom and have to refrain from subversive attacks against the democratic system.

The hatred of conservatives, libertarians, and fundamentalist christians for democratic and secular government is merely a frustrated rage directed against the one power that prevents them from establishing their own dictatorial, anti-democratic systems in opposition to the rights of the people. Private power always seeks to dominate. It has to be restrained or there can be no democracy at all and no freedom except for the privileged few.

Chapter 12. Republican Fascism (Corporatism)

The philosophy of the Republican economic system after the Civil War was social darwinism buttressed by Sir Francis Galton's eugenics notions. Social darwinism was a foreign import invented in England by Herbert Spencer and taken up in the United States by conservative politicians and commercial exploiters as a cover and justification for their rape of American democracy and their exploitation of the American people for a profit. That alien philosophy was imposed on this country after the Civil War as the country was being rapidly developed and industrialized. The whole continent was taken over and controlled by the robber barons; and the Republican politicians worked for them and used the machinery of government to assist them in their pillage of every resource.

In 1882, Herbert Spencer visited the United States and was royally entertained and feted by the rich and their Republican supporters. Andrew Carnegie, Andrew Mellon, and John D. Rockefeller in particular were intensely supportive of Spencer and his social darwinist philosophy, almost to the point of worship. Thereafter, the Republican Party shaped its philosophy to incorporate the social darwinist ideas of Herbert Spencer complemented by Galton's eugenics ideas. The robber barons saw these ideas as justification for their predatory commercial practices. From that time on, the Republican Party acted as the political arm of American capitalism.

It was Herbert Spencer who invented the term "survival of the fittest" to epitomize his belief that humanity was divided into two distinct parts —

the fit and the unfit. The fit consisted of the wealthy and the eminent. Their competitive success under the rules of western capitalism was supposed to be proof that they had the right to rule over those who were not successful and who were therefore inferior or unfit. The way to improve the race, according to Spencer, was to allow or even help the unfit to die out. Thus, governments must do nothing to help or protect working people, the sick, the hungry, the homeless, the handicapped, the morally undesirable, the unruly and disobedient, the lawless, and the abjectly poor. The only purpose of government was to insure order and protect the persons and property of the rich against the poor masses.

Jean Baptiste Lamarck believed in the spontaneous generation of life forms and in the inheritance of acquired characteristics. Herbert Spencer got his notions about the competition for survival between the fit and the unfit from Lamarck, not from Charles Darwin. Spencer applied his "survival of the fittest" conceptions to social, political, and economic life. Spencer's views complement and overlap the biological conceptions of that other Englishman, Sir Francis Galton, the man who invented the idea that only deliberate breeding and sterilization can improve the human race.

These companion ideas hold that those of superior character and intelligence will rise to the top and the inferior will sink to the bottom and die out unless misguided governments help them to survive and propagate. Acquired moral character was heritable, said Spencer and Galton. Good characteristics such as "civic prosperity" and "civic worth" can be cultivated by human effort but only if the strivers have the right stuff to begin with. They can then pass their acquired characteristics down to their offspring. Environment and education cannot make the unfit fit.

Spencer said that nothing must be done to interfere with the evolutionary process. Governments must not enact social legislation designed to help the poor. The weeding out of the unfit (the physically and intellectually feeble) must not be interfered with or the progress of the human race will be retarded. Those "not sufficiently complete to live" should be allowed to die. Incompleteness was physical infirmity, disease, handicap, lack of self-control, misbehavior under society's rules, low intelligence, etc. He said the "purifying process" will eliminate "nature's failures."

Sir Francis Galton provided biological "proof" that the race can only be improved by sterilizing the unfit. The Republican Party eagerly swallowed these ideas and used them as guides for their governance. By the early twentieth century, at least thirty-three of the forty-eight states had adopted sterilization programs. In 1927, the Supreme Court upheld the Virginia sterilization law thus approving sterilization as a legitimate state government undertaking. At least 70,000 unfit people were sterilized under these laws. These programs lasted until the 1970s.

Galton said that unfit persons who insisted on procreating were "enemies of the state." He said that laws should prevent the unfit from inheriting fortunes, and endowments should be provided for the fit. He said it was unreasonable to oppose the gradual extinction of the unfit. He said that extinction under the right laws would "work silently and slowly" to improve the race through competitive struggle.

Thus, in the nineteenth century, the conservative ideology of the Republican Party, was shaped by social darwinist and eugenicist ideas. Though today the language has been sanitized and concealed behind various conservative and libertarian bromides, the core belief remains the same. Today's Republicans use the terms "successful" and "unsuccessful" rather than the terms "fit" and "unfit." It is a deception. These ideas were and still are used to justify and support the "competitive struggle" of the free enterprise system. If economic competition is fierce and brutal, said Spencer, it will improve the race in the long run. If powerful business leaders crush their competition, that will accelerate progress and efficiently eliminate the unfit.

This is why Republicans oppose practically all legislation that helps working people, the poor, the hungry, the homeless, the sick, the old, the young, the disadvantaged, the degraded, the down and out, etc. Spencer opposed all social legislation and all regulation as do today's Republicans. This is why they demand "small government" and oppose any government expenditures to help ordinary citizens or even to protect the environments in which they live. It is why they oppose public education, public radio, public television, public parks, national forests, mail delivery, municipal sanitation, vaccinations and milk for school children, food stamps for the hungry, and all health and retirement systems for the common people. Spencer opposed all government actions except the administration of justice or police power. So do the Republicans.

The above words accurately describe many of the characteristics of the fascist nature of the Republican Party. However, the first and central characteristic of fascism was shaped in Italy. The man who first used the term "fascism" in a political context was Benito Mussolini. Indeed, Mussolini seems to have coined the term "fascism." In the 1920s, he formed his "black shirt" party and called it the "Fascist Party." He took control of Italy in 1922 under that rubric. He and his party were much admired in the Western world, especially in the United States. When asked what fascism was, he replied, "Fascism should more properly be called corporatism, since it is the merger of state and corporate power." Hitler gained power over Germany in 1933 by imitating Mussolini. He called his movement the "brown shirts" and adopted the fascist philosophy. However, the Germans called their party the Nazi Party. Franco in Spain and Salazar in Portugal also formed fascist parties and took control of their countries with military support from Italy and Germany. These parties all got considerable support from political and religious conservatives as well as from monarchists. Thus, the original and core definition of fascism is corporatism.

Fascism has other characteristics as described in the first part of this chapter. Thus, fascism is social darwinist and eugenicist. It is also intensely nationalistic and calls itself "patriotic" at the drop of a hat. It is suspicious of other countries and of immigrants. It is police statist and militarist and it talks incessantly about state security, identifying itself as the only real protector of the people from foreign attack. It is often eager for war and conflict because it wants to conquer and dominate others. It descended from the christian religions; the first four fascist countries, and many since then, were Catholic. And it is sweepingly exceptionalist in that its followers believe that their race, their religion, their economic system, and their social life are superior to all others.

In an earlier book (*Republican Treason*), I described the Republican Party as being fascist and therefore treasonous. That book even irritated liberals because they shrink in horror from any seemingly "extreme" accusation against the Republican Party. They think it is a kind of reverse McCarthyism and fear they will be called bad names and will lose elections if they sound like accusatory Republicans. They reject the term because it is redolent of Hitler's atrocities. I think the term is also redolent of Stalin's atrocities and of this country's atrocities against others, massively so in Vietnam and Iraq. In any case, the term "fascism" is broad enough to cover far more than the behaviors of Hitler and Stalin. In truth, it includes nearly everyone who stands in opposition to democratic liberalism. Indeed, I think that divine kings and their aristocracies were fascist. They ruled the earth for thousands of years and the power of those kings included absolute political and commercial control and frequently religious control as well. Kings were absolute rulers and their royal blood came from god, they said; they owned everything and they had a sacred right to rule, a claim also made by George W. Bush. Vice President Dick Cheney's use of the term "unitary presidency" to describe his and Bush's joint rule over this country encompasses that claim. Supreme Court justice Antonin Scalia salutes the arrangement of governments under god and sneers at democratic governments for not being submissive to his god's rule.

I don't by any means accept the notion that my charges are extreme or inaccurate. I think they are coherent, well supported, and absolutely accurate. Everyone knows the Republican Party is the big business or corporatist party. In fact, they themselves brag about their intense support for business interests and their strong dislike for working people and their unions; and, of course, they attack the Democrats for being hostile to corporations and supportive of working people. They are outraged at all consumer organizations as well and regard environmentalism as communistic. Their "grow the economy" and "trickle down" beliefs fit the corporatist profile very well as does their never-wavering support for tax breaks for the rich, for capital gains tax cuts, and for the complete elimination of taxes on inherited wealth and indeed on all unearned income. They want to privatize everything public except military and police power and nowadays even that is being contracted and privatized. They are outraged at even the slightest regulation of any corporate entity. They use violent language to attack everything public including democratic government itself. Their vicious words of hatred for liberalism and democratic government sound exactly like the jeremiads of Hitler and Stalin against liberalism and democracy. The Republican Party is clearly fascist and it is no sin to say so.

CHAPTER 13. CORPORATE TRIUMPHALISM

In January of 2010, five extremist Supreme Court justices, deciding a question specifically waived by the petitioner, held, in *Citizens United v. Federal Election Commission*, that corporations, being persons, have a constitutional right to spend as much money as they like on commercials supporting or attacking candidates in an election.

Chief Justice John Marshall called the corporation an "artificial being, invisible, intangible." Thomas Jefferson said we must "crush in its birth the aristocracy of our moneyed corporations, which dare already to challenge our government to a trial of strength and bid defiance to the laws of our country." Indeed, Jefferson wanted an amendment to the U.S. Constitution that would prevent commercial companies from becoming monopolies, stop them from dominating specific industries, and keep them from becoming so big they could control government. Theodore Roosevelt asked for public financing of elections and said to Congress, "All contributions by corporations to any political committee or for any political purpose should be forbidden by law." He signed the Tillman act that, in 1907, banned corporate donations to federal campaigns. Unions have been barred from spending on federal campaigns for more than 60 years and corporations for more than 100 years.

Santa Clara County v. Southern Pacific Railroad was an 1886 case about the taxation of railroad fence posts. The railroad argued that section 1 of the 14th Amendment required that the railroad be treated like "anyone else."

However, section 1 refers only to "persons" and "citizens" when it requires "equal protection of the laws" and forbids that "any State deprive any person of life, liberty, or property." Nevertheless, the conservative justices of that time agreed with the railroad. Then, in a head note to the case, the court reporter wrote "corporations are persons within the intent of the clause in section 1 of the 14th Amendment to the constitution." In a later case, Justice William O. Douglas said that the Santa Clara case "armed [corporations] with constitutional prerogatives never imagined or intended by the founders." In the Citizens United case, Sonia Sotomayor said the court should reconsider the Santa Clara case that "gave birth to corporations as persons instead of expanding the privileges of corporations." She added, "that was the court's error to begin with." During the hearings, Justice Ruth Bader Ginsburg said, "A corporation, after all, is not endowed by its creator with inalienable rights."

In *First National Bank of Boston v. Belloti* in 1978, Justice Lewis Powell, himself an extreme corporatist and Chamber of Commerce maven, found support in Santa Clara for a majority decision that nevertheless said, "Our consideration of a corporation's right to speak on issues of general public interest implies no comparable right in the quite different context of participation in a political campaign for election to public office." William Rehnquist, a dedicated conservative, wrote a dissent in which he warned, "It might be reasonably concluded that those properties [of corporations], so beneficial in the economic sphere, pose special dangers in the political sphere." Rehnquist also questioned whether paper entities "have a constitutionally protected liberty to engage in political activity." John Paul Stevens, in his dissent from the *Citizens United* case, pointed out that the majority opinion, written by Justice Anthony Kennedy, was able to cite only one past relevant decision, the Belloti decision, that, of course, contradicts Kennedy's decision.

In his State of the Union speech of January 27th, 2010, Barack Obama said, "Last week, the Supreme court reversed a century of law that I believe will open the floodgates for special interests — including foreign corporations — to spend without limit in our elections." From the audience, Justice Samuel Alito sneered and lip-synched his disagreement. A few days later, Chief Justice John Roberts joined the Republican Party in attacking Obama for daring to disagree with the decision. *The Nation* magazine of February 15, 2010, reported, "Already the Chamber of Commerce is promising to unleash the 'largest, most aggressive' election-season spending spree in the organization's history. Chamber officials promise to 'highlight lawmakers and candidates' who toe the corporate line and 'hold accountable those who don't.'" To do this, they intend to spend $50 million targeting 40 congressmen and 10 senators who oppose the Chamber's pro-corporate agenda.

In a *New York Review* essay of February 25, 2010, Ronald Dworkin wrote, "The nerve of this argument — that corporations must be treated like real people under the First Amendment — is in my view preposterous. Corporations are legal fictions. They have no opinions of their own to contribute and no right to participate with equal voice or vote in politics." In an editorial of February 15, 2010, *The Nation* wrote, "As Lisa Graves, a former Justice Department and Senate Judiciary Committee attorney, puts it, 'We have to rebuke the court's arrogant decision and make sure the law puts Americans before corporations.' Graves...backs an amendment stating, 'No corporation shall be considered to be a person who is permitted to raise or spend money on federal, state, or local elections of any kind.'"

In a February 15, 2010, column in *The Nation*, Patricia J. Williams set forth a critique about the legal claims that corporations are persons and money is speech. She wrote:

> In 1976...*Buckley v. Valeo*...allowed individuals unlimited spending in pursuit of political ends...*Citizens United* allows corporations that very same grace, and then some.
>
> It is a strange moment in jurisprudence...the inanimate entity of the corporation itself will now enjoy a range of First Amendment benefits not limited by principles of debate or substance...constrained only by the size of its treasury in deploying whatever technological bullhorn has the greatest chance of drowning out everyone else.
>
> Hence, the questions on many minds are why "freedom" (as in speech) has become the functional equivalent of "expenditure" (as in money) and why on earth corporations are considered "persons" to begin with....
>
> A corporation...is not only not human, it is property. A corporation has no natural life span, it does not vote and many are multinational. Corporations...are necessarily exclusionary...[a corporation] doesn't change its nonexistent mind or respond with compassion or feel empathy. Thus, "corporate citizenship"...is...different...from citizenship founded on a constitution of enfranchised individuals ... united in allegiance to an ideal of community, an egalitarianism of society, the mutual shelter of a nation....

> It takes either the most simple-minded or the most cynical state of
> mind to conclude...that corporations are entitled to the same...civil
> and dignitary rights as actual, fully endowed people.

*

The Civil War was a fight between systems of Southern agricultural corporatism (plantations) and Northern industrial corporatism (commercial companies). Of course, it was also a fight over human slavery. Southern ownership was based on chattel slavery, the actual and literal ownership of human minds and bodies. Northern ownership was based on wage slavery or at least servanthood. In both configurations, what was important was the ownership and profitable use of human labor. In this configuration, Northern wage slavery was merely a relaxed version of Southern chattel slavery. In the South, a slave was "personal, moveable property." In the North, a slave was free to get a job and move from master to master by his own will.

This Northern version of human slavery was certainly better than the Southern version but, in the end, it was as controlling and exploitative as the Southern version. Indeed, the Northern version was much less paternal, much colder, and much more profitable. Southern plantation owners could sell their slaves. Northern owners of commercial companies had only to fire them with the snap of two fingers. They were thus made homeless and jobless all at once. Their only recourse was to seek another job, if one was available. If no new job was available, the fired person was entirely disconnected from society and livelihood. No owner or boss owed him anything at all and, until recently, no government owed him anything either. He was a non-person and an alien or tramp in his own country. He was mere meat to be devoured by the elements and the vicissitudes of cold economic fate. He was jailbait and the enemy of policemen and respectable, employed citizens.

After the Civil War, Southern plantations (and Northern farms) were often turned into agricultural corporations, owned from a distance by rich bosses. Small farmers were wiped out by the agricultural corporations and not only in the South. Slowly, independent farms disappeared and the Northern version of wage slavery was imposed on almost all farms. Most on-site farmers do not now own their own land as in olden times. There are no sheltering plantations, only giant conglomerates issuing orders from afar. The Civil War was a great turning point in the employment history of this country. From then on, the corporations were in the saddle and they rode on the backs of working people and consumers. The Republican Party put them in the saddle and kept them there. More and more, the Supreme Court has enabled them. Those corporations now have all of the rights of human beings, says the Court, indeed far greater rights than does any human being or any collection of human beings, including even a whole nation of working people.

Furthermore, this magical and total power, placed in the hands of corporations, is not even slightly in the hands of the people who work in the bowels of the corporations; these mere employees own nothing of the business and have no rights or any voice. It is the corporate rulers at the top who control all of the money and make all of the decisions, and these are the people who have been blessed by the Supreme Court with this new and all-encompassing power. This decision was a literal coup, one of the greatest in human history. Now, our "democratic" political system has been turned over to the corporations without any stint of control by working people, consumers, or the general public. They already had all of the economic power; now they have the political power too. This country has not been truly democratic for a long time thanks mostly to the Republican Party but now it has been turned into a slave state. Neither Hitler nor Stalin ever dreamed of such totalitarian control or of such wealth and privilege based on nothing but corporate greed locked in place by a legalistic behest from on high.

For all practical purposes, a corporation is a dictatorship. Thus, the Supreme Court has delivered massive power to a collection of dictators, that is, to a handful of top-level corporate decision makers. These decision makers have no more respect for the views and the rights of citizens generally than they do for those of their own employees. As said before, employees have no say in the economic policies, practices, or decisions of the organizations for which they work. They will now have no say in the political decisions of their employers; with this decision in place, corporate control of employees will increase and there will be a tremendous chilling effect over all voters everywhere. Does anyone doubt that corporations will suppress and punish those of their employees who differ with corporate leaders about candidates and issues? Indeed, they do it now but this decision will multiply internal disagreements, pressures, and conflicts. What the conservative judges want is total corporate control over the American electoral system and an end of worker and consumer resistance to the dominance of their bosses and manipulators. This decision is a strike against democracy and for tyranny.

Kennedy, in his decision, makes the astonishing claim that "shareholder democracy" can protect shareholders who disagree with a corporation's political behavior. In fact, shareholders are so dispersed, so disconnected, and so ill informed that they have very little control over the behaviors of the corporations whose stock they hold. Neither employees nor shareholders run the corporations and it's laughable to claim they do. CEOs and Boards of Directors do so, and, when there is a single or family owner, that's where all the power is.

In another bizarre distortion, Kennedy says, "If the First Amendment has any force, it prohibits congress from fining or jailing citizens, or associations of citizens, for simply engaging in political speech." Does he think these corporate "associations of citizens" (a term made up by him) are free and independent political groupings covered by the term "citizens" in the actual constitution? Does he think a group of working people, compelled by their economic system to work for some corporation in order to survive, are on the same footing as fully voluntary or independently and rightfully established associations of citizens. Does he believe that even an elected mayor of a town (or any public official) should be free to spend money from the town's treasury to support or oppose political candidates or issues he doesn't agree with while the citizens themselves are denied any choice at all in such matters? That is the arrangement his decision forces on all of the workers (associates) in corporations; they have no say in how the money they helped earn will be spent by their unelected bosses in political campaigns. Or does Kennedy believe that, somehow, those corporate associates appoint or elect their own bosses or at least approve of them and their ideas?

One wonders with amazement if Kennedy believes corporations are socialist organizations (economic democracies) rather than the monarchial collectives they really are? Does Kennedy actually believe that these corporate associates share power equally or at all with the owners and top managers of the corporations? Does he believe that, when the rulers of the corporations support or oppose any political figure, any cause, or any idea, that they are fairly and nobly representing the people over whom they rule and not themselves and their own interests alone, often against the will and the welfare of their associates?

Kennedy seems to think that there really is such a thing as "democratic capitalism." Well, there isn't. Corporations are ruled from the top. They are hierarchical and they brook no opposition from their employees or their stockholders. Every corporation and company has an organization chart. Take a look at one if you want to see where all the power is. Even the military is no more authoritarian than a corporation.

Ronald Reagan declared that democratic government is the ultimate evil and that claim has been the Republican Party's and the corporate world's mantra ever since. Quite obviously, it has also become the decision-making philosophy for five of our Supreme Court justices. The Reagan "revolution" is complete. Why not just do away with representative government altogether. Let the corporations decide everything, make all of the appointments, and control all of the budgets. After all, we are told by the tea party boys and girls and the militias that government is totally incompetent, costs too much, and has no right to provide programs or services useful to the American people or any regulations or laws to protect them from corporate abuses and corruptions.

Does anyone sane believe the Gore v. Bush or the Citizens United decisions had anything at all to do with the Fourteenth Amendment (or the First Amendment)? The Thirteenth, Fourteenth, and Fifteenth amendments were called the "freedom amendments" for a reason. They were occasioned by the determination of the "radical" Republican congress to end slavery and all of the inequities and discriminations of the states against the national rights of former slaves and, for that matter, the whole people. Since then, conservative Supreme Court justices have often jerked those provisions around sideways and backwards to expand the powers of corporations while, at the same time, ignoring the abuses of states, especially in the South, against real citizens. Now, we have five conservative Supreme Court justices going far beyond any of those previous abuses of law; and they are making their mischief in gross contradiction of principles that they themselves claim to be devoted to — original intent, states' rights, strict construction, and limits on oppressive power, though, of course, they believe that oppression always comes from government and never from private corporate power.

In a book called *Republican Treason*, there is a chapter called "Cashocracy." That term came from the rich Texas oil tycoon, H.L. Hunt, who used his 300 radio stations to support Barry Goldwater's 1964 presidential campaign and also used those stations to advance his belief that "democracy" should be based on a system of cashocracy: the more money you have the more votes you should get. Now, the Supreme Court says the more money you have the louder and the more far-reaching your voice and your influence should be, a near implementation of Hunt's cashocracy. They say the corporations are as alive and as deserving as any citizen and that they are deprived "people" whose freedom has been denied until now by the tyranny of evil liberals and democrats.

They insist that money is speech but don't admit that this idea means that corporations will have far more freedom of speech than ordinary citizens or even workers unions, consumer advocacy groups, and environmentalists (real associations of citizens) all lumped together. Conservatives, libertarians, and other Republicans don't and never have liked democratic government (the only democracy there is). Instead, they love what they call "democratic capitalism." They think that their "shop and buy" system is the only system that should be allowed in this country.

What most people regard as social democracy, they regard as communism or, at least, socialism. Thus, they are determined to force us all to live under their system of predatory, unregulated capitalism. The Citizens United decision comes at a frightening time for the Friedmanite, "free enterprise" Republicans. They see the People enraged at their system because of the Great Conservative Recession of 2007, a near repeat of their Great Conservative Depression of 1929, both set off by several decades of wildly irresponsible worker exploitation and citizen abuse by the rich. The robber barons of the Gilded Age were scarcely more predatory and corrupt than our Reaganite and Bushite cheaters and stealers of today. They see a black man in what they regard as their White House and feel that their whole world is coming to an end. The Supreme Court thinks it can rescue them from the dastardly Democrats and their "socialism." Thus, the Republican Party and its adjuncts have mounted a huge campaign of accusatory McCarthyism, their old standby, in an effort to spread fear and hate across the land. They hope that, with the help of their Supreme Court and endless overseas wars, they can recover or at least prolong their old conservative order.

Chapter 14. Christianism

The christian religion is the largest religion in the world. It has over two billion members, almost one third of the world's total population. Of course, it is not really one religion but many. Few of the sects agree on much of anything at all and very few christians agree with or obey the supposed words and teachings of the man they claim as their founder. The sects are more various than the seeds in the fields. Sadly, most of them have always believed in holy wars, forced conversions, inquisitions, slavery, economic injustice, political dominance over others, and the worst kinds of cruelty imaginable including torture, abuse, persecution, and outright murder in the name of their sect. They are not an admirable lot but there are a few good ones. Nowadays, the christians and capitalists have united; many of them call themselves "free-enterprise christians." Initially, the christian religion was highly communistic. It seems now to have squared the circle. I don't see any improvement.

Wikipedia describes christianity as "a monotheistic religion centered on the life and teachings of Jesus of Nazareth." This is the way the christians see their religion but it is a fanciful view. For example, the christian religion isn't monotheistic.

Christianity is as polytheistic as were the many pagan religions in earlier times. The different christian sects of today have almost nothing in common other than their pretense that they all believe in the same god.

The Catholic religion is made up of a whole horde of gods. The major gods are called the father, the son, and the holy ghost and, as impossible as it is, they are supposed to be both separate from one another and united in a sort of three-sided god head. Then, the Virgin Mary is herself a god every bit as important as the other three. In fact, she is the most important of all to many members of the Catholic horde, especially among the Latins. The lesser gods are called saints; they have powers over particular pieces of the religious pie and can deliver miracles and answer prayers just as well as any of the four major gods.

The Protestants have an enormous variety of gods, usually but not necessarily only two for each sect. No christian sect believes in just one god as they all pretend they do. At the least, each such sect believes in god the Father and Jesus the Son and most of them also believe in a vaguely defined holy ghost. Some Protestant sects have gods that resemble one another but most of these gods are very different and they require different beliefs and different behaviors from their followers.

For christians to pretend that they all believe in the same god is absurd. There are thousands of quite different gods under christianity. The pretense that everyone believes in the same god is just a way of trying to bind people together so they won't attack and kill one another at every disagreement about the nature of their gods. Our world is not monotheistic; it is vastly polytheistic. This fact should be absolutely clear to anyone with an ounce of intelligence. Peoples' beliefs are easily corrupted for political purposes. Accordingly, almost no one ever admits out loud that each separate sect has its own god and that such gods are all different from and antagonistic to one another.

I dislike organized religion because of its murderous history and its invariable determination to impose itself on others by harassment and force. However, there are a few good people among the religionists. For example, if published accounts can be believed at all, Jesus Christ was a good person. The christians claim to admire Jesus and say that they take him as their model. Few of them can be believed. They are nothing like Jesus and pay no attention at all to his words and actions. Still, some do try to follow his example.

Not much at all is known about Jesus Christ. The words he is said to have spoken, according to the gospels, are very much in dispute even among christian scholars. Nevertheless, he appears to have been a good and decent man. If his actual words and actions were anything like those reported, he might be a good model to follow. Unfortunately, today's christians — especially the evangelicals — are extremely vicious, destructive, and immoral people and they are secretly contemptuous of Jesus and everything he believed and said.

Many of those who define themselves as christians today are completely unaware of the true nature of christianity and the character of Jesus. Quite obviously, Jesus and all of his early followers rejected the possession of wealth and the ownership of property as good or even permissible conditions of christian behavior. Jesus did not believe that anyone could be both wealthy and christian. He urged his followers to give away all of their property and said that a rich man's chances of getting to heaven were no better than a camel's chances of getting through the eye of the needle.

He also urged his followers to put off their families so they could serve the needs of god instead. Jesus did not believe in family values nor did he spend "quality time" with his own family or very much time at all. He did not hate prostitutes, robbers, homosexuals, lepers, or even those who attacked him. Unlike today's christians, he was tolerant, liberal, humanistic, relativist, communistic, and even secularist. No one knows what he looked like but, if the pictures imagined and painted by his later supposed followers are representative at all, he was a bearded radical in sandals and dirty clothes and he was a peacenik and a pacifist.

Modern christians, especially the fundamentalists, the evangelicals, and the traditionalists, are the exact opposite of Jesus in every way. Even worse, they quite literally hate and want to assault and even kill all of those who are truly similar to Jesus in dress, character, belief, and behavior.

Can anyone imagine that the right-wing christians are anything like Jesus or even christian at all? Consider the characters, words, and behaviors of Jerry Falwell, Pat Robertson, the Bakers, Oral Roberts, Jimmy Swaggart, Jesse Helms, Pat Buchanan, Oliver North, Chuck Colson, J. Edgar Hoover, Joe McCarthy, Anne Coulter, Jeanne Kirkpatrick, Rush Limbaugh, Glen Beck, Bill O'Reilly, Tom DeLay, Phyllis Schlafly, Cal Edwards, Richard Nixon, Ronald Reagan, and the members of the Bush family. If these people are christians then so are satan, beelzebub, and the red devil.

Was Christ a family man? Not on your life! The early christian version of Christ never made him a family man. He had disciples, followers, men who were inferior to him in every way. He was the boss and the big man. He rejected his own family — mother, father, siblings — and went off alone to find followers and to invent his new religion or, more likely, to reform his old jewish religion. Jesus was a loner. He most certainly didn't believe in family values or traditions or convention. In fact, he didn't believe in any of the "values" of his time and he didn't accept standard morality. He wasn't a family man, an organization man, or a patriot. The christians of today in no way resemble Christ. In truth, they reject everything he was and everything he believed in and stood for. Today's christians are about as unchristian as it is possible for anyone to be.

The religious-right christians are not real christians at all. They do not heed the biblically inscribed words of Jesus even a little bit. They are aggressive, violent, arrogant, intemperate, intolerant, cruel, and often murderous toward those who disagree with them. It is liberal christians like Jimmy Carter, Dean Smith, Desmond Tutu, and Martin Luther King Jr. who genuinely try to imitate and be like Christ. Among the several billion people who call themselves christians, very few are true christians. The apocryphal Christ was admirable. Most other christians are not.

The fundamentalists and evangelicals are not christian at all. This is especially true of the thirty or forty million Americans who adhere to the preachings of the dominionists. Their preachings have been described as examples of christian fascism, a charge that I think is clearly true. They describe themselves as "free-enterprise christians" and, like their great hero, Ronald Reagan, they very much believe in getting rich. They despise the poor, the sick, the hungry, and the homeless but, most of all, they despise liberalism and democracy. They regard the Constitution, the Bill of Rights in particular, as unchristian and evil. They say they are going to overthrow the government and impose their version of christianity on everyone else by force of arms. They are also going to require every citizen to give the churches ten percent of his and her income. The government will be abolished entirely except for the military and police forces and any agencies that support and service their religion and their commerce.

They mean to use the police at home to enforce their christian program and the military overseas to force the conversion of all other peoples. Those who refuse to join their religion will be exterminated. There will be no personal liberty and no sin will be allowed. Deviation and dissent will be viciously punished. Liberals, progressives, homosexuals, adulterers, and unbelievers will be killed. These dominionists believe the world is full of sinners, demons, and witches and that there are "controllers" and other evil and magical people out there threatening them.

They say that Jesus is one of their warriors and that Ronald Reagan and George W. Bush are saints and saviors. Quite clearly, Bush shares their belief system and has given them billions of dollars of taxpayer money to do with as they choose. In truth, he bought their votes in the 2004 election. George Bush is the first out and out theocrat to ever be president of this country. Let's hope he is the last.

It's truly astonishing that the members of the press refuse to believe what they see before them every day. Bush and his staff have manufactured an incredible mass of extreme lies and the press has accepted most of those lies without resistance or qualification. Even the abuse, rape, torture, persecution, forced exile, and murder of millions of innocent Iraqis are ignored or dressed up as normal and just actions designed to defend the United States and spread democracy throughout the world. Make no mistake. Fascism is alive and strong in the homeland.

Fundamentalist christians believe you are oppressing them when you won't submit to their dogma and won't allow them to rule your life and the lives of your children. They complain bitterly about the separation of church and state believing, as they do, that the state has no right to decide anything or do anything without the approval of their god as transmitted to us by them. They demand that all public school children be forced to say prescribed christian prayers every single day of their lives and demand that no church activities ever be regulated or taxed or inhibited no matter how far those activities depart from the confines of religion. They have long imposed a rigid religious test on all elected politicians and indeed on all public officials. They routinely oppress and persecute everyone who is not a christian and even those who do not share their particular brand of christianity. And yet they present themselves as the victims of liberals and secular humanists and pretend that they are martyrs under siege because of their godly belief and practice.

Christianity is and always has been an attacking religion. It was successful because it proselytized and its conquests were always carried out by force of arms. The christian empire was established under the sword and it always was ruled by force and coercion. The christian tyranny finally lost its military power because the empire came apart, split into many pieces because of doctrinal differences. Like the communist empire, it disintegrated but its demise was not nearly so peaceful as that of communism. The christians continued to attack one another, in the field and in the pulpit, for hundreds of years, indeed far into the twentieth century. And beyond.

The various revolutions against the divine right of kings and the rise of the Industrial Revolution all greatly weakened the power of the christian empire and deprived it of direct control over military and police power. Now, it has little direct political power but it still has great coercive influence. It continues to proselytize with every breath, of course, but now it can only imprison, torture, and kill you with the help of a not always cooperative political power.

When, on June 26, 2002, the Court of Appeals for the Ninth Circuit outlawed the phrase "under god" in the pledge of allegiance, what it was really outlawing was *forced prayer*. The 1953 intrusion of those words into the pledge made it impossible for any citizen to honestly declare his or her allegiance to this country without also embracing the monotheist god of the christians. As always, the court's affirmation of the right of a citizen to be patriotic without being a christian caused the christians once again to express their bitter hatred of "liberal judges" and their utter contempt for the very idea of religious liberty and the prospect of showing some small respect for the rights and the consciences of other people. Toleration and civility are not among the christian virtues.

The court said that the words "under god" were an endorsement of monotheism. Those words also quite clearly refer to the christian god. Other religionists do not commonly use the name "god" to refer to their deity. The muslims call their god "Allah," the buddhists worship the Buddha, the hindus Vishnu or Krishna, and the jews refer to Yahweh or Elohim or refuse to name their god at all. There are as well numerous deistic and pantheistic gods as well as polytheistic ones not to mention the millions of people who believe in no god at all. Does anyone doubt that the christians would foam at the mouth and march on Washington if anyone required them or their children to pledge allegiance or pray to Allah or Vishnu or Yahweh?

Make no mistake: The christians do not like non-christians and want to isolate and harass them by forcing them to publicly identify themselves as non-christian over and over and over again; then, knowing their names, the christians can label them as sinful and disreputable people in need of correction. The christian objective is to force conversions through public embarrassment, shaming, insult, threat, and outright violence. Coupling a patriotic pledge with a declaration of belief in the monotheist god is a way for the christians to tar disbelievers as unpatriotic and even treasonous. This McCarthyite tactic is especially brutal when it is directed against vulnerable children.

Historically, the christian effort to force daily school prayers out of the mouths of children was only partially successful and so, fifty years ago, they snuck their god into the pledge of allegiance as a step toward establishing their religion and supporting their preposterous claim that the United States is a christian nation. They want to exclude non-christians from citizenship altogether and they want to take names and deliver punishments. As always, being cowardly, they make school children their number one target.

What's wrong with "voluntary" school prayer or a godly affirmation concealed in the pledge of allegiance? Well, to begin with, it can't be voluntary. Approved prayers ordered up every day by the authorities, conducted by them on public property, and involving a captive audience of children with private beliefs and differing backgrounds cannot be voluntary. Announcing to a gathering of such children that they can avoid saying those prayers, or hearing them, by leaving the room is absurd. It is only a way of embarrassing and coercing children who may not share the religious beliefs of their classmates.

To apply this kind of pressure to a child every single day of his or her school life is offensive and cruel in the extreme. Can anyone possibly doubt that believing teachers, classmates, and parents will taunt and criticize those who are different from them? It happens now to jewish, muslim, and atheist children, especially in backward places like Alabama, Mississippi, West Virginia, Oklahoma, and the Carolinas.

No teacher or other school official has any right to say a single word to a school child about his or her religious belief or disbelief. Even children — especially children — have a right to guard their private belief against the prying eyes and ears of government officials, including teachers. People of any age or station have the right to absolute privacy regarding matters of conscience and belief. To demand public words and acts that reveal the heart of a child, or a grown-up, to would-be religious molesters like the christian fanatics so intensely determined to lay their forced prayers on every child every day is barbaric and vicious.

Every school child and every other citizen should be taught as a civics lesson that he or she has an absolute right of conscience and privacy with regard to matters of religious and political belief. And each child should be taught that those who try to pry open the minds and reveal the beliefs of children, or anyone, for the purpose of pressuring or converting them is guilty of a tyrannical and unacceptable act, an act of child abuse, an act of oppression and bad faith, an un-American and unchristian act, indeed an act that ought to be made criminal and ought to be punished by imprisonment.

Freedom of religion has little or no meaning unless it allows citizens to keep their belief or lack of it to themselves. The issue of forced prayer in public schools or forced obeisance to god in the pledge of allegiance reveals the tyranny of christian conservatives determined to force their beliefs on every helpless school child and indeed, if given a chance, on every citizen everywhere. Forced prayer in school and elsewhere is not about the right to pray which has never been prohibited in or out of school as long as it remains private and unorganized. It is about the power of christians to cram their religion and their prayers down the throats of everyone else by forcing organized, public displays of their religious rituals on property that does not belong to them personally.

Christianity has always been repressive and totalitarian. It has always assaulted nonbelievers, destroyed their churches, their relics, their altars, their images, their books. It has always sought to conquer everyone on earth by converting them, willingly or unwillingly. It has always used coercion, threat, censorship, suppression, violence, and slaughter to force others into the christian straight jacket. It has never tolerated any difference or deviation it had the power to change into servile obedience.

Today, christians have less military and police power than they once had but they continue to proselytize and coerce different others, to pressure and punish non-christians, to grab after political power that they mean to use as a weapon against anyone who does not obey their moral rules and prohibitions. All christians are the bitter enemies of personal freedom. They are all severe tyrants by definition and they are out to subvert democracy and destroy the rights of everyone who does not accept their god and obey his orders as defined and legislated by them.

In America, christianity and capitalism are always on the hunt. The free enterprise spirit is the proselytizing spirit. Both of these religions want to conquer or convert everything they see around them and everyone. They get their energy from their fervent desire to exterminate those others who stand against them in their imaginations if not in the real world. They see all those others as enemies. They see the world as their rightful possession and everyone not with them as alien. To be a traitor or sinner is to be anywhere outside their belief system. They are ready at every moment to wage war and seize what is rightfully theirs; and they believe that everything is rightfully theirs including the minds and bodies of every last person on earth.

Christianity and capitalism have had an alliance for a long time but, at times, they oppose one another. This doesn't happen often, though. They need one another to conquer and control the world. A few christians actually believe that the rapaciousness of commerce is sinful and a few of the more enlightened capitalists believe that the crude superstitions of the christians are boorish. However, for the most part, they tolerate one another and eagerly compromise their belief systems to accommodate their allies. Together, these two religions absolutely control the western world and everything in it. Anyone who disagrees with their dogma or gets in the way of their profits or their dogmas is marginalized, vilified, imprisoned, persecuted, or killed.

In recent decades, christians have been trying to revise history so they can take credit for democracy and the idea of freedom. It's as if today's nazis were to claim credit for themselves and for Hitler as opponents of jewish persecution. Christianity not only was not democratic but stood always in violent opposition to even the slight possibility of democracy or any freedom whatever for people, least of all for heathen and other unbelievers.

Until just a few centuries ago, the christian churches pretty much owned the world "known" to Europeans, and everyone in it. No one had the right not to be a christian. Unbelief was punished by persecution, repression, imprisonment, torture, and death. Even the faithful had to be extremely careful not to offend anyone powerful or depart even an inch from the prevailing dogma. For six hundred years, for example, the christian churches tortured or brutally murdered millions of witches even though witches never ever existed. These were not trivial events, mere "mistakes," or aberrations. The worst of communism was certainly better than the worst of christianity and its abuses didn't last nearly as long.

It's true that christianity in the twentieth century was less abusive and tyrannical than it had been before but that improvement wasn't due to any change in christian dogma, practice, or moral intention. The christian churches slowly and reluctantly retreated from their power to harm others only because of the advance of freedom and knowledge. A greater rationalism came into the world mostly in the form of increased literacy, as science and the democratic idea began to advance. Rationalism was always opposed by religion.

The way the christian argument goes, the early christian leaders were willing to take anyone into the church and that is supposed to be proof of democratic practice by the churches. In fact, converting others by any means available, including force, is a way of conquering the world, not a way of establishing and practicing democracy. Proselytizing is a way for an individual or an organization to acquire power and take over the lives and the fortunes of others. Militant proselytizing is intolerant, arrogant, and tyrannical by every measure. It is a way of showing contempt, not respect, for the belief, the conscience, and the dignity of others. Nothing is more offensive than being told you are a great sinner and that you are doomed to suffer through all eternity because you don't believe precisely what some frothing fanatic is babbling about his superior being, belief, and condition.

When the early christians gained power, they began to attack, coerce, and kill those who disagreed with them. They also demanded that the Roman state raise up their religion and suppress all others. They were determined to destroy every belief different from theirs, to smash all the "false" idols, to destroy all the artifacts, symbols, and rituals of others, to forbid on pain of death any alien ceremony or tribute to the old gods still dear to millions of people.

Many christians believe that prayer has a magical effect on the person praying and even on the world at large. Those who pray are, they say, good people and those who don't are bad people. Furthermore, prayer transforms bad people into good people and reduces or entirely eliminates immoral and criminal acts. Prayer is a way of influencing god, a way of persuading him to decrease the amount of evil in the world and to increase the amount of good. This is why fundamentalist christians believe so fanatically in forced school prayer. They also want to post the Ten Commandments in courthouses, post offices, schools, and indeed nearly everywhere. They believe their spoken words and their written pieces of paper are all magical and that forcing them on others will make everyone into christians.

What fundamentalist christians really want is a world in which everything and everyone is christian. Those things that aren't christian must be made christian and those people who aren't christian must be converted, condemned, or killed. But this attitude comes from the Old Testament, where christians pick up the jewish god who calls himself a "jealous god" and dooms everyone who doesn't believe in him to the pit of hell and eternal damnation. This god is not only jealous but also cruel and unjust. He regularly condemns children and other weak mortals to misery, suffering, disease, and death. In fact, he quite often kills them himself. Christians pay lip service to the mild and forgiving teachings of Jesus but they do not believe in tolerance for non-christians, not even for christians whose views on certain details may differ from theirs. Thus it is hard to see why they bother to invoke "Jesus Christ" at all.

Their hybrid jewish–christian god sends pestilence, disease, war, starvation, and sudden death to those who ignore his words or refuse to join his church; and his followers even help him mete out his vengeance and rage against sinners. Christians are always on the hunt. They are willing to take you in if you submit to their god, confess your sins, and swear eternal obedience to their rules.

Some New Testament christians see Jesus as a figure who rebelled against these aggressive teachings and emphasized instead the tenets of the ancient Greek culture and philosophy. The Greeks didn't believe in one god; in fact, they tolerated many different belief systems concurrently and the basis of their philosophy was scientific, not dogmatic. Much of what was Greek in Western understanding was suppressed by christianity. It was the muslims who preserved this knowledge and even added to it. Later, this knowledge came back to the West from the muslim world.

However, the root of christianity remains in judaism and, when it split from jewish belief, it embraced pagan thought and ritual and combined them with old jewish myths to make the new religion of the Holy Roman Empire.

Christianity warred against the books, libraries, folklore, rituals, and beliefs of nearly everyone else in the world and wiped out enormous amounts of human knowledge. Christians have tried to disappear everything that was not christian and they have tried to convert, oppress, or kill everyone who was not christian. Though their killing power has been reduced, their intolerance and proselytizing militancy continue today.

Awhile back, the pope apologized to the jews, but he was only sorry for the "inadequate response" of the flock to the holocaust. The holocaust grew out of christian hatred, pretty much originated by the Catholic Church. Hitler was a Catholic and his anti-jew hate came from the long crusade of the Catholic Church against jews. The pope not only denies that Hitler was a prince of the Holy Church but even claims that he and his nazis were atheists and that they used the holocaust to create Catholic martyrs. It is not unusual for popes to lie but not many of them have lied to make themselves and their church out to be protectors and friends of the jews and actual enemies of the nazis.

Antisemitism was invented by christianity and it was and still is at the very heart of the christian system of belief. Christianity has always been a militant, marauding force. It has always sought to exterminate and to replace other belief systems. It used political and military power when it had political and military power. When it lost its power to dictate its dogma to all others within its reach by the force of arms and dogma, it turned to other, humbler methods.

It still proselytizes today and it still condemns opposing belief and tries to destroy it. It does not believe in tolerance for different others or in religious freedom. It still coerces the belief of its own adherents and tries to compel the belief and behavior of everyone else. It still condemns and damns those who deviate from its main doctrines and it still attacks scientific inquiry and political liberty in detail. It still wallows in the deepest superstition and still disciplines those of its officials and members who try to lead it toward liberation for the poor and the oppressed. It opposes all forms of sexual freedom and any form of gender equality. Its high officials still wear rich robes and wave golden scepters and they also point and accuse when anyone disagrees with their policies or challenges their privileges and power. Everyone is still required to bow down to them and kiss their hands. The Catholic Church is a remnant of a corrupt and evil system of divine kings and princes and it tries its best to maintain as much of that system as it can.

There is a Catholic institute called Oremus that is working to "bring back Latin in the Mass, the altar faced away from the people, adoration of the Host, and Gregorian Chant." As for preaching in Latin, why not? Catholic dogma is senseless anyhow. Why not present it in a dead language that nobody understands anymore? It's too bad we can't persuade all Catholic officials to speak only in Latin in all of their pronouncements and communications. As for facing away from the people, that's what christianity has always done.

In the case of the protestants, maybe we can get them all to speak in tongues, the language of the insane. The religiously addled ought to be permanently disconnected from everything that's real in the world. They have been building their towers of babble for centuries. Unfortunately, we now have one of them in the White House and he expresses his contempt for the "reality-based" world. Sad to say, he uses his delusions as excuses for abusing, raping, torturing, exiling, and mass-murdering hundreds of thousands of innocent people.

A country cannot be both christian and free. Christians do not believe in religious freedom and, quite often, not in political freedom either. All of the christian religions are proselytizing religions; they all seek to convert everyone with a belief different from theirs, and they do this because they are certain that their religion alone is right and all others wrong and sinful. Thus, any christian with power must use his power to force the conversion of others. It is his god's will that he do so and anything less is sinful. All of the christian sects are tyrannical by nature and, to one degree or another, they all insist on a theocratic government, one that compels belief or, at least, does everything in its power to spread the faith by force of law and political and social pressures.

CHAPTER 15. SECULARISM

In the first chapter of this book, I said just about everything that needs to be said about the definition of atheism. I said it was simply a disbelief in a god or a system of gods, nothing more. However, atheism does have natural alliances: with science, with reason, with history, with liberalism. Many but not all scientists, rationalists, and historians lean toward atheism because their occupations and life-views are based on evidence rather than belief without evidence, otherwise known as "faith."

There is no atheist belief in pogroms, utopias, churches, sects, rites, rituals, dogmas, sacred texts, miracles, prayers, chants, jihads, crusades, saints, angels, gods, devils, heavens, hells, limbos, purgatories, ghosts, after lives, or any of the other detritus of religious faith and practice. Atheism is simply a disbelief in religion.

Atheism is not a program or a political system. It does not have and cannot have any dogmas or goals. It is simply a refusal to accept a dogmatic belief in a god or a system of gods. It is nothing more and nothing less than that. Atheists don't have churches or political parties. They have never tried to organize themselves into groups or enterprises. They have written no manifestos and have no bibles or rules of order. They have never had an army and have never assaulted or oppressed anyone. They are not missionaries or evangelists and they do not proselytize or preach. They do not assert a belief in anything at all as a condition of atheism. Atheism is simply disbelief. Of course, atheists may believe any number of things about the world, good and bad, but none of them are related specifically to atheism nor do they depend on atheism for any support.

Liberalism is informed by the three systems mentioned above (science, reason, and history) but many liberals are christians just the same. The supposed words and behaviors of Jesus Christ described in the gospels inspire and inform them. In fact, Christ himself was liberal right to the core.

Atheism and secularism are related but not identical to one another. Atheism is disbelief. Secularism is a practice or stance more than a belief or disbelief in anything. The dictionary defines it as religious skepticism or indifference and also as the idea that religious considerations should be excluded from civil affairs and public education. Secularism should be viewed as a stance of civic neutrality and as a necessary condition for an open society, one based on broad tolerance toward public and shared areas of life. Separation of church and state is fundamental to the idea of secularism and essential to any system of religious freedom.

Secularism must also be defined as a counterpoise to religion. Like atheism, it lacks content and has no program beyond the neutrality it offers. No one can worship or even swear allegiance to any secular dogma because there is none. It offers a neutral space for individual choice and decision, a haven for the unreligious and also for those believers who support tolerance for different others. Above all, it is a communal umbrella of protection for all believers and nonbelievers. It asks for nothing except mutual respect and an end of aggressive, invasive, and assaultive proselytizing.

Secularism does not offer an alternative system of belief. Being secularist doesn't prevent you from being religious but it does prevent you from forcing your religion on others. Secularism is not the brother of atheism as many christians claim. Rather, it is the father of democracy and individual liberty. Although several theocratic states (Israel, for example, and the former Soviet Union) have claimed to be secularist, it is not really true. The christians even claim that the United States is a christian nation but that isn't true either. No democratic country can be anything but secularist in its attitude toward religious and political belief.

In recent years, there has been a disturbing effort (even by some liberals) to smear atheism and secularism as twin evils that inspired Hitler, Stalin, Mao, Pol Pot, and other such monsters. There have even been articles in *The Nation, The New York Review of Books,* the *American Prospect, the New Republic,* and naturally in many rightist publications that vilify atheism and secularism in the interest of the christian religion. The quotes that follow are fairly typical.

In an essay in the November 20, 2006, issue of *The Nation*, Eyal Press (a good liberal for sure) says, "But there's also no shortage of secular people who have propagated murderous ideas through the years. Hitler hardly mentioned god, and Pol Pot, Stalin, and Mao never mentioned god at all." Clearly, Press is not a very careful historian.

In a book review of January 11, 2007, in *The New York Review of Books*, H. Allen Orr attacks Richard Dawkins for "his war on religion" and says, "Dawkins has a difficult time facing up to the dual facts that (1) the twentieth century was an experiment in secularism; and (2) the result was secular evil, an evil that, if anything, was more spectacularly virulent than that which came before." After condemning Stalin and Mao for persecuting, torturing, and killing the religious, he goes on to say, "But Dawkin's inability to see the difference in severity of their sins — one of orders of magnitude — suggests an ideological commitment of the sort usually reflecting devotion to a creed." Orr himself can't count, measure the magnitude of, or face up to the thousands of years of religious persecution and murderous violence directed against unbelievers and different believers by the religionists. Indeed, aside from capitalism, religion is by any measure the most murderous force to ever exist on earth.

In the pages of *The Nation*, October 8, 2007, a Canadian named Ian Hacking, calling himself a Darwinian, spits venom all over atheism and presumably secularism as well. He bitterly attacks "the arrogant religion baiters — yes, Richard Dawkins, but others are worse..." Hacking provides the mildest kind of loving criticism of the anti-Darwinians even while he presents himself as an objective scientist who believes in and loves the christian religion and thinks it is warmly wonderful in contrast to disgusting atheism. He agrees with a christian sympathizer named Philip Kirchner that Americans need god because life in the U.S. is "so cruel and competitive... that Americans need extra consolation." He says of this Kirchner, "his heart is in the right place, unlike the current crop of atheist propagandists."

Hacking virtually foams at the mouth in expressing his hatred for the "virulent atheists" and their "loathsome arrogance." He adds "those who think that Genesis is just another old book should marvel that its authors got it right, in the very beginning." He claims to be on the side of "the people" and says, "I do have a lot of respect for popular skepticism" and adds, presumably in support of the peoples' disapproval of atheists, "The people do not trust those who present themselves as elite."

Contrary to the above sneers and false accusations, nazism and communism were nothing like atheism or secularism in their structures or their ideologies. In fact, the real source of both of these isms was the christian religion, not atheism or secularism. Nazism was directly christian; communism was a christian heresy. The evidence is clear.

Hitler was a lifelong Catholic. His rule was openly and murderously christian. His book, *Mein Kampf*, was inspired by Martin Luther's vicious, violent, racist, and antisemitic tomes. Hitler killed six million jews for christian reasons. He killed additional millions including secularists, atheists, liberals, progressives, and democrats. He bragged that he had exterminated atheism in the name of his christian god. He was no atheist and he was no secularist. In a speech in 1944, he said, "I am a pious man and believe that whoever fights bravely in defense of the natural laws framed by god and never capitulates will never be deserted by the lawgiver."

Hitler was born a conservative christian and remained a devout Catholic throughout his life. In 1941, he told General Gerhard Engel, "I am as before a Catholic and will always remain so." In power, he subsidized the christian religion, forced school prayer on children, ordered the teaching of religion in the schools, put priests in official positions, and said that state loyalty derived from the truths of christianity.

When Joe Stalin became the dictator of the Russian Empire, he imported social darwinist and eugenicist ideas from the christian world but claimed he was applying them in a marxist manner. Therefore, he set out to suppress, imprison, or kill the unfit so that the "new man" of the communist utopia could emerge from the carnage through heroic competitive struggle and right-thinking conformity. Like the nazis in Germany and the free-enterprise christians in the United States, Joe Stalin saw history as a fight between the fit and the unfit. Stalin and Hitler are now dead and their empires are gone but the salvationist christians in the United States still reign.

Like Hitler, Stalin had a strong christian background. He was raised in a "priest-ridden" family in Georgia and became a dedicated seminarian. Thus, he began as a religious fanatic as did many of the old Bolsheviks. Mikoyan and Yenukidze were also seminarians, Voroshilov was a choirboy, Kaganovich was a devout jew, and Beria's mother was so intensely worshipful that she went to a church to die near her god. When these men rejected their christian or jewish beliefs, they replaced them with communist beliefs.

Stalin's first contact with the communists (the Bolsheviks) did not occur until 1905, long after his character had been formed by his christian upbringing and by the treatment he got from his christian teachers and supervisors. Like Hitler, Stalin was manufactured by the christian religion.

When, in the Great Terror of 1937 Stalin was about to kill his close followers and friends, he said to them, "Maybe it can be explained by the fact that you lost faith." Stalin also said, "The Russian people need a Tsar whom they can worship and for whom they can live and work." He later told Beria that the "enemy of the people is not only one who does sabotage but one who doubts the rightness of the Party Line. There are many of them and we must kill them." The communists believed as much in the inerrancy of the words of their saints (Marx and Lenin) as do the fundamentalist christians in the inerrancy of their bible and the words of their priests and preachers.

Communism was a religion, especially when it was new, and its very close resemblance to fundamentalist christianity and mohammedanism is striking. Its leaders allowed no dissent or doubt and required the abject submission of adherents on the pain of torture and death. It was driven by religious fervor, and it proselytized very much in the fashion of christian missionaries preaching to the unbelievers. Its afterlife was the magical and distant "workers' paradise" that would be achieved eventually by the sacrifices of true believers waging crusades against sin and heresy. Like the christian and muslim religionists, the communists also hated secularism and sought to destroy liberalism and its "weak-kneed" respect for the rights of the people and for such abominations as tolerance and individual conscience. They too were racist and antisemitic and they also tried to co-opt and corrupt science in the interest of their dogma.

Communism is based on a blind faith in intense utopian dogmas, not at all on history or anything scientific or objective. Some other religions (buddhism, deism, pantheism etc.) do not claim to have specific or definable gods either and the ones that do make this claim (christians, jews, muslims, hindus, etc.) have vague, divided, misty, and inexact gods. For them, the word "god" is a ghostly and rather empty word but it plays a kingly or dictator role in the complicated systems of belief and behavior imposed on gullible religionists by their all too human rulers. Communists kept the belief system intact but threw the word out.

Atheism and secularism simply were not a source of or an inspiration for nazism or communism. Hitler's nazism came directly from and was an expression of christian belief, both Catholic and Protestant, and he and his followers always said so. Stalin's communism very much resembled medieval christianity in its tyrannical repressions, punishments, enslavements, and violence toward dissidents, deviants, and unbelievers. Communism itself was a heretical religion derived from christianity and capitalism and it imitated those systems in almost every respect though, of course, it had its own cultural configurations.

Atheism and secularism are different things altogether. Neither has a set of dogmas and neither is based on faith or force. They impose nothing on anyone and ask for nothing other than tolerance and neutrality with respect to freedom of belief and expression for all people.

Chapter 16. Socialism

Unfortunately, millions of people the world over believe that communism and socialism are one and the same thing. This is completely untrue. Socialism is the real alternative to Soviet and Chinese "communism" and also to Western, especially American, capitalism.

Environmentalism is socialist in that it treats the land, the air, and the water as public possessions, not private ones. Public parks and national forests are socialist lands. Bringing electricity and other utilities to rural populations is a socialist idea. All things that serve public interests rather than private ones are socialist.

Promoting consumer rights is socialism. Unionism is socialism. The social security system is socialist. So are Medicare, Medicaid, and the food stamp program as are child labor laws, the minimum wage, the eight-hour workday, industrial safety, public roads, public radio, and public television. Socialism is economic democracy and public control of all the things that directly affect the great majority of citizens. Public control is democratic control and it stands squarely in opposition to private and autocratic control over the lives of citizens.

Capitalism is economic authoritarianism by definition. What it seeks is private and tyrannical control over the work of others. Capitalism is not merely the ownership of property but it is the use of property to control others. Acquiring property does not make anyone a capitalist. Using it to control others for a profit does.

There have always been arguments about the definition of socialism. To make any kind of historical or political sense, I think it must be defined as economic democracy. At the root of socialism is the idea of cooperation, of collective action for the common good. Obviously, democracy cannot be anti-cooperative or anti-collective and remain democratic. For the most part, democracy is a political process, socialism an economic one; but the two overlap and reinforce one another.

Democratic movements like workers' unionism and citizens' consumerism are direct forms of socialism. Michael Harrington described socialism as a true decentralization, a system of worker self-management, of participatory democracy at the production level. The ultimate purpose of socialism is to prevent the few from ruling the many through systems of work. Leszek Kolakowski, the Polish philosopher, said, "Democratic socialism has no prescription for the total salvation of mankind. It only has ... an obstinate will to erode by inches the conditions that produce avoidable suffering, oppression, hunger, war, racial and national hatred, insatiable greed and irrational envy."

Socialism is anti-hierarchical and anti-authoritarian. Some of its utopians envision a world of workers, all equal, toiling side by side for the common good, with no owners or managers or bosses to rule or abuse anyone. Everything is voluntary. Workers work as much as they want to. Consumers consume as much as they need to. The state has withered away leaving only a collection of voluntary cooperatives. Forlorn hope! However dreamy and unrealistic this is, the vision is certainly humane and democratic in the most literal sense.

Why do politicians, journalists, and historians try to draw a distinction between socialism and welfarism? Among other things, socialism is welfarism. Before marxism, there had always been a familial or nurturing element in socialism. Probably it came from early tribal history, especially before the invention of agriculture and private property. Socialism can be seen as the economic expression of tribalism. Tribalism was collective, cooperative, egalitarian, and democratic; food, shelter, safety, and health were all collective and cooperative matters.

We need to redefine the terms we use to describe the economic and political world we live in. Capitalism is the means by which the few use the work of the many to enrich and empower themselves. Capitalism is not primarily about the ownership of property; it's about the control of work.

Socialism is economic democracy, not economic equality. The notion of economic equality imposed by the state, much less an absolutely rigid equality, is totalitarian as well as ridiculous. It is bossism that has to be eliminated or at least reduced, not differential rewards fairly and proportionately based on differences in effort and output. Of course, there should be a much greater equality than that provided by capitalism, but that will be the natural result of economic democracy.

Of course, property is an issue. To have true economic democracy, the people who work in a factory must control the factory and its bosses with their votes. In other words, the bosses should work for the workers and be subject to demotion and firing at the will of the workers. To have true economic democracy, large businesses would have to become cooperatives directly controlled by workers and subject to broad policy direction by the people generally. Small businesses should be left to function independently as they do now.

A system like this wouldn't be that hard to achieve in purely practical terms. The economic functions and mechanisms now in place wouldn't change enormously. At a given factory, for example, workers might well vote initially to keep some or all of the bosses in place and might also vote to keep the same policies, business practices, and pay structures in force. In the long run, of course, there would be a large and nonviolent transformation.

Naturally, the great problem is that the current economic power structure would never allow such a cooperative system to be established without the application of force. No one believes that such a system could be achieved by peaceful means. But it is not as utopian or extreme as some might think. It would not overthrow all existing economic practices and it would not seek to transform fallible human beings into the "new man" envisioned by utopians. The state would not wither away. Anarchism would not emerge. People would not become angels. They would not become less selfish and they would not stop exploiting one another. Democracy is a great and equitable system and it can make life far better and much fairer than it is now. However, it cannot change human nature and it cannot create a perfect world or a noble one.

The central insight of socialism was that, under capitalism, the worker has no control over his work and, therefore, little general control over his own life and its environment. When you work eight or more hours a day, sleep another eight so you can go on working, and use the remaining eight to prepare for work, travel to and from work, and feed, clothe, and nourish your body so it is able to keep on working, there isn't much time left for any other purpose. And when all of this is more or less dictated by business owners and bosses, then life loses its autonomy and the worker is forever locked into a closed system from which he cannot escape, since he has no power and no independence of his own. Under these circumstances, even relatively good pay and an abundance of consumer goods are not tremendously satisfying.

Socialism has always existed in the minds and words of working people. They have always complained about their bosses and rulers. They have always known that they were being used for somebody else's benefit and they have always longed for control over their work so they could better control their own lives and advance their own personal interests.

The conservatives rigidly insist that the political system in the so-called communist societies was socialist, that it failed, and that anyone who disagrees is making excuses for socialism. The reason they insist so fanatically on this view is because they are afraid of socialism or any alternative to their beloved religion of capitalism. They want the entire world for themselves; economic democracy is the last thing they want to see.

The term "socialism" has been badly tarnished by the cold war. With both the communist countries and the capitalist opposition proclaiming that the cold war was a struggle between capitalism and socialism, the absence of any real socialism was ignored. However, it really doesn't matter whether or not the term "socialism" is used in the coming battle between the capitalist authoritarians and the economic democrats. In the long run, the authoritarians cannot win unless they establish a total dictatorship over the people of the world. Of course, that is just what they are trying to do right now with their free-market globalist system of dominance and control.

If the authoritarians are to continue in control then, eventually, even the present Western forms of economically manipulated political democracy will have to be destroyed. Before that can happen, however, advances in computer information systems and a decreased need for human labor will force democracy on every culture. Power will inevitably shift from property owners and bosses to consumers and workers. Physical labor and the time demands of work will decrease and, more and more, the economy will come under the control of individuals and small groups of citizens working together for their mutual benefit. Corporate capitalism will disappear and economic democracy will become a reality. This may take a hundred years or more but it will happen.

In 1865, close to eighty percent of the American people lived on farms. How industrial could that have been; how capitalist could it have been? The farmers weren't capitalists just because they owned the land on which they farmed. By my definition, capitalists are people who control the work of others, not merely people who own property. A few of the farms had hired hands but most were family farms. In any case, the relationships between farmers and their few hired hands certainly weren't typically capitalist. If capitalism is understood as a system in which the few control the work of the many, then it can't include family farms or even small businesses. It seems clear to me that farms and businesses worked by the people who own them are more socialist than capitalist. Any sane definition of socialism includes the idea that the people who do the work also own the work and its product. The real distinctions between capitalism and socialism are nothing like those invented by cold warriors.

Another example of the confused definitions and functions of our capitalism are insurance systems, including health insurance; these systems are, in fact, a clever combination of capitalism and socialism. Their advertised purpose is to provide benefits and protection to members for some specified misfortune such as accident, ill health, theft, injury, or death. Benefits only go to those who, by chance, suffer loss; and so the system is a kind of collective welfare scheme in which the many members share costs but only the few get any benefits. From each according to his premium to each according to his policy, so to speak.

In function, insurance systems are entirely socialist or cooperative. What makes them also capitalist is that their ultimate purpose is to make a profit for an authoritarian owner who makes all the decisions about "his" company including even its existence. The owner is the absolute master of the enterprise and the receiver of all of its profits. He decides the way in which benefits are to be distributed and to whom as well as the amounts to be paid. He hires and fires all workers, originates and fixes all operating policies, and decides whose membership to accept, reject, and discontinue. To be sure, his decisions are not entirely arbitrary but that is only because the members and society in general force him, through laws and regulations, to respect some of the claims and some of the rights of members and employees. Even so, he often evades his responsibility in order to maximize his profits.

If the ownership of such a company is made democratic (that is, shared equally by its members), then it ceases to be capitalist even though, in every other way, it may function exactly as before. What distinguishes capitalism from socialism is not the organization of a business or the making of a profit but the use of the labor, the money, the health, and even the lives of the many to benefit the few. Without an authoritarian owner, there is no capitalism.

All wealth comes from the collective condition of those in a given political unit, not from isolated, individual accomplishment. People succeed only because many others allow them and help them to succeed. All success comes at the expense and rests on the shoulders of other people. It is the poor and the lower orders who make the rich rich. No one becomes rich or even moderately well off in an economic, social, and political vacuum. The systems of money and commercial exchange are common creations of society as a whole. Some few succeed because their fellow citizens and their ancestors created and maintain a system that permits them to do so. Wealth is never earned alone. It is never entirely individual and it is never entirely deserved by those to whom it migrates.

It ought to be clear to anybody that capitalism is an economic system that benefits the few at the expense of the many; it is a completely undemocratic system of privilege and exploitation. It's just horseshit to pretend that economic democracy can't possibly work and that it is, therefore, utopian and unachievable. It's easily achievable and it doesn't require a complete restructuring of society. What it does require is democracy in the workplace, i.e., worker ownership of all large businesses and a system of voting for the appointment and removal of managers and executives as well as voting on all important issues. No system of centralized power in the hands of owners and bosses is needed and neither is any system of centralized government bureaucracy.

Even under the best conditions, working for someone else's benefit is oppressive. However, the best conditions have rarely ever existed in the history of work. Rather, working people have almost always been brutally exploited, worn out, injured, and often killed by their work or, more directly, by their bosses. Bossism is by far the most murderous force ever to exist on the face of the earth. Work has injured and killed many, many more people than war. Millions have suffered, sweated, and died so that a few could live rich lives.

Opposition to the ownership of property is not the be all and end all of socialism. Absolute economic equality is not the aim and the purpose of socialism. Socialism is not economic centralization as so many conservatives pretend; rather, it is the ultimate decentralization with the worker owning his own work at the factory level and everywhere else. Socialism is not state planning though, under a real socialist system, some mechanism of coordination would undoubtedly be necessary to assist independent cooperative enterprises and individual workmen. Such mechanisms would have to be democratic or they would not be socialist; of course, they exist under capitalism and in government now but they are not now democratic.

If any system of socialism is ever established on earth, it will not resolve all problems or be free of error and failure any more than capitalism is. It will not be perfect or utopian. Unlike capitalism, however, it will not claim that there is magic in the economic machine or that the system is self-correcting and ordained by all the gods. If such a system is ever established, rather, it will be democratic by definition and it will put power in the hands of working people and their families. It will take power out of the hands of owners, bosses, and politicians and it will result in much greater equality and stability than now exists. And most important of all, it will serve the everyday interests of human beings rather than those of the beneficiaries of bottom lines, production numbers, and profit margins. Life will be better simply because people will all be free of the fanatical obsessions, aggressions, and compulsions of capitalist greed and of the irrational competitiveness that drives the industrial enterprise.

By definition, it isn't possible to be egalitarian without being democratic. If everyone is equal, then everyone has an equal vote on all important issues; and that spells democracy. However, the kind of equality wanted by ordinary human beings is not any absolute material equality but fair reward based on a system put in place by a democratic vote and an ethic of fairness. No one with any sense believes that democratic voting is always fair but what else is there short of dictatorship. What people really want in their work is a sense of decency. Perfection is not in the cards but something a lot more just and satisfying than the competitive rat race is certainly possible.

The Soviet Union was not the embodiment of "actually-existing socialism" or any socialism. There has always been and there remains one fundamental, simple, sensible definition of socialism and that is economic democracy. No non-democratic or antidemocratic economic system can be described as socialist. All of the economic systems established by communism were antidemocratic; under it, workers did not control their work in any way whatever. It cannot be repeated often enough: communism was a form of capitalism, not a form of socialism.

Socialism will continue but perhaps other names will be used for it. The democratic impulse will continue in the working lives of human beings. They will continue to resist those who own them and control them. They will continue to insist, if sporadically and intermittently, that they be given control over their own work and their own lives. There will be strikes, political movements, revolts, reforms, and advances. And there will be plenty of failures.

The emphasis on any future socialism needs to be on economic democracy, not on some system of imposed economic equality. In and of itself, economic equality is meaningless; but economic fairness is of enormous importance. Of course, fairness demands a substantial level and degree of equality but not an arbitrary one, not a rigid one, not an automatic one, not one imposed from above. There needs to be room for initiative and differential reward based on effort and achievement. Unless there is, there can be no fairness and no real equality.

Workers should be able to earn extra income and benefits by their own extra effort and talent. However, those extras must be commensurate with the degree of extra effort and achievement. No one can ever "earn" hundreds or even thousands of times more wealth than the next guy. It isn't possible. Indeed, it's hard to see how one person can work even two or three times more hours or expend two or three times more energy than the next guy. As for talent and achievement, neither comes in large multiples. There should be limits on reward and wealth. Obviously, democratic government — that is, voting by the whole people — is the only fair and appropriate way to establish the guidelines, rules, and limits for society's system of rewards. Let people earn extra wealth but not at the expense or the very survival of others. In any society, everyone should be able to live a dignified, decent, healthful life and no one should be able to benefit himself at the expense of the humanity and even the existence of another.

Naturally, there should be a minimum level of material support for every citizen. That must be the first priority of the economy. No one should be without adequate shelter, clothing, food, and medical care; and, at the basic level of sustenance and care, there should be absolute guarantees for everyone. And, of course, there should be equal treatment for everyone but with a care for any difference in condition. A rich society like ours can easily afford to meet all of the basic needs of its citizens but it cannot be done by indirection, that is, by charity drives or private capitalist money systems that give first, and usually sole, priority to profit, privilege, and luxury for the few. Neither can it be done by rigid egalitarians out to stifle all difference and punish all ambition and all acquisitiveness.

Greed is evil when it exploits others through systems of unfairly rewarded work or authoritarian work control, but some difference in economic reward is good and necessary. Such difference in reward must be just; it must not be extorted through the power of ownership and great accumulated wealth. The problem is in the extremes. Wealth must not be too great and there must be no avoidable poverty and suffering caused by economic want.

The death of communism was a huge advance for socialism. Because the communist regimes went beyond re-distributing wealth and implemented various degrees of totalitarian and repressive measures, and because Western capitalists used the evils of communism to scapegoat socialism, there is now a widespread belief that socialism is dead. It is not so. Socialism is more alive now than ever. Western, and now Eastern, capitalism may extend their control over people and the work they do, but eventually the abuses of capitalism will cause the world's citizens to take more economic power into their own hands, whether through revolution or evolution.

In fact, Western capitalism is thoroughly infiltrated now with socialist mechanisms and processes. Welfarism is socialism. Unionism is socialism. Consumerism is socialism. Environmentalism is socialism. All of these movements are but different means of reducing the controls of owners and bosses over citizens' work and the fruits of their labor. All are hostile to the abuses of capitalism and all are fanatically hated by the corporatists and their supporters. The future is tending toward economic democracy, that is, the control of work by workers, consumers, and ordinary citizens. The commercial interests cannot continue to dominate the people indefinitely. Capitalist authority will weaken. Democracy will win.

CHAPTER 17. DECONSTRUCTING REPUBLICANISM

The conservatives and the libertarians both hate liberalism because it favors the constructive use of government to help ordinary citizens live decent lives and because, to this end, it supports civil rights, human rights, and the rights of working people. Both bitterly oppose the liberal's supposed belief in relativism and equality and also claim that the rights liberals have been advancing ever since the American Revolution are destroying the social and political order. The advocates of both conservatism and libertarianism believe in the rule of an upper class of rich men raised up to nobility by their ownership of money and property; and they believe that the lower orders have a patriotic and christian duty to obey the rules of the property owners and bosses with no interference from the government, unions, consumerists, environmentalists, civil rightists, pacifists, or any dissidents whatever.

The conservatives and the libertarians (Republicans all) don't usually admit openly that their belief system is intensely authoritarian and antidemocratic, so deeply so that it can only be called totalitarian. Their burning contempt for civil rights and the rights of working people, for toleration and some measure of equality, and for the very idea of human rights can only be seen as tyrannical and oppressive in the extreme.

The threat to the social and political order comes from the conservatives and the libertarians, not from the liberals who are merely representing the values and traditions of the American Revolution, a revolution against the divine rights of King George and his English aristocracy. The Revolution was not waged for independence alone but also for a democratic order that posited the equal and natural rights of citizens as against the political, social, economic, and religious order of the world's divine tyrants. The American Revolution was the most radical uprising ever and it and the French Revolution marked one of the great breaking points in human history, the point at which the divine rights of kings and their upper-class aristocratic tyranny began to be overthrown all across the world. The conservative and the libertarian movements are merely heavily disguised throwbacks to that old despotic order.

When all is said and done, the conservative propaganda against American liberalism and the democratic government of the United States contradicts and indicts itself at every turn. The conservatives' own words are deeply hostile to America and the West. Traced to their sources, the ideas behind those words reveal themselves to be fascist and tyrannical. The real enemy, within and without, has always been fascism in all of its guises. Stalinism, nazism, and conservatism are and always have been the enemy and, despite much propaganda to the contrary, those three isms blend together closely and, sometimes from seemingly different directions, they all attack liberalism and democracy and pretend that they and they alone represent the true American way.

The words used by the conservatives to damn liberalism and democracy reveal just how absolutist and authoritarian the conservative movement really is. The conservatives regularly condemn American society itself with certain key words that they sneeringly repeat over and over again as evidence of the evil nature of liberalism and democratism. Those accusatory words are relativism, tolerance, equality, rights, racial justice, gender fairness, equal opportunity, collectivism, secularism, modernism, permissiveness, regulation, centralization, public, socialist, free, progressive, populist, politically correct, etc., etc., etc.

Republican conservatives describe everything in Manichean terms — good versus evil, the Republican Party versus the Democratic Party, capitalism versus socialism, conservatism versus liberalism. This may be a useful rhetorical device, one I use myself, but the Republicans reverse the normal terms of the argument, at least as they are seen by traditional Western democrats. For the Republicans, authoritarianism is good and democracy is evil, responsibilities are good and rights are evil, aristocracy is good and equality is evil, moral outrage is good and tolerance is evil, military attack is good and negotiation is evil, absolutism is good and relativism is evil.

Republicans have a harsh, bitter, rigid view of the world and they are always prepared to hurt and even kill those who disagree with or stand against them. They even condemn their own allies when they dare to deviate a jot from the prevailing conservative dogma. Conservatives are an unhappy, resentful lot; they loudly announce, as a matter of policy, that "Those who are not with us are against us"; and they regularly smear everyone in opposition as evil, communistic, or terroristic.

GOVERNMENT HATE

When the conservatives rage against the democratic government of the United States, it's not just a partisan tactic. They really do hate their own government (even when they are in charge of it) but, even more, they hate the very idea of democracy. For at least the last half-century, they have been using a strange subterfuge to conceal their contempt for their own country's democratic system. They claim that the founders of our country set up a "republic" rather than a democracy and that our present system of government is illegitimate. Somehow, it has degenerated and been taken over by the "democratists." Even more strangely, they claim that the Republican Party is named after this original republican idea and that the Democratic Party is named after a later democratic corruption of that idea. This weird nominalism or naming exercise seems to have come from the John Birch Society but there may have been some earlier origin.

At any rate, this claim defies all dictionary definitions and history as well. Of course, it is only an evasion designed to confuse the people and to keep them from knowing the straight truth about Republican elitism and authoritarianism. Republicans know the people will reject them if they ever find out the true nature of their anti-democratic belief. Their jerrybuilt system is a recent invention and it has been shaped by conservatives to accommodate all kinds of ideological mumbo jumbo including Southern racism, the doctrines of privatization, deregulation, devolution, forced christian religious practices, and the absurdity of preemptive attacks designed to force "democracy" on other people against their wills.

PRIVATIZATION AND DEREGULATION

Privatization is an attack against democratic government. Its purpose is to remove all power from democratic hands so it can be placed in private hands. The Republicans are trying to destroy as much governmental power as they can. They do not want the people of this country — or any country — to vote on any commercial issues whatever.

Another closely related part of this Republican subversion of democratic government is deregulation. If everything is privatized and nothing private can be regulated in any way by democratically elected officials of the government, there can be no democracy at all. There can only be a private world forever immune from any restraint or direction by democratic or popular instruments. Voting in such a system is completely senseless. This system is known as fascism. What I am saying is not a matter of opinion. It is a matter of overwhelming fact. Democracy cannot survive massive privatization and deregulation. These two Republican devices have but one purpose: the destruction of democracy and the disarming of the people so they can be exploited and manipulated by private power alone.

Thus, there is a bitter fight today between those who support public enterprise and those who support private enterprise; and, sadly, the privateers are winning. Bit by bit, democracy is being destroyed by the Republican Party. Many members of the Democratic Party — especially those who belong to the quisling DLC — are helping the privateers in their attacks against the democratic government of the United States.

The Republican alternative to democratic government is corporate authoritarianism or fascism, the exact system championed by Hitler and Mussolini. We are almost there and, with the Republicans now entirely in charge of all three branches of government and with their huge multiplication of military and police power, there is no one to oppose the totalitarian might of these corrupters and subverters. Right now (the early 2000s), this country is in greater danger than it ever has been before and the greatest danger is internal, not external. It is not terrorism but Republicanism that threatens to destroy America.

CONSUMER AND WORKER RIGHTS

Another facet of the Republican and commercial attack against democracy is the effort to suppress the rights of consumers and workers. Consumer and labor organizations are private and voluntary groups that work against the commercial abusers in the interests of their members and indeed in the interests of all citizens. These private organizations are democratic in their formation and function although they are not a formal part of government. Unlike the Chamber of Commerce, the Better Business Bureau, the National Association of Manufacturers, and dozens of other organizations that represent the commercial interests only, consumer, environmental, and labor organizations represent ordinary people, that is, the overwhelming majority of the people. The Republicans are trying to outlaw these organizations or at least to pass laws that rob them of any right to "interfere with" business interests. They are even trying to "reform" the system of tort law so that juries will not be allowed to decide issues regarding damages done to ordinary citizens by abusive and dishonest business practices. And they have passed many product "disparagement" laws that prevent citizens or citizen organizations from ever saying a negative word about any commercial product no matter how accurate or truthful such words may be. All of this is a direct attack against the democratic rights of the people of this country.

CHURCH AND STATE

And there is still another attack against the rights of the people, this one against the separation of church and state, in favor of forced school prayer, and, in fact, universal forced public worship in all of its ugly forms. There are, as well, efforts to clear the way for religious advertising and proselytizing on all public property. This may be the most tyrannical and the most dangerous of all of the Republican assaults against the rights of the people because religious freedom is among the most personal and private of all rights and it is the easiest to misrepresent and abuse.

Supreme Court justices Rehnquist, Scalia, and Thomas claimed that the First Amendment does not prevent the government from favoring religion over non-religion. In other words, they claim that the government *can* discriminate against and even attack the rights of nonbelievers. If the government can discriminate against nonbelievers, then obviously it can also discriminate against *certain* believers, that is, the ones it defines as not *true* or proper believers. This can only mean the establishment of a government religion, one that includes and excludes citizens by fiat.

Even Billy Graham long ago gave up his claim that the constitution does not guarantee "freedom from religion" but only "freedom for religion." How-

ever, with the encouragement of Supreme Court justices, such religious big-
ots as Elizabeth Dole and Joseph Lieberman have now taken up Graham's
old cry against religious liberty. There is no doubt that a state religion is
now being established bit by bit and that unbelievers and heretics are under
threat of exclusion from full citizenship.

The rage aroused in the fundamentalist christians by the Republicans
is a real threat to religious freedom because these christians are part of a
substantial majority (a falsely perceived one, I believe) that has very little
respect for religious deviation or dissent. If the Republicans succeed in their
subversions of religious freedom, persecution and civil strife are sure to follow. Then, it won't be long until the christians start persecuting and killing
the nonchristians just as they have always done when they have had enough
political power to do so. After that, the many christian sects will attack one
another over doctrinal differences.

What the christians choose to ignore is that they are not one religion
but many. The different sects have vastly different dogmas, different rules
of behavior, and different definitions of their various gods. There is no way
they can live together in peace and without trying to "save" the members
of contending sects through coerced conversions and militant propaganda
campaigns. The christian sects cannot live together without violence as
they have proven time and again throughout their history in Europe and
everywhere else.

Proselytizing christians want to impose their religion on everyone else.
They say that their god tells them to become missionaries — "fishers of
men" — and they dedicate themselves to luring or forcing others away from
what they consider the evil and sinful ways of other religions and belief systems. Unless you believe just what they believe, you are living in sin and
error and they think they have to save you from yourself and from whatever
non-christian creed you adhere to. You are wrong and immoral because you
do not agree with them and obey them when they tell you what their god
demands of you.

They actually believe that they are being objective and morally upright
when they try to seize control over you and your conscience. They want
to own you and they demand that you think what they think and believe
what they believe. Their religion is right and moral because it is theirs and
not yours. There is no arrogance and no egomania greater than that of the
proselytizing christians.

Though they pretend they do, these christians do not respect or tolerate the beliefs of different others and they are fanatically determined to gain the upper hand at any cost, including coercion and force. Christianity is an aggressive, violent religion that has always tried to conquer the world and to impose itself on every living organism and institution in existence. It is totalitarian by any and every measure.

If christians practiced their various religions in their churches, at home, on their private property, and even quietly and unobtrusively in public, there would be no clash between them and those of us who do not share their belief. But this is something they can never do. They are not capable of neutrality or even civility. They are determined to testify and condemn, to proselytize and convert, to rage against and attack the sin they claim to see in the world and in the lives of all of those different from them. They are determined to conquer us all down to the last resisting child.

They despise the idea of democracy because it requires tolerance and respect for the private beliefs of all. They claim to believe in religious freedom but they do not. Over and over again, endlessly, they tell us that their god is the one and only king of this and every other country and that we have no right to disobey any of his rules as formulated, stated, and interpreted by them alone. They cannot bear the freedom of others, their right to keep their beliefs to themselves, their right not to be bombarded by christian propaganda just about every hour of every day. True fundamentalist christians are not nice people. They are not even decent people. They are always on the attack and frequently they are tyrannical and brutal in the name of their unjust, murderous god.

Law and Regulation

In another one of their odd self-contradictions, the Republicans say they love law and order but hate regulation. Somehow, the first is moral and the second immoral. The reason for this, of course, is that the Republicans think they need law and order to control the unruly masses but object to any controls at all on the upper class that owns the businesses affected by regulation, namely them. They want to force morality on the people but don't want any morality at all applied to them and theirs.

What we're talking about here and elsewhere is a class struggle between the few who own most of the wealth and property and the rest of us who are forced to work for them and obey them. They think they are our mothers and fathers, morally and economically. They stand above us because capitalism has appointed them as our masters. They think that capitalism is our moral system as well as our economic system and, for many of them, it is also a pure and unchallengeable religion. According to them, it does not make mistakes and it does not need any restraint or correction — ever.

In the end, there is no difference between laws and regulations except for their targets. What's good for the democratic goose ought to be good for the capitalist gander. There can be no democracy or any order without laws *and* regulations. A decent society has to be regulated but laws and regulations have to be fair. Civil rights and economic rights have to be defended against private abusers and it is democratic government that must do this job. The Republicans are going to have to get over the notion that no one has the right to restrain them. It is always the rich and privileged few who cause revolutions and guarantee violence. That is just where we are headed unless the Republicans are forced to show some respect for the rights of citizens.

EQUALITY

Aside from the idea of democracy itself, nothing arouses the contempt of Republicans more than the concept of equality. Time and again, they rage against equality claiming it is "unnatural" and entirely hostile to their concept of liberty. It is their contempt for equality that leads them to oppose civil rights and human rights. In fact, they have been waging an intense campaign against rights generally ever since Reaganism showed its oppressive head and began to pack the federal courts with anti-egalitarians. It's astonishing that they believe liberty is reserved for the rich alone and that liberty *and* equality cannot be compatible.

Concealed just behind the Republican contempt for equality, there stands the ogre of racial and genetic superiority. Almost without exception, the Republicans argue, directly or indirectly, that crime and poverty are inherent traits and not conditions of environment. They claim that the poor cause their own poverty and nothing at all can or should be done to help them. Likewise, they claim that criminals are bad seed and that rehabilitation always fails. Furthermore, they believe that these undesirables must be severely shamed and punished for their bad character and that the government must never be allowed to help them in any way. They should be allowed to die out or to kill one another off. Of course, the "successful" and the "fit" must be protected from them through the use of a strong and ever-present police force. Capitalism and christianity provide the only formal and legitimate tests of the fitness of citizens, and the racially and economically impure must be helped to fail those tests.

Though it is concealed from the public by the media, this country sterilized thousands of impure citizens throughout the twentieth century and intimidated millions more. This sterilization policy came from the conservative and christian value system. Many Republicans supported this policy as did almost all Southern Democrats. At bottom, nearly every Republican alive today opposes the concept of equality and believes that, for one reason or another, there are inherent differences between the upper and lower classes and races.

Republicans see equality as the enemy of liberty. The motto of the French Revolution was "Liberty, Equality, Fraternity" and that is why the Republicans hate the French Revolution, and the French people, so much. They say they hate it because of The Terror, which killed several thousand, but it's quite clear that what they really hate is its destruction of the old royal aristocratic order and the rise of the democratic ideals of liberty and equality. The revolutionaries thought that liberty and equality went together and were entirely compatible and, deep down, most Americans agree.

To believe in equality is to believe in equal rights for all citizens. Republicans like to claim, rather idiotically, that equality means the assumption by government that every citizen has equal physical strength, equal brain power, equal skill, equal creative power, equal imagination, etc. and that, therefore, all rewards must be the same. Hard pressed by the civil rightists, they changed their argument somewhat and began claiming that they believe in "equality of opportunity" but not "equality of outcomes." In other words, they believe in a kind of narrow procedural equality as long as there are no positive outcomes. In fact, voting rights, busing, and affirmative action, for example, were all procedures designed to increase real opportunities for minorities. The Republican Party opposed them all. Thus, it does not favor any kind of equal opportunity.

It should be noted that voting is merely a democratic procedure, not an outcome. Busing was a method or procedure used to get blacks to white schools so they could take classes and compete with the white kids. It was not an outcome. Affirmative action was a method or procedure for placing minorities in jobs or colleges. Then, as workers and students, the minorities had to work for their own outcomes. Affirmative action itself was not an outcome.

In any case, equal opportunity is largely meaningless unless there are a reasonable number of positive outcomes. Liberals believe that, given a fair chance, minorities will quite often succeed. Republicans claim they don't believe this because they just *know* that minorities are incompetent and defective; but, quite obviously, they fear that it might be true. Therefore, they do everything in their power to stack the deck against any more than a tiny, token number of equal outcomes.

Today, even the Republican Party has a few tokens of its own. With hardly an exception, these tokens claim to be superior and heroic talents who succeeded on their own without any help from civil rightists. Being good Republicans, they too rage against equal opportunity claiming that it demeans minorities and casts a shadow over their own wonderful achievements. It's too bad they don't believe in civil rights. Given the great talents they claim to have, they might be of help to their own people instead of working so diligently for the privileges of white men.

LIBERTY

What kind of liberty is reserved for the privileged class alone? Republicans always define liberty in terms of money and property; and they mean quite literally that the rich should have liberty and not anybody else. If liberty is defined as freedom from restraints or control by others, then, of course, money, property, and influence can buy liberty of a kind. If only the rich can afford this liberty, though, then most people will never be free. Although Reagan and such other strange people as Ayn Rand and George Gilder claim they can, the hard reality is that only a small portion of any society can be rich. The rich rise on the backs of working people and consumers and all profit is a taking. Entrepreneurs don't "create" wealth. They extract it from the labor and consumption of their fellow citizens. There must be (or should be) a mathematical formula somewhere in economics that explains profit. It would show workers and consumers on one side of the equal sign and profiteers on the other. The workers and consumers give; the profiteers take.

Under the word "liberty," my dictionary says, "1. Freedom or release from slavery, imprisonment, captivity, or any form of arbitrary control, and 2. The sum of rights and exemptions possessed in common by the people of a community, state, etc." Thus, liberty is "possessed in common by the people" and cannot be reserved for the rich alone. The first definition says liberty is "freedom or release from slavery, imprisonment, captivity or any other form of arbitrary control." The use of money and property to exert control over people is "arbitrary control." When all is said and done, the Republicans don't believe in liberty any more than they believe in equality. They are political and economic authoritarians who invent numerous lies to conceal their real belief system and justify their privilege.

Without reservation, the Republicans want inequality. They want anti-democracy. They want wealth and privilege for the few and supine obedience and hard work for the laboring masses. They demand servility from the lower orders and they justify it all with the fantastic claim that they love liberty and believe in merit when what they really believe in is a totalitarian state massively dedicated to the dominance of their wealth, their privilege, their religious dogma, and their very own values and virtues. They believe in a two-class system with them alone in the top class.

RELATIVISM

A man named Ralph Estling, posing as a skeptic, attacks relativism as "the hell of pseudo- and quasi-science" and goes on to say that we mustn't "confuse relativism with relativity." Actually, relativism fits very nicely with Einstein's ideas about relativity. There *is* a scientific and philosophic concept behind the notion of relativism and, generally speaking, it stands in opposition to absolutism. Republican conservatives claim that relativists are people who treat ideas as if they were "neutral" or of "equal value." Of course, that is precisely the scientific attitude, at least at the initial stages of its investigative undertakings. Indeed, it is also the attitude of scientists at all times that truth is tentative and forever open to question. It's true that scientists ultimately decide "some ideas are better than others." However, even after scientific laws have been established and made operational, competent scientists still try to keep "open minds" — that bugaboo of the anti-relativists — about the nature and character of the laws, the facts, and the truths they see, or think they see, around them in the real world.

The Republican conservative anti-relativists don't like science and reason very much and have always been hostile to Einstein, Darwin, Galileo, Bruno, and most other scientists. They are comfortable with dogmatic religion but not with the uncertain and provisional nature of scientific truth.

What's odd, of course, is that these enemies of science and reason live their lives almost entirely in a world made by scientific discovery and development. They can't escape it. Still, they try to purge it from the schools and from government and often associate it with communism, socialism, and liberalism. Well, it *is* liberal — and relativist. Thank god! If there is one.

COLLECTIVISM AND INDIVIDUALISM

In their usual arbitrary way, the Republicans pit collectivism against individualism and centralization against devolution or states' rights. They claim that collectivism is the communist and socialist way while individualism is the American and capitalist way. I think that their definitions and comparisons are screwy and self-contradictory. Surely, majority voting is collectivist. That's what *we* do, not what the nazis and communists do. Can democracy possibly be anything except collectivist? This country was the first great mass democracy in the world and most of the time our population has been stable, docile, and obedient. Those traits aren't individualistic. We have plenty of individuals but, in large, we are a collectivist society, even a conformist one.

Presidents, popes, dictators, generals, CEOs, and police chiefs are individualists. The people controlled by them are not. Being an individual implies a certain stand-aloneness, a certain uniqueness, a certain nonconformity, a certain upper-classness. People of high rank can afford to be individualistic; there is nobody to force them into line. Working people have to conform to the rules of their bosses. If they become too individual on the job, they get fired and, if they become too individual in the streets, they get locked up.

And so again, some conservatives claim to support individualism, which they associate with capitalism, as the opposite of collectivism, which they associate with communism. But some others (Robert Bellah, Robert Bork, William Bennett, Edmund Burke, Joseph de Maistre) attack individualism and condemn it as a characteristic of liberalism. They see it as an embrace of material gratification and an attack against christian morality. They also see it as an attack against the legitimacy of authority and an improper justification for dissent.

On the other side, liberals believe in majoritarian vote but also believe that certain personal and individual rights must be protected against majoritarian coercions, no matter how many people want to violate those rights. The liberals thus try to reconcile individualism with democracy and collectivism. The conservatives just wallow in self-contradiction and liberal-hate.

We have more laws than anybody. Our police force is probably the biggest in the world. We have more prisoners in our jails than anyone else. We have more military power than anyone ever has had and one of the biggest armies around. We have enormous wealth, almost entirely in the hands of our upper class, which controls our own citizens and the people of the world with its money. Now, we have a president (Bush) who insists on conquering the whole world through unprovoked, indiscriminate, preemptive attacks so he can control all of its resources for the profit and comfort of our upper class and in the interest of his own political ambition. How much individualism do these leaders and their followers allow at home or abroad? They want obedience and they have deployed the police and the army so they can control us all in detail, freedom and individualism be damned.

CENTRALIZATION

Centralization is another Republican mantra. They were told all about "socialist centralization" by such people as Hayek and Friedman. The Soviet Union was indeed centralized but not much more so than the Western countries, especially the United States. Hayek pointed the capitalist finger at "central planning" as the basis of communist rule. What Hayek and Friedman objected to, of course, was *government* planning, or government anything. They did not object to private planning and made no mention of the overall levels of extreme centralization and planning in a corporatist country as against the overall levels of centralization and planning in a state capitalist country like the Soviet Union.

I have never heard of a large or medium-sized corporation in this country that didn't have a headquarters or central office, probably even numerous regional offices as well. I have never heard of a factory that didn't have a front office. All of these offices plan and plan and plan. I seriously doubt that there was even one tenth as much planning in the Soviet Union as in the United States during any common time period. I would also bet that there were more than ten times as many central offices, regional offices, front offices, and the like in the United States as there were in the Soviet Union. All of this nonsense about centralization is meaningless as are the various Republican theories about the superiority of local power to national power and the absence of planning as a great enhancer of morals and a proof of freedom. Coercive controls are as easy to impose by corporate headquarters as by the commissar's office.

Devolution is just another name for states' rights. The Republicans came up with it because states rights was a term closely and negatively associated with Southern racism, one of their beloved but concealed dogmas. Being tricky and dishonest in this maneuver as in all others, Newt Gingrich pushed this idiotic term into the public arena. The Republicans figured that if they couldn't grab all of the federal power for their private concoctions, they could at least push it down to the several state houses, counties, and cities where it would be so diffused as to be ineffectual and easy for the Republican Party and its rich clients to control.

National power is not necessarily or even usually more despotic than local power. In fact, local power is more likely to be despotic since it is closer and can be more invasive and more personally offensive than a distant power that could care less about the personal lives and habits of distant and unknown citizens. Local power might be warmer and friendlier at its best but it will surely be more jealous and injurious at its worst. Anyway, who wants warmth from government? This is just another Republican game of mumbly peg. It has no valence and can't be made into a sensible or even an intelligible policy.

As for the notion that socialism is centralization by definition, it's all balderdash. Ludwig von Mises, Friedrich von Hayek, and Milton "von" Friedman were responsible for the preposterous claim that socialism is a system of centralized economic planning that leads inevitably to tyranny. In fact, socialism is the ultimate decentralization, a means by which the worker, singly or in voluntary association with other workers, exercises control over his own work and the product of that work. It is capitalism that centralizes all authority, all planning, and all profit in the hands of a central owner (often a single owner) who exploits the work of others solely for his own profit and privilege. Centralized planning and control are the very essence of capitalism but the conservative ideologues pretend that capitalism is, somehow, a system of rugged individualism that is the true expression of democracy.

Work is for the People

One definition of tyranny is the arbitrary control of the many by one or a small number of authoritative figures. A factory owner or other business owner is such a figure. Has anyone ever heard of a factory owner being elected by the workers in the factory or even by the general population? Has anyone ever heard of a factory owner conducting a referendum on his policies and business practices or on anything at all? If language means anything, then quite obviously it is the owner in whom all of the authority is centralized and it is the owner who is the tyrant, not workers controlling their own work and acting in voluntary association with other workers in their own interests. Socialism is obviously democratic by definition and capitalism is obviously anti-democratic. It is impossible for any rational person to draw any other conclusion.

After all, work is for the people. If a business can't charge its customers a fair price and pay its workers a living wage, then it has no right to exist. Work is for working people and consumers, not for owners and bosses. Making a big profit is not the purpose of organized work. The only legitimate reason for organizing work in the first place is to establish a shared community in which people can help one another live better and more securely. They can accomplish this by providing goods and services to one another in free and fair exchanges that don't exploit or abuse either the workers or the consumers. This cannot mean a commerce unregulated by the democratic instruments of the community. It cannot mean dog-eat-dog competition and it cannot mean the triumph of the profit motive over the needs of ordinary people. Work must serve the requirements of the people first and the profits of the bosses last.

Absolutism

Conservatives believe that life and morality cannot proceed without a fixed set of dogmas and a powerful authority to enforce those dogmas. Francis Fukuyama says. "If nothing can be true absolutely...then cherished values like human equality have to go by the wayside as well." For the moment, let's leave aside the fact that neither Fukuyama nor any of his fellow conservatives ever have believed in human equality and let's just say that, in fact, we all live by operational or provisional truths most of the time. You can call those truths inductive generalizations or commonsense assumptions based on experience and tested by time or whatever you will but you can't reasonably call them absolutes. Indeed, there *is* a core of accepted knowledge in every culture but there is no holy mandate to treat that knowledge as absolute, fixed, eternal, and sacred; in fact, over time, no culture has ever clung to absolutist doctrine and survived for very long. Absolutism kills too many people and makes too many enemies.

Because, at last, we cannot know the absolute truth, we have to live our lives tentatively and uncertainly. Absolutism may provide a feeling of security for some but it is oppressive and tyrannical by definition and the more rigid and certain it is in concept the more brutal it is sure to be in practice. Tolerance of the different beliefs, actions, and words of others is necessary to human decency and even to the most elemental requirements of democratic civility, practical cooperation, and useful human discourse. And yes, tolerance, equality, and democracy are all relativist in a sense but that does not mean that liberals consider all values to be neutral and equal. In fact, they consider liberal values to be superior to conservative values, indeed consider conservative values destructive, cruel, and despotic.

TOLERANCE

In your private sphere, you have a right to believe anything you want to believe and you have a right to do whatever you will as long as it doesn't intrude on or hurt others. In the public sphere, however, you are required to behave with enough tolerance so that others can live peaceful and unthreatened lives. You cannot impose your ideas or values on them and you cannot attack them or punish them for disagreeing with you. This means you have to be tolerant of ideas that you may not like. It means that the public polity has to remain neutral with respect to certain matters of private conscience and discreet moral practice, no matter what you think of them. This is what's called "minding your own business" and "tending your own crops." We liberals suggest that you conservatives should pay some serious attention to these maxims for a change.

It's easy enough to come up with logical-sounding arguments about the need for absolute ideas regarding the nature and certainty of truth but, in fact, such arguments cannot be logical. They can only be digressions into tyranny. Excluding most of the evidence cannot be a logical act. If you have a fixed idea and insist it is the only possible truth for now and forever, you are merely preparing the ground for slaughter. We don't know everything and never will. In fact, we know very little with any degree of certainty and know nothing at all worth the brutality and sterility of imposing it on others against their wills. Life is a continuing struggle for truth and human liberation. One of the best ideas we humans have ever had is the idea of democracy. Where absolutism prevails, there can be no democracy and little free choice. Democracy requires tolerance, civility, and a belief in the value of private conscience, un-coerced thinking, and free speech. Sad to say, the anti-relativists among us are too anti-democratic to be of any use in our quest for a better world.

THE REPUBLICAN ATTACK AGAINST LIBERAL AMERICA

The word "relativism" is an important word for the Republican attackers. It serves as an euphemism for tolerance and leads to a whole host of other words and concepts that stand for ideas that they detest. Relativism leads to tolerance, tolerance leads to racial and gender justice or civil rights, civil rights to human rights, and all of these lead to the general idea of rights and to democracy itself. Thus, when Republicans attack relativism, they are attacking everything that term stands for and leads to. They don't want the American people to know, without confusion, that the Republican Party stands massively against tolerance, civil rights, and the democratic government of the United States. They don't want them to know, in the end, that Republicans are the ones who are unpatriotic and un-American. They are the ones who hate what America stands for and they are the ones who "blame America" first, last, and always. They are the subversives and the traitors and they are the enemies of Western civilization.

I say this to the Republican conservatives. You can't make liberals out to be absolutists Bill-of-Rightists and relativists at the same time. You can't make them out to be communist oppressors and the "inventors" and "manufacturers" of "new rights" for the people at the same time. You can't say that they are both permissive and tyrannical, that they believe all values are neutral and equal and, at the same time, say that they believe in and follow the Stalinist line. And you can't rage against regulations to limit commercial abuses and then pass intensely punitive laws to repress the moral abuses you claim to see in the population at the same time. You can't impose your own censorious and punitive absolutes on everyone else and claim you are the apostles of freedom and you can't, at the same time, accuse liberals of being tyrannical because they show too much respect for rights and equality and tolerance and democracy. Unless you are utterly insane, you cannot equate liberalism and democratism with crime, communism, and terrorism and you can't blame these concepts and America's governmental institutions for your own abuses against your fellow citizens. In other words, you can't "blame America" for your own bizarre hang-ups and twisted ideas. And, at last, you can't degrade liberals with the deepest hatred imaginable, drive them out of their jobs and out of office unjustly, falsely accuse them of treason and every crime known to humankind, threaten to jail them and kill them on sight, and then claim that they are somehow showing an outrageous "disdain" for you.

CHAPTER 18. ZIONISM

In 1917, the Balfour Declaration stated that the British government supported the creation of a national home for the jewish people in Palestine. At
that time, there was only a tiny jewish presence in Palestine. In 1922, the
League of Nations referenced the Balfour Declaration in the mandate it gave
the British to oversee Palestine. In 1936–37, Great Britain's Peel Commission
recommended a two-state solution in Palestine requiring the compulsory
transfer of populations. A British white paper in 1939 rejected that recom-
mendation and the British government sought to limit the massive jewish
immigration it had previously allowed because it was causing resentment
and unrest. In reaction, zionist terrorists launched attacks against the British occupation forces and the Arabs in Palestine. Great Britain referred
the matter to the United Nations and the UN, manipulated by the United
States, recommended that Palestine be divided between the jews and the
Arabs with the United Nations retaining control over the city of Jerusalem.

In 1887, all but 5 percent of the population in Palestine was Arab. In
1920, less than one tenth of the population was jewish and jews owned less
than 7 percent of the land. Then there was a massive influx of jews driven by
a zionist plan to establish a state by "facts on the ground." Even so, by 1947,
no more than ten percent of the land in Palestine was owned by jews and
most of that land had been covertly purchased from Palestinians as part of
the zionist plan to establish a homeland by private means. The jewish population was still less than one third in 1947 when the Allied powers, appalled

by the Holocaust and eager to provide an outlet valve for their own jewish populations, decided to accommodate the zionist demand for a jewish homeland by giving them 53 percent of Palestine. The zionists celebrated and prepared to take control of their new state.

The Palestinians and all the Arab peoples were outraged; they demanded a single state and removal of the flood of jewish migrants that were invading what they considered their own territory. On May 14, 1948, the British mandate ended and the Jewish Agency, under Ben-Gurion, declared the creation of the state of Israel. Harry S. Truman immediately recognized the new state as did Joseph Stalin. Then 850,000 jews rushed in, most from the Arab world. As a result, 711,000 Palestinians were driven off their land and out of their ancestral homes. Some sixty years later, the Palestinians are still stateless and homeless.

The Arab League planned to invade as the British left. The Arab Liberation Army and village militias opposed jewish militias and a professional, well-armed jewish force called the Palmach. After the British departed, the Arab economy quickly collapsed. The jews had a good deal of money from the Jewish Agency, an independent tax source. More than 100,000 Palestinians were driven out in the early stages. By May of 1948, 150,000 more were evicted and driven out. The jewish force destroyed most of the Arab villages along the route between Jerusalem and Tel-Aviv. Czechoslovakia violated a UN Security Council arms embargo and supplied the jewish state with critical military hardware. The UN declared a month-long truce. Large numbers of jewish immigrants began arriving; most of them were World War II veterans and people released from the camps. Naturally Israel, having the best resources, gained the upper hand and won the war. By 1949, Israel controlled 78 percent of the land, not counting the West Bank left to Jordan and the Gaza Strip left in Egypt's hands, both of which Israel would seize in the 1967 Arab–Israeli war.

The Jordanian Arab League refrained from helping the Arab forces but instead focused on occupying the West Bank and East Jerusalem. In March of 1949, a permanent ceasefire went into effect and Israel's borders, along the Green Line, were established. Thus, between 1947 and 1949, over 700,000 Palestinians were driven from their homes by Israel. Refugees who left Palestine were settled in refugee camps and, except for Jordan, the Arab states denied them citizenship.

It was hardly surprising that the world's jews should have wanted a homeland to which they could migrate so they could escape the persecutions and expulsions they had suffered for nearly two thousand years at the hands of the christian and, much less often, the muslim countries. In fact, the muslim countries often welcomed jews expelled by the christian nations. However, Palestine did not belong to the jews; they had themselves been expelled by the Romans twenty centuries earlier. Furthermore, the British and the other World War II allies didn't own Palestine either; they had no right to give land owned and occupied for centuries by Palestinians to people who had no moral or legal claim to it, most of whom had never lived there at all.

The jewish claim was based on the preposterous religious notion that the jews were god's "chosen people" and that he had given them the "promised land" three or four thousand years earlier. Though there was no direct connection, of course, this claim very much paralleled Hitler's claim that his people (the Aryans) were a superior people under the approval of the christian god and that he had a right to seize the lands around Germany to gain "living space" for them.

Secretary of State George C. Marshall and many others opposed the establishment of a jewish state right in the middle of a contiguous area overwhelmingly owned and dominated by muslims and Arabs, seeing it would cause endless conflict and instability. The new zionist state has spent its entire history, more than sixty years now, attacking the Palestinians so as to expand its borders and establish itself as a mighty world power, a "greater Israel." Israel has been and continues to be a bone in the craw of just about every one of the one and a third billion Arab and muslim peoples who totally surround Israel; they live in fear of the Israelis' vast military power, created and supplemented by American power, including hundreds of illegally developed nuclear bombs.

As Israel grabs more and more Palestinian land and sends hundreds of thousands of "settlers" to occupy that land by armed force, Israel's leaders claim they are protecting their security, complain bitterly about the Palestinians' resistance, and slyly tell everyone that they are "establishing facts on the ground" by advancing relentlessly into Palestinian lands. Sad to say, history has often determined land rights based on conquest and without any consideration for the rights of the dispossessed. Force and religious dogma are the only claims Israel has ever had for its aggression. However, as unjust as Israel's establishment and expansion have been, it would be unthinkable to now dismember Israel and force it out of the country it has created. Just or not, the world is stuck with Israel. So are the Arab and muslim peoples.

However, it is not unthinkable for the world powers to force a solution on Israel and Palestine. The Palestinians have waited and suffered enough. Now is the time for a solution and only the United States, Israel's protector and enabler, has the power to force a solution. Unfortunately, American presidents have always refused to act against Israel's unjust aggressions, indeed have supported them with enormous handouts of money and military equipment.

With each passing year, Israel is inviting its own destruction. Even as Israel kills more and more of them, the Palestinians are multiplying and will soon outnumber the Israelis unless the government of Israel comes up with a "final solution." With the help of the United States, Israel might be able to exterminate all of the Palestinians or drive them out but they cannot conquer the entire Arab and muslim world. Israel is now a pariah throughout most of the civilized world and it will be so remembered forever in the pages of history as will the United States for its unrelenting help to Israel's unjust project. Israel and the United States are the aggressors in Palestine. There can be no possible doubt about that.

Israel cannot continue to exist without massive economic and military support from the United States. If the United States had the courage and sense to cut off all aid to Israel until it withdraws all of its settlers from Palestinian land, then a settlement would become possible. However, any American denial of funds has to be absolute. As for the details of a settlement, that should be placed in the hands of the United Nations. For the sake of stability, a fence could be erected all along the Green Line and the UN could patrol it and control all movement between the new state of Palestine and Israel. Likewise, the city of Jerusalem should be controlled by the United Nations. Something similar would be required for Gaza since it is geographically separate from the West Bank.

The UN and the United States should immediately recognize the existence of a new Palestinian state within the borders of the Green Line and around the existing borders of Gaza. The borders between Israel and Syria (the Golan Heights) and the still-disputed borders between Israel and Lebanon would be handled as separate matters; they should be much easier to settle after the new Palestinian state has been established.

There can be no "right of return" for the Palestinians, however just such a move would be. Israel is determined to be a theocratic state, a jewish state, as wrong and racist as that is. Despite claims to the contrary throughout the Western world, Israel is not a democratic state. It has periodic elections, has a parliament, and limits the terms of its top leaders. However, only jews have full rights of citizenship and Israel absolutely refuses to be fully secular. Secularism is a precondition for true democracy. Israel is not democratic and neither are any of the Arab and muslim states. For that matter, the United States itself is no longer a fully democratic country either. Its fanatical and indiscriminate anti-communism and now its even more sinister anti-terrorism have utterly crippled democracy here, enriched the military–industrial–media complex, and threatened peace and justice everywhere in the world. Israel has played an important role in corrupting democracy in the United States.

Z Magazine, December 2009, described what high school graduates said in an October 6, 1988 letter they sent to Prime Minister Benjamin Netanyahu announcing their refusal to serve in an occupation army, their belief that the settlement policy is "racist in principle," and their disagreement with the claim that Israel is "the only democracy in the Middle East." They ask, Can a government that controls the lives of millions of people who did not take part in elections be called a democracy? Can military rule of a civilian population be considered anything other than a "dictatorship"?

If Israelis want to live normal lives without being subjected to suicide attacks and without seeing their government launching massive and disproportionate military retaliations, then they have to allow the Palestinians to live normal lives too. The US, aided by the UN, can force a settlement and could have done so a long time ago. It need not ask any permission from Israel or the Palestinian authorities in the West Bank and Gaza. The solution, whatever the details, has to be forced and, of course, it must be just in the eyes of the world. If these two countries have to be maintained in a suspended but non-violent condition for years to come, so be it. The citizens of both countries — Israel and Palestine — should be able to live peaceful and unthreatened lives within the borders established for them by the world community.

Furthermore, Israel's neighbors should be able to live their lives in a normal fashion without constant threats and bombings from Israel. Settlement of the Palestinian problem along these lines will not eliminate the hostility between Israel and its neighbors but it will lessen the immediate problems and prepare the way for further diplomacy. Many Arab and muslim states are in unstable condition and the future looks bleak. However, if the US stops trying to force a Bush-style of totally phony "democracy" on those countries, some form of representative, but perhaps not fully democratic, government might be justly encouraged and supported by the West.

It should be openly recognized that what Bush was pushing in Iraq was not democracy but only a form of predatory capitalism disguised as democracy. The Republican Party does not believe in democracy, a fact the American media absolutely refuses to acknowledge. Fake democracy has long been a guise used to cover American aggressions against others. Exceptionalism was never based on anything democratic. Rather it was based on salvationist commercialism and missionary christianity.

I don't know how the zionists or the muslims or the hindus can be persuaded to establish truly secular (that is, tolerant and religiously neutral) governments. Such governments need not be fully democratic in the Western sense but they do need to be sensibly tolerant toward other belief systems. They could be jewish, muslim, or hindu according to necessarily reduced definitions; but, if they insist on abusing their own citizens — especially women and children — then the outside world must act to restrain them. This cannot mean violent war. Such wars always kill the innocent and make matters worse. There are other pressures and punishments.

Only a modicum of secularism can provide the conditions for cooperative living and at least some small freedom and security for citizens. In the meantime, the United States has no business trying to force its belief systems on others. It should encourage and reward democratic actions and especially secular ones but it must stop its aggressions and threats. This applies not only to religious issues but also to commercial (that is, capitalist) issues. The camouflaged aggressions of "neo-liberalism" have to stop. They are as tyrannical as are any of the other religious and ideological aggressions discussed here. Furthermore, American politicians and journalists must stop corrupting the meanings of words like "democracy" and "secularism" in order to justify unjust wars and interventions.

ISRAEL ON THE ATTACK

Extracted below from a Herbert P. Bix article in the May 2009 issue of *Z Magazine* is a summary description of some of Israel's recent behavior toward the Palestinian people:

> The Gaza assault began with a massive surprise air attack in broad daylight on December 27, 2008....

> The non-combatant, uninvolved population...had no place to hide. According to the Palestinian Center for Human Rights, in the three weeks between December 27, 2008 and January 18 the IDF killed not 1,300 as first reported but "1,434 people, including 960 civilians, 239 police officers, and 235 fighters." Of this number 288 were children and 121 women: a further 1,606 children and 828 women suffered injuries. Israeli soldiers trapped Palestinian civilians in their homes and apartments and murdered them when they attempted to leave bearing white flags. Israeli army tanks and snipers deliberately targeted women and children, hospital workers, ambulance drivers, doctors, medics, mobile clinics, clearly marked hospitals, the UN school in the Jabaliya refugee camp, and the UN university....

> The resulting physical destruction was enormous and impossible to justify in any way, let alone on grounds of "self-defense": over 4,000 homes completely destroyed, another 21,000 badly damaged, an estimated 5,000 to100,000 people rendered homeless, forced to live in tents provided by the UN under concrete blocks.... With Israel sustaining 10 military and 3 civilian deaths, even the most casual observers of the conflict found the 100 to 1 "kill ratio" shockingly lopsided....

Writing at an early stage of the Gaza assault, Noam Chomsky observed that "Israel could have security, normalization of relations, and integration into the region. But it very clearly prefers illegal expansion, conflict, and repeated exercises of violence, actions that are not only criminal, murderous, and destructive, but are also eroding its own long-term security." He then added, "Those who call themselves 'supporters of Israel' are in reality supporters of its moral degeneration and probably ultimate destruction."

Chapter 19. Imperialism: Killing Iraq

According to the dictionary, terrorism is the use of violence by an individual or group to coerce a government for some political reason. This term is not ordinarily used to describe violence by governments themselves but governments are far more dangerously violent than mere individuals and groups can possibly be. Some say terrorism should be defined as a tactic only. In any case, you cannot wage war against anything so abstract. Those who use such a term as an excuse for waging war are disguising their real purpose. They are asserting a right to use massive state violence indiscriminately. They are claiming wide authority for wanton and haphazard aggression against an undefined or falsely defined enemy.

Thus, they issue dire warnings against claimed threats from "evil doers" so they can tighten their grip on the resistant behavior of their own citizenry. They know that informed people will resist indiscriminate and unjustified attacks against false enemies but that the gullible are easily stampeded. That's why they lie with such extremity about the sins of those they seek to destroy and that's why they conceal their real purposes. They want war and they invent masses of lies to conceal their real aims. They pass laws against those who seek to restrict their fervor and restrain their violence to narrower, more rational ends. They resort to alien and sedition acts and to dishonestly labeled "patriot" acts. They announce that those who are not with them are against us all. They even violate the laws of their own country and say they are doing so in the name of security and extreme danger. Of course, they present no evidence for their claims and they hurry their wars along to avoid any informed challenge. Quite often, they threaten, imprison, abuse, and smear those who oppose or criticize them. What they are claiming for themselves is the right of dictatorship, the right to oppress, harm, and kill others outside the requirements of any established law. They call this totalitarian construction a "unitary presidency."

The above narrative describes the behavior of the Bush–Cheney government after the September 11th attack against the United States by al Qaeda. Instead of focusing American power against al Qaeda itself, the Bush–Cheney government launched a wide-ranging and misdirected attack against "terrorism." They said they were attacking fifty to sixty other countries in their war against terrorism. Bush called it a "crusade." They named Iran, Iraq, Afghanistan, Syria, and Korea as the "axis of evil." Without quite saying so, they also made it clear that they were including all of the enemies of Israel, in short, everyone in the Middle East except that great friend and business partner of the Bush and Cheney families, Saudi Arabia. As fantastic as it may seem, nearly all of the September 11th attackers were from Saudi Arabia including the gang leader, bin Laden. Just as strange, the Bush family was hosting the bin Laden family at the time of the attack after which they helped them leave this country secretly. Yet, they launched their attack against Iraq, a country that had nothing whatever to do with the September 11th attack against the United States and had no terrorists at all within its borders.

The Bush–Cheney government received at least forty warnings about the likelihood of an al Qaeda attack but ignored them all. Their own security adviser, Richard Clarke, was criticized and finally moved from his job by Condoleezza Rice for pestering the top staff in the White House and the Vice President's office by constantly warning them of a coming terrorist attack by al Qaeda, and "only al Qaeda" as he said. The government was heavily pressured to attack Iraq by neoconservatives and right-wing zionists. Indeed, Bush and Cheney were eagerly planning an attack against Iraq long before September 11, according to Bush's own Treasury Secretary, Paul O'Neill. Thus, the retaliatory attack against al Qaeda was deliberately muted by Bush and Cheney so the bulk of the military could be held back for an attack against Iraq instead. The September 11th attack was obscenely used as an excuse for a world war against "terrorism" and very specifically for an attack against Iraq.

Clearly, one purpose was to create a wider war against a weak enemy so Bush and Cheney could have a second term by pretending to be heroes who won a war against a mighty foe, in truth, a largely helpless Iraq. This is just what Reagan did with his unjustified sneak attack against tiny, unarmed Grenada. And it was what H.W. Bush did with his attacks against both Panama and Iraq. Those wars were deliberately instigated for internal political reasons. Presidents invariably gain public support when they attack someone. No American president has ever lost an election during a war. After September 11th, the only real enemy we had was a criminal gang, al Qaeda, consisting of about twenty thousand members worldwide, most of them in Afghanistan. There was no justification whatever for a war against a large portion of the entire muslim and Arab world. The war was manufactured and all of the reasons given to justify it were falsifications.

Bush and Cheney attacked Iraq precisely because they knew Iraq was extremely weak. They wanted an easy target. They knew full well that Iraq could not possibly have any appreciable number of weapons of mass destruction, any nuclear program, or any delivery system. Furthermore, they knew that bin Laden and Saddam Hussein could not be allies or collaborators, indeed knew that they had always been enemies and that there were absolutely no al Qaeda members in Iraq. The evidence of this last fact and of Iraq's weakness was overwhelming. There was no reliable contrary evidence at all. The entire story was manufactured. Only the extremely stupid believed it at all.

How could Iraq be a threat to the United States or anyone? With Reagan's enthusiastic support, it fought an eight-year long war against Iran, a much bigger country. It lost more than half a million men in that war and exhausted itself. It was bankrupt and pitifully weak. Then, two years later and encouraged to do so by the H.W. Bush administration, Iraq attacked Kuwait for stealing its oil and because it desperately needed to replenish its resources. On the pretense that he was defending Kuwait, "H.W." Bush sent a 700,000-man army against an unresisting Iraq army of less than 180,000. He killed several hundred thousand Iraqis, most of them while they were retreating. Saddam began to destroy his weapons of mass destruction, and they were all gone in short order. "H.W." Bush left Saddam in power but instituted a sanctions policy accompanied by an endless bombing campaign against Iraq's civilian population.

Bill Clinton continued that campaign of extreme violence against the civilian population for the next eight years. It killed more than a million Iraqis, half of them children under five years of age. Then, in a very short time, "al Qaeda attacked the United States" and killed almost 3,000 innocent American civilians. Knowing full well that it was a lie, the new president, George W. Bush, blamed Iraq and set in motion plans to attack the innocent people of Iraq still again. In the buildup to the war, Bush and his staff launched an incredible campaign of extreme lies so fantastic and so far out of touch with reality that no one capable of reason could possibly believe them. No country so endlessly abused and assaulted could possibly be capable of posing a serious threat to anyone at all. What followed was a massacre of hundreds of thousands of Iraqis, almost certainly close to a million, and a policy of savage abuse, rape, torture, expulsion, and persecution.

And so, the Bush–Cheney attack against Iraq was the latest in a whole series of barbaric acts by the United States against that country. In the first place, the Americans were at least partly responsible for the rise and cruel rule of Saddam Hussein. Then, there followed the wars described above. As said before, the Bush–Cheney attack on Iraq was based on a campaign of lies so extreme, bizarre, insistent, and groundless that they revolted the whole world. In addition to the mass murders, nearly five million were expelled. The excuse for all of this mayhem was "terrorism." This brutality was directed against a population of only twenty five million. How can anyone rational doubt that this conglomeration of violence amounts to a policy of genocide? And now we have Barack Obama refusing to investigate, accuse, or prosecute the criminals responsible for these outrages. He is even helping them to cover up and conceal their crimes and their identities.

Though Saddam Hussein's rise to power, supported by the United States, began earlier, Saddam's greatest support began with Ronald Reagan and the Republican Party. Starting with his 1980 campaign against Jimmy Carter, Reagan's manipulations and deceptions regarding Iraq and Iran were seminal in the creation of subsequent atrocities. Two of the building blocks that put Reagan and H.W. Bush in power, openly on the side of Saddam Hussein and secretly on the side of the Iranian mullahs, were the so called "October Surprise" conspiracy and, six years later, the Iran–Contra conspiracy. Below is a somewhat speculative discussion of those two scandals. They were, in clear fact, the same scandal begun during the Reagan campaign in 1980 and continued for six years until 1986 when the so-called Iran–Contra conspiracy was exposed.

Reagan almost certainly won the election against Jimmy Carter in 1980 because some Iranian students seized the staff of the American embassy in Teheran and held it hostage throughout the campaign. The president of Iran, the Ayatollah Khomeini, was not responsible for this act though he did nothing to stop it. Carter did not cause the rage of the students. The people of Iran, especially the young, were intensely anti-American because, more than two decades earlier, Dwight Eisenhower had overthrown democracy in Iran by using the CIA, housed in the embassy, to subvert democratically-elected Mohammad Mossadegh and restore the dictatorship of the Shah. Carter got the blame and both Ted Kennedy and Ronald Reagan ran smear campaigns against him saying he was a coward and a weakling for not attacking Iran militarily. Kennedy called the Carter campaign a "Rose garden campaign." Reagan and his followers sneered at Carter, called him a coward, and demanded that he attack Iran.

During the fall months of that campaign, Reagan's staff began to loudly warn that Jimmy Carter was trying to pull an "October Surprise" by obtaining the release of the hostages in time to help him win reelection. They seemed to want the whole world to know about their fear that the hostages would be released. Khomeini then did precisely what Reagan wanted by going to great lengths to delay the release until just a few minutes after Reagan was sworn in. Many wondered if there had been an arrangement between the Reagan campaign and Khomeini. It was hard to believe that Khomeini would favor a man who was attacking Carter for not dealing more harshly with him and the hostage takers.

Gary Sick, a security specialist in the Nixon, Carter, and Reagan administrations, wrote a book about the "October Surprise." Sick's book said that the Reagan campaign, working through rogue elements in the CIA, the military, and through the Israeli government, had, in effect, stolen four plane loads of weapons from the American military which were then sent, through Israel, to Khomeini in Iran. Ongoing military aid to Israel was the cover for this arrangement. President Carter and his government knew nothing about the trafficking between Israel and the Iranians. Sick claimed the weapons were a payoff to Khomeini by the Reagan campaign that wanted him to hold the American hostages until Reagan had been safely elected. Sick called this a "political coup" that "bordered on treason." Some of the speculative and perhaps shaky details in Sick's book about meetings between the two parties were disputed and used as an excuse to undermine the central thesis of his claim. Was the Iran–Contra conspiracy six years later, finally admitted by Reagan, simply a continuation of a Reagan campaign arrangement with Khomeini, whether or not it was set up in a specific meeting mentioned by Sick? Or was Sick a great prophet who alleged what hadn't happened yet?

It seems clear to me that Saddam Hussein was maneuvered into his wars against Iran and later Kuwait by the United States. Ronald Reagan supported Saddam's attack against Iran full out and did so publicly. His pretended hostility to Iran, during his campaign against Carter, was one of the reasons for his friendship with Saddam. In fact, even while Saddam was using gas against the Iranians, Reagan publicly announced that there was no way he would let Saddam lose his war. He and George H.W. Bush then gave Saddam billions of dollars in credits which he used to acquire more weapons of mass destruction, advance his nuclear program, and enlarge his delivery systems, with many of the supplies sold to him by American firms at the urging of the Reagan administration. Reagan also gave Saddam access to American intelligence information about Iran. Reagan could have ended that war by slapping Saddam Hussein on the wrist, but Reagan wanted the war. In fact, it was a very bad war for Iraq. Iraq was one third the size of Iran and less powerful militarily. I don't believe that Saddam would have launched his attack in the first place without American assurances of support. The result was that over a million people died in the war, roughly half on each side. The war lasted eight years, depleted war supplies, and drained the treasuries of both countries.

The Iran–Contra conspiracy was exposed by a Middle Eastern newspaper in 1986. It revealed that Reagan had long been secretly supporting and supplying Iran even while he was openly supporting Iraq. In response to the scandal, Reagan and his Attorney General and long-time enabler, Ed Meese, decided on a damage control effort. They called a press conference and admitted the main outline of the charge. Thus, they were admitting Reagan's completely bizarre behavior regarding Iran, a country he claimed was an enemy. Moreover, why was he, as president, secretly doing just what he was suspected of doing, as a private citizen, during his campaign back in 1980? What was his motive? The press, eager to be helpful to Reagan, speculated that his motive must have been bribing Iran to get its help in arranging for the release of various hostages being held by other Arab and muslim countries. The press made no mention of the October Surprise incident. Unlike the single hostage problem under Carter, none of Reagan's more-numerous hostage problems were highlighted by the press. Members of Reagan's team quickly agreed with the press speculation but Reagan himself refused to concede that it had anything to do with the hostages. After three or four confused efforts to explain his motives, he finally said that he really didn't understand his own motives and actions but it must have been about the hostages. Was it about *his* 1986 hostage problem or was it about the 1980 campaign? Was Reagan still rewarding Khomeini for his help in making him president? Even though there was a very limited Iran–Contra inves-tigation, one thwarted by the Republican Party, Israel, and Iran, none of this was ever seriously examined. After the 1986 revelations about the Iran–Contra plot, it seems certain that the Reagan campaign of 1980 was guilty of the treasonous plot described then by Gary Sick.

*

To better track the course of this long war against the innocent people of Iraq by the United States, I am listing below a number of quotations about the war from books, newspapers, and magazines interspersed with my own remarks and speculations.

RONALD REAGAN

 • In 1982, Ronald Reagan removed Iraq from the State Department list of terrorist countries and canceled Carter's human rights policy.
 • In November of 1983, Reagan issued Directive 114 which said that he would do "whatever is necessary and legal" to help Iraq win its war with Iran even though he knew from official documents that Iraq was using chemical weapons "almost daily" against Iran and that Saddam Hussein was trying to build a nuclear bomb.

> On Dec. 20, 1983, "Ronald Reagan was...giving aid and weapons to both Iran (secretly) and Iraq.... In 1982, Ronald Reagan had taken Iraq off the list of nations that sponsored terrorism. That allowed a floodgate of U.S. 'aid' to go into Iraq. The Reagan administration was actively encouraging manufacturers to sell to Iraq and Saddam Hussein was aggressively buying everything he could get his hands on from the United States.

> "Ronald Reagan dispatched his special envoy to Iraq with a hand-written letter from Reagan to be given to Saddam Hussein, with a clear message that what Washington wanted was to restore normal relations.... So when the envoy (Donald Rumsfeld) arrived in Bagh-dad, not only did he have a handwritten letter, but he also gave Sad-

179

dam Hussein a pair of golden cowboy spurs, as a present from Ronald Reagan. He shook Saddam's hand, called him 'Mr. President,' and had a meeting that the Iraqi foreign minister described at the time as being about 'topics of mutual interest.' [Shortly] allegations started to emerge about Iraq's use and possession of chemical weapons."

> — Jeremy Scahill, interview by David Ross, *Z Magazine*, November 2002.

"When April Glaspie went to Baghdad as U.S. ambassador in early August 1988, Iraq's war with Iran was into its eighth year and had become one of the deadliest of all time. The casualties of this conflict, which had begun when Iraq invaded its neighbor in 1980, were estimated as high as 1 million soldiers and civilians, possibly the highest toll of any war since World War II."

> —Don Oberdorfer, *The Washington Post Magazine*, March 17, 1991.

"Imagine if you were Iranian and watched the boys in your neighborhood board a bus for the front, never to return. Imagine staring in mute horror at the television screen as Saddam rained chemical weapons down on your boys, his death planes guided by U.S. satellite photos. Fast-forward about fifteen years. Now you are watching faded video footage of Donald Rumsfeld shaking Hussein's hand, smiling at the butcher who made our capital's cemetery a city. Now you are listening to President George W. Bush.... Do you believe him?'

"When the Iran-Iraq war stuttered to a truce eight years later, more than a million people on both sides had died. An entire generation of Iranian men had been obliterated..."

> —*Iran Awakening: A Memoir of Revolution and Hope*, by Shirin Ebadi, book review by Reza Aslan.

"The *Miami Herald* ran a front-page story that said Oliver North had been assigned to the White House (under Reagan) to work in FEMA on the development of an executive order that was to say, 'In the event of military activity by the United States in Central America or anywhere in the world, if a significant number of people objected, 1. The Constitution of the United States shall be suspended, 2. A military government shall be established, 3. The courts shall be suspended and military tribunals established, 4. Camps shall be established where any person who disagrees shall be detained.'"

> —Arthur Kinoy, Rutgers professor, interview, *The Progressive*, October 1992.

"There is a need for 'breaking the law from time to time' and a need to change the law 'that prohibits American officials from working with murderers' and a need to change the 'executive order, dating

to 1975, prohibiting any official of the American government to con-
duct, order, encourage, and facilitate assassination.'"

> — Michael Ledeen, one of Ronald Reagan's Iran–Contra schem-
> ers, *Partisan Review* article, cited by Sidney Blumenthal in *The
> Washington Post*, February 16, 1987.

"Director of Central Intelligence William Webster openly called
on Congress to provide the CIA with greater latitude—including
the right to assassinate foreign leaders. (An executive order signed
by President Ford in 1976 and strengthened by President Carter
in 1978 prohibits any U.S. participation in assassination attempts,
though the Reagan Administration clearly violated this order when
it bombed Muammar Qaddafi's residence in 1986.)...George Bush has
endorsed Webster's call."

> — Comment, *The Progressive*, December 1989.

"'All wars...are based on national myths, most of which are, at their
core, racist,' he contends. They are racist in that they assert the inherent goodness of "us" and the evil of "them." This black and white
thinking allows us to kill the enemy without conscience, while cel-
ebrating our success in slaying without mercy those who oppose
us...we have our own terrorists — such as the Nicaraguan *contras*
and the late Jonas Savimbi, whom Ronald Reagan referred to as the
Abraham Lincoln of Angola...The Reagan years, he contends, helped
to resurrect this 'plague of nationalism.'"

> —*War is a Force That Gives Us Meaning* by Chris Hedges, review by
> Joseph Nevins, *The Nation*, November 18, 2002.

"Hawaii, Cuba, Philippines, Puerto Rico, Nicaragua, Honduras,
Iran, Guatemala, South Vietnam, Chile, Grenada, Panama, Afghanistan, Iraq: What do these 14 governments have in common?

"You got it. The United States overthrew them.

"And in almost every case, the overthrow can be traced to corporate interests....

"Actually, the United States has been overthrowing governments
for more than a century,'" Kinzer said in an interview.

He documents this in a new book: *Overthrow: America's Century of
Regime Change from Hawaii to Iraq* (Times Books, 2006)....

"[T]he Kremlin had not the slightest interest in Guatemala at all
in the early 1950s. They didn't even know Guatemala existed. They
didn't even have diplomatic or economic relations.

"The leader of Iran who we overthrew was fiercely anti-communist. He came from an aristocratic family. He despised Marxist
ideology.

"In Chile, we always portrayed President Allende as a cat's paw of the Kremlin. We now know from documents that have come out that the Soviets and the Chinese were constantly fighting with him and urging him to calm down and not be so provocative towards the US. So, in the first place, the Soviets were not behind those regimes...."

The United States had a hand in many other overthrows, but Kinzer limited his cases to those where the United States was the primary mover and shaker.

—Russell Mokhiber and Robert Weissman, interview, *Asheville Global Report*, May 3, 2006. Source: Focus of the Corporation.

H.W. Bush and Bill Clinton

• In 1990, President George H. W. Bush overrode a congressional block on trade credits to Iraq that the Democratic Congress had imposed because of Saddam's use of poison gas against Iraqi Kurds.

"In the 1950s under President Eisenhower, the Dulles brothers (John Foster in the State Department and Allen at CIA) began locking down U.S. hegemony around the globe and perfected the hate-the-commies rhetoric that justified the U.S. war machine for decades....

"In 1961, Iraq leader Abdul Karim Quassim spoke out very strongly for the return of Kuwait. Miller reports that the Baghdad CIA station chief gave the order to kill Qassim to an aggressive young hustler named Saddam Hussein. Saddam did the job very well, killed and tortured other radicals and trade unionists and began his rise to power in the Baath Party with our backing.

"By 1975, the Pentagon had refined plans for our military emplacement in Saudi Arabia and our takeover of the Persian Gulf coast....

"In mid-1990, we pushed Saddam's trigger. Secretary of State James Baker sent the message to Saddam, 'We have no interest in your border dispute with Kuwait.' Saddam took the bait and moved his forces to the border of Kuwait. Miller reveals that the night before Saddam entered Kuwait both the U.S. and the Soviet ambassadors left Iraq 'for vacation.' Saddam moved into Kuwait, we stomped on him and the rest is history."

—William Jakobi, guest commentary, *Asheville Citizen–Times*, July 22, 2005.

"It is becoming increasingly clear that George Bush, operating largely behind the scenes through the 1980s reelection, initiated and supported much of the financing, intelligence, and military help that built Saddam's Iraq into the aggressive power that the United States ultimately had to destroy."

—Ted Koppel, *Nightline*, June 9, 1992.

"We do not have any defense treaties with Kuwait and there are no special defense or security commitments to Kuwait."

—Margaret Tutwiler, State Department spokesperson, in reply to a question at a press conference.

"David Hoffman reported that the 'Bush administration in the weeks before the Aug. 2 invasion was gripped by inertia and indecision over whether to get tough on Saddam.' Around the same time, we learned of the meeting at which the U.S. ambassador to Iraq, April Glaspie, told Saddam that his dispute with Kuwait was an 'Arab–Arab' matter about which Washington had 'no opinion.'"

—Richard Cohen, column, *Washington Post*, April 30, 1992.

"Baker denied that there was any U.S. hostility toward Iraq.... Tariq Aziz asked Baker ...to approve new U.S. credit guarantees for Iraq food purchases from the United States.... Bush overrode congressional objections to continuing U.S. Export–Import Bank financing for commercial transactions with Iraq....

"On April 12, five U.S. senators — led by Bob Dole — made a now-famous visit to Saddam in Mosul....Dole told Saddam...that Bush had assured him personally only 12 hours earlier that he was pleased with their visit and that 'he wants better relations, and the U.S. government wants better relations with Iraq.'"...

—Don Oberdorfer, *The Washington Post Magazine*, March 17. 1991.

"Preparation for the (first) gulf war was well in hand before Secretary of State James Baker announced that its *principal* rationale was 'jobs, jobs, jobs.'"

—Christopher Hitchens' column, *The Nation*, August 19/26, 2002.

"Saddam Hussein's government is well known for its human rights abuses against the Kurds and Shiites, and for its invasion of Kuwait. What is less well known is that this same government had also invested heavily in health, education, and social programs for two decades prior to the Persian Gulf War. While the treatment of ethnic minorities and political enemies has been abominable under Hussein, it is also the case that the well-being of the society at large improved dramatically...Before the Persian Gulf War, Iraq was a rapidly developing country, with free education, ample electricity, modernized agriculture, and a robust middle class. According to the World Health Organization, 93 percent of the population had access to health care."

— Joy Gordon, article, *Harpers*, November 2002.

"I broke with the administration on Nov. 8, when President Bush abruptly doubled American forces in the Persian Gulf and headed toward war with Iraq instead of giving sanctions a chance to work. I still believe it was unnecessary to kill tens of thousands of Iraqis and heavily damage Baghdad. It was an easy victory but an awful price to inflict on the soldiers and the people of Iraq for the sins of their brutal leader....

"It also seems incoherent to me that Mr. Bush authorized the sale of high tech equipment to Saddam, which he converted to chemical warfare. It seems equally incoherent to me that the Bush administration told Saddam a week before the Iraqi dictator invaded Kuwait that our government would not become involved in an Arab border dispute."

—George McGovern, letter, *Washington Post*, March 8, 1991.

"The day before Iraq sent its troops pouring into Kuwait, the Bush administration approved the sale of $695,000 worth of advanced data transmission devices to the Iraqi government, according to U.S. government records.

"The sale was just one item in $1.5 billion in advanced U.S. products that the Reagan and Bush administrations allowed Iraq to buy from 1985 to 1990."

—Stuart Auerbach, report, *Washington Post*, March 11, 1991.

"Every Iraqi leader, from the British-imposed king in 1921...regarded Kuwait as an integral part of Iraq. Kuwait had been set up as an imperial outpost by the British on the eve of World War I.... most Iraqis believed that Kuwait was rightly and legally an Iraqi province."

—William K. Polk, essay, *The New York Review*, February 18,1999.

"On July 16, foreign ambassador Aziz sent a letter to the Arab League.... Kuwait was charged with 'twofold aggression' [for manipulating the market] and for 'stealing' $2.4 billion in Iraqi oil from an oil field that straddles the Kuwait–Iraq border."

—Don Oberdorfer, essay, *The Washington Post Magazine*, March 17, 1991.

"And in this same period the Pentagon refined the plan for U.S. military takeover of Middle East oil fields....

"We cleverly set up this bogeyman: State Dept. officials led Saddam to think he could get away with grabbing Kuwait...Small wonder Saddam concluded he could overrun Kuwait. Bush and Co. gave him no reason to think otherwise. Thus, we deliberately triggered the '91 Gulf war, the staging operation for our current disastrous entry into Iraq."

—William Jakobi, Guest Opinion, *Asheville Citizen Times*, June 21, 2006.

AUG. 12, 1990 — IRAQ INVADES KUWAIT.

"Bush began preparing for war shortly after the Iraq invasion of Kuwait and refused to respond to at least five Iraqi offers of negotiation between August and January 15, the deadline for Iraq to leave Kuwait. On that date, *The Washington Post* reported that the Administration feared a 'nightmare scenario' under which 'the beginnings of a credible Iraqi withdrawal could make it impossible for Bush to launch military action.' A 'nightmare scenario' recurred when the Soviet Union attempted to broker a peace settlement in the days before the ground offensive. But though the Soviet plan would have removed Iraq from Kuwait, Bush would have none of it. He...insisted that the killing continue."

—Allen Nairn, Reflections, *The Progressive*, May 1991.

"We called the story 'Flacking for the Emir' and published it in *The Progressive* May 1991 issue. One of Arthur E. Rowse's disclosures was the role Hill & Knowlton played in disseminating 'Perhaps the most widely publicized accusation against Iraq' — a charge that Saddam Hussein's soldiers had brutally allowed Kuwaiti babies to die after removing them from their incubators at three hospitals....

"The story about the incubator atrocity had originated with 'eyewitness' testimony before a Congressional committee by a fifteen-year-old Kuwaiti girl, identified only as 'Nayirah,' who wept as she told of seeing fifteen babies dumped to their deaths.

"The horrifying charge...later embellished to a total of 312 babies, was frequently mentioned by President Bush and members of Congress in the debate over whether to start shooting. Rowse reminded Knoll that this charge, as my article for *The Progressive* reported, was firmly disproved by reporters who visited the hospitals after the war....

"Apparently, it wasn't news that a high-priced PR firm had successfully peddled a fabricated story, but it was news that the firm had used an ambassador's daughter to do its dirty work."

—Erwin Knoll, Memo from the Editor, *The Progressive*, April 4, 1992.

"January 17, 1991 — U.S. launches war to repel Iraq from Kuwait. Conflict ends Feb. 28."

—*Public Citizen News*, May/June 2003.

"The day the Baghdad shelter was bombed, killing hundreds of people, the Pentagon lied and said it was an Iraqi army command center, even though, as the *London Independent* later established, the Pentagon actually believed they were bombing a shelter for the families of the Iraqi elite....Leslie Gelb, the *New York Times* columnist... said viewers should not be 'too quick to believe (their) eyes' because, he explained, the smoking bodies they saw being hauled up from underground (presumably including those of the tiny, charred children) might be those of civilians who had been working for the Iraq military....

"During the war's final days, when the Iraqis were out of Kuwait, militarily crushed, and desperately trying to surrender, Washington kept attacking nonetheless (and not just on the 'Highway of Death as the road to Basra became known, but also in Baghdad itself.) White House officials lived in 'fear of a peace deal,' wrote columnists Rowland and Robert Novak, who applauded them for their 'eagerness to avoid peace and confront war.'"

—Allen Nairn, Reflections, *The Progressive*, May 1991.

As George H.W. Bush and Saddam Hussein were screaming at one another through the public air, the Soviet president, Mikhail Gorbachev, on February 21, 1991, arranged a withdrawal of Iraqi forces from Kuwait in accord with United Nations directive 660 and Bush's insistent demands. Bush angrily rejected Gorbachev's arrangement. Quite clearly, Bush wanted a war no matter what.

At 5:35 PM on February 25, 1991, Radio Baghdad announced the withdrawal of all Iraqi troops from Kuwait. Saddam announced that the withdrawal would be completed the next day. President Bush denounced the statement as an "outrage" and a "cruel hoax." The withdrawal began anyway in the early afternoon of February 26th when approximately 2000 vehicles began to move up the two northern roads toward Iraq. Many Kuwaiti eyewitnesses agreed that the withdrawal began at this time. There were a good many civilians in the convoy; included were quite a few Palestinian civilians who feared to remain in their homes in Kuwait because Yasser Arafat, head of the PLO, had angered the Kuwaitis by siding with Saddam in the dispute between the two countries.

The US forces were thirty-five miles away from Kuwait City and there was no military engagement or any effort by the Iraqis to regroup or prepare for battle. In fact, it would be thirty-six hours before any American troops arrived in Kuwait City. Nevertheless, Bush announced that the Iraqis were "continuing to fight" and said that there was "no evidence" of withdrawal. He said he would continue "to prosecute the war" and added, on February 27, 1991, that "no quarter" would be given. The Hague Convention of 1907 states that it is illegal to declare that no quarter will be given to withdrawing troops. At this point, the massacre from the air had already begun even as White House spokesman, Marlin Fitzwater, was saying the US would not attack Iraqis leaving Kuwait. In a military briefing from Saudi Arabia, Colin Powell repeated Bush's statements and boasted about his intention to destroy the enemy.

The two parallel northbound roads from Kuwait were filled with miles-long streams of vehicles surrounded by deep sand. There was no possibility of escape and the withdrawing Iraqis did not expect an attack from the air by a large swarm of American aircraft. The planes trapped the long convoys by disabling the vehicles in front and behind and then by pounding away at the defenseless human beings below. One pilot said, "It was like shooting fish in a barrel." Another described it as "a turkey shoot." One of the squadron leaders, Frank Sweigart, said the victims were "basically just sitting ducks." So many planes swarmed over the helpless people that air controllers had to divide the "killing box" in half to avoid mid-air collisions. An Army intelligence officer said, "Even in Vietnam I didn't see anything like this. It's pathetic." Strikes originating from the aircraft carrier, USS Ranger, were being "launched so feverishly" that pilots were grabbing "whatever bombs happened to be closest." With loud music playing in the background, the crews were stuffing the planes with bombs as they raced back and forth between the mother ship and the helpless quarry.

The air strikes continued night and day until every living thing had been destroyed. On the inland road, 450 people did survive to surrender. Among these were a 60-year-old reservist and two 13-year-old children. There were no survivors at all on the 60 miles of the coastal road. Every vehicle was blasted, twisted, burnt, riddled with steel fragments. Fried and blackened bodies lay strewn about, some still sitting, some leaning against charred metal. Cluster bombs and 500 pound bundles of death had ripped open vehicle after vehicle and spilled their human remains and their possessions across the surface of the road and out into the sand of the dessert. Thousands of people were massacred.

When the US Army did finally arrive on the scene after the slaughter, the soldiers took out their cameras to record the carnage and went searching through the mass of dead bodies and the huge mounds of burnt and twisted metal for souvenirs to take home to their families. US Army sergeant Ray brown said, "I got a little sick when I saw this." Later, General Schwarzkopf would say, in a *Newsweek* article, that he wondered "How long the world would stand by and watch the United States pound the living hell out of the Iraqis without saying, 'Wait a minute — enough is enough.'" This massive extermination was clearly deliberate and planned. Bush and his generals decided to kill all the Iraqis they could kill while they had the chance. The intention was to prevent any possibility of withdrawal. Rick Atkinson of the *Washington Post* wrote, "The noose has been tightened and no escape is possible."

In Riyadh in Saudi Arabia, the American central command was worried about public opinion. They represented the slaughter on the two roads as great tank battles with streams of retreating Iraqi soldiers trying to regroup to fight the Americans. In fact, the Iraqis were never engaged by ground forces at all since no American troops were anywhere near and would not reach Kuwait city for another day and a half. The strewn household goods and the destroyed civilian vehicles were described by the army as loot stolen from Kuwait. One wonders: Why would a maneuvering army be carrying household goods and family possessions and why would soldiers be driving cars and vans and busses? The Iraqis had been in Kuwait for six months and now, all of a sudden, they had looted the place so they could carry their loot into battle? Civilians, including women and children, were a part of their army? The Iraqi army had arranged itself in long lines on two parallel roads north to Iraq so they could be easily bottled up, knowing they could not take to the sand and escape? What kind of battle plan was this?

The *Washington Post* and most other media outlets did their best to help Bush and his generals represent the massacre as a legitimate battle. One of the *Post* stories claimed that only 200 to 300 Iraqis were killed on the two roads with a few more being captured by the absent American army. Other stories described the supposed brutality of the Iraqi occupation without mentioning the highways of death at all. One story even claimed the Iraqis were headed west on the two north–south roads. But some of the stories were not so accommodating. One section of a *Post* story was headed "Shaping World Perception." Another *Post* story said that the Army explained that its spokespersons needed to use forceful language to portray Iraq's claimed "withdrawal" as a fighting retreat made necessary by heavy allied pressure. The *Post* added this: "In fact, however, tens of thousands of Iraqi soldiers in and around Kuwait City had begun to pull away more than 36 hours before allied forces reached the capital" and added, "they did not move out under any immediate pressure from allied tanks and infantry, which still were miles from Kuwait City." In the *New York Times*, Maureen Dowd said of the war, "Mr. Bush decided that he would rather gamble on a violent and potentially unpopular ground war than risk the alternative: an imperfect settlement hammered out by the Soviets and Iraqis that world opinion might accept as tolerable."

George H. W. Bush repeatedly said that his sole objective was removal of the Iraqis from Kuwait. But, the war was completely unnecessary to accomplish that objective since Iraq was already withdrawing when Bush sent his air force on its extermination campaign. Saddam Hussein had invaded Kuwait over an oil dispute with the advance approval of Bush and then, when Bush and the UN ordered him out, he began to withdraw only to have Bush launch a senseless attack. At the end of the war, Bush encouraged the Kurds and the Shias to attack and overthrow Saddam. When they tried to do so, Saddam used American-supplied helicopters to slaughter them as the American army sat and watched. Bush refused to protect the rebels. Then, incredibly, Bush refused to remove Hussein from power although, in effect, he had already surrendered unconditionally. Clear objectives?

The atrocity committed by George H. W. Bush at the highways of death was a war crime; it was one of the worst and most dishonest massacres in the modern history of warfare. The U.S. Army's disinformation campaign covered it up and the media collaborated supinely with the politicians and generals. Standards of legality and decency that were contemptuously violated were set forth in the Geneva Conventions of 1949, Common Article III, as well as in the U.S. Field Manual of 1956. As mentioned earlier, the 1907 Hague Convention governing land warfare also outlawed such atrocities as the ones perpetrated by the George H.W. Bush administration at the highways of death in February of 1991.

—Compiled by Joseph Burrell from various newspaper and magazine reports.

"Pentagon smugness, never in short supply, hit a sewer-line low when a smiling Gen. Colin Powell said that his forces have 'lots of tools. And I brought them all to the party.'

"It is a party — a drunken one turning sadistic. Relentless aerial bombardment — lately about as surgical as operating on a cornea with machetes — is a systematic destroying of Iraq's electricity, water and sewage facilities. That, plus blowing up bridges and obliterating neighborhoods, is called 'softening up' the enemy.

"On February 13, back the fearless warriors went, this time to obliterate with smart bombs what the Pentagon called an Iraqi 'command bunker' but which the world now knows was sheltering hundreds of civilians trying to make it through another hellish night. Scores of noncombatants — women and children — were slaughtered.

"Regardless of what Saddam Hussein is doing to Iraqis, the sadistic ritual of daily bombing by the U.S. military is in keeping with its picking fights — in Grenada, Libya and Panama — with enemies expected to be done in quickly.... After a month in the gulf, the United States is now involved in war for war's sake, war for the fun of it, war as a party that brings smiles to Gen. Powell....

"After a month of obliterating Iraq, and now downtown Baghdad, the U.S. air war has been revealed as a coward's war."

—Colman McCarthy, column, *Washington Post*, January 17, 1991.

"Throughout the war American news organizations ran tally boxes of the casualties, listing in one column how many American soldiers had perished and in another column how many Iraqi tanks, APCS, and planes had been 'killed.' There was no mention of Iraqi deaths....Powell's famous declaration about the Iraqi army — 'we're going to cut it off, then we're going to kill it'— neatly edited out all consideration of the enemy's humanity.

"There has not been released, about this war fought in the video age, a single foot of film depicting anything resembling combat involving human beings [100,000 plus civilian dead]. Military censors went crazy when one field commander let reporters watch a gun camera video from an Apache gunship that snuck up on an Iraqi squad. In the tape, terror-stricken teenagers rush wildly in all directions as cannon rounds from the helicopter, which they can't see, slice their bodies in half. The video was quickly withdrawn from circulation. When I asked a senior Pentagon official why, he replied, 'If we let people see that kind of thing, there would never again be any war.'"

> —Gregg Easterbrook, book review of various books by and about General Norman Schwarzkopf, *The New Republic*, September 30, 1991.

"Late last fall, the Census Bureau assigned a 29-year-old demographer to update the government's population estimate for Iraq....

"How many Iraqis died during the war and its aftermath? The answer, officially taboo in the Bush administration, was indispensable to Beth Osborne Daponte's calculations. In January, when a reporter asked for her estimates, she told him: 86,194 men, 39,612 women and 32,195 children died at the hands of the American-led coalition forces, during the domestic rebellions that followed, and from postwar deprivation.

"Wednesday evening, after weeks of turmoil during which she was removed from the Iraq project and her files disappeared from her desk, Daponte was told she is to be fired. Barbara Boyle Torrey, her boss at the Bureau's Center for International Research, wrote that Daponte's report included 'false information' and demonstrated 'untrustworthiness or unreliability.'...

"The White House and Pentagon consistently have sought to suppress discussion of Iraqi casualties, directing analysts and military officers not to provide estimates or professional judgments....

"'I think that Beth is collateral damage in the government's campaign to avoid discussing the question of Iraqi casualties,' said William M. Arkin, a former intelligence officer who now does military analysis for Greenpeace. 'I think this is an ugly case of retribution....

> —Barton Gellman, report, *The Washington Post*, March 6, 1992.

• Of the 296 men and eight women who died since the U.S. mobilization for war began on Aug. 7, an estimated 182 died in "non-hostile" incidents, deaths attributed to equipment failures, accidents and natural causes. Of those, 106 were killed before the war erupted Jan. 17.

• To sum up, 114 Americans died in the war and (at least) 158,000 Iraqis, a ratio of 1 American to 1,388 Iraqis. A just war?

"The United States and its allies assembled a mighty force — about 700,000 troops — in the Persian Gulf during the fall and winter of 1990 to take on a formidable foe. Saddam Hussein's Iraq, we were told, had more than 500,000 troops poised to engage in combat, and some of them were elite units — remember the superhuman Revolutionary Guards? — endowed with legendary fighting skills....

"Now, slowly, belatedly, some of the facts come seeping through the bottom of the bloody barrel. Turns out, according to a bipartisan report from the House Armed Services Committee, that there weren't 500,000 Iraqi troops after all, but only about 180,000. That means that the United States and its allies had about a four-to-one edge — 'a very significant advantage,' as House Armed Services Chairman Les Aspin put it. It also means that the war turned into a turkey shoot — a random slaughter of a never-to-be determined number of Iraqis. (The House estimates that 120,000 Iraqi soldiers fled or were killed during the ground assault.)"

—Comment, *The Progressive*, June 1992.

When the war ended on February 28th, Bush refused to remove Saddam, withdrew American troops, and explained why in the following statement:

"To occupy Iraq would instantly shatter our coalition, turning the whole Arab world against us and make a broken tyrant into a latter-day Arab hero...assigning young soldiers to a fruitless hunt for a securely entrenched dictator and condemning them to fight in what would be an un-winnable urban guerila war. It could only plunge that part of the world into even greater instability."

—George Bush Sr., from his book, *A World Transformed* (1998), cited in the *Asheville Global Report*, April 10–16, 2003.

"The so-called fighting stopped only 25 days ago, but that has been enough time to show that President Bush has not a clue about what to do with his victory. Liberated Kuwait, choking on the fumes of its burning oil wells, is indulging in an orgy of recriminations; Iraq, with 100,000 dead, and according to the United Nations, bombed back to the 'pre-industrial age,' is racked by disease, want and civil war; Saudi Arabia is gratefully reverting to feudalism, and Israel to intransigence on the Palestinian question. The only thing arguably improved is Bush's standing in the polls....

"Now, in liberated Kuwait, ghastly atrocities are occurring, but a curious detachment has set in at the White House. Palestinians and Iraqis are being subjected to 'routine torture' of 400 to 500 people taken to detention centers and tortured and beaten."

—Mary McGrory, column, *The Washington Post*, March 26, 1991.

"An independent human rights organization has accused the Kuwaiti government of repeated, flagrant human rights abuses over the last six months — including rape, torture and extrajudicial killings — and says that the Bush administration bears responsibility because it defended Kuwait's actions....

"'We have to use torture to make them confess,' one military officer was quoted as saying. 'They would not confess without the use of force,'...

"The report noted a July 1 press conference in which President Bush said he understood the Kuwaitis' feelings of rage and added: 'I think we're expecting a little much if we're asking the people in Kuwait to take kindly to those that had spied on their countrymen... that had brutalized families there and things of that nature.'

"'It is difficult to imagine a more forceful apology for abuse,' Middle East Watch said of Bush's remarks.'"

—Ted Robertson, report, *The Washington Post*, September 11, 1991.

"One of the reasons we went halfway around the world was to kick the Iraqis out of Kuwait. We returned to that small country the most precious gift anyone can give: the gift of liberty."

—General Norman Schwartzkopf, speech at the U.S. Naval academy in May of 1991.

It's astonishing that the Bush administration should have claimed, in the first Iraq war, that it was fighting for the liberty of the people of Kuwait. In fact, of the 2.1 million people in Kuwait, only 825,000 were allowed to be citizens at all. The others were humble servants to the rich upper class.

Many of these servants without rights (called Bidoon) were born in Kuwait but were of the wrong ancestry to be allowed citizenship. Others were imported from Saudi Arabia, Iraq, Iran, Algeria, Tunisia, Sudan, Somali, and Palestine to be servants. Kuwait was not a democratic country or even a decent one. The Kuwaitis themselves did almost no work; the stateless servants did everything, even professional and technical work. The upper class in Kuwait was probably the richest and the most privileged in the world.

When Iraq invaded, all of these stateless people became suspects to the Kuwaitis. It made little difference whether or not they had collaborated with the Iraqis. Their ancestry and low class indicted them. Many were imprisoned, abused, and tortured; others were expelled, including even people who had always lived in Kuwait and had no country of their own to go to. Quite a few were killed. Palestinians in particular were suspect. The simple truth is that, despite Saddam's torture and selective brutality, even Iraq treated its ordinary citizens better than Kuwait did its bidoons.

—Compiled from various newspaper and magazine articles by the author.

"The real problem, of course, is the Palestinians. Of the 450,000 Palestinians of Kuwait, many have been here for decades; they made the country work. 'The people who know how to run things, the people who always did the work here, were almost all Palestinians,' said one U.S. official involved in the reconstruction. 'They were the judges, the doctors, the dentists, practically all the engineers, all the middle managers.' ...a Red Cross official marveled at his difficulties in establishing a coherent relief system. 'The people we are dealing with have no concept of the mechanics of actually getting jobs done,' he said. 'They are very good at talking and sitting and drinking tea all day, but they don't have a clue about things like how to get a lorry from point A to point B.'"

—Michael Kelly, *The New Republic*, April 8, 1991.

"In 1998 bin Laden asked an American journalist, 'Was it not your country that bombed Nagasaki and Hiroshima? Were there not women and children and civilians and noncombatants there? You were the people who invented this terrible game, and we as muslims have to use these same tactics against you.'

"'The function of propaganda,' Hitler wrote in *Mein Kampf*, 'is not to make an objective study of the truth,' but to incite. Bin laden regards himself as an instigator."

—Raffi Khatchadourian, essay, *The Nation*, May 15, 2006

Lesley Stahl: "We have heard that a half-million children have died (from the sanction against Iraq). I mean, that's more children than died at Hiroshima."

Madeleine Albright: "We think the price is worth it."

"No Flag is Large Enough to Cover the Shame of Killing Innocent People."

—Parade banner in Taos, NM, February 15, 2003, cited in a *Z Magazine* interview with Howard Zinn by David Barsamian, May 2000.

"In the fall of '98, Clinton...launched 200 cruise missiles to hit those sites....

"The Washington Times, a conservative paper, ran an article that began: 'The White House orchestrated a plan to provoke Saddam Hussein into defying the United Nations inspectors so President Clinton could justify air strikes, former and current government officials charge....'

"The Conservative Caucus in Vienna, Va., went into high gear with a list of 10 reasons to oppose war with Iraq, not the least of which was 'Clinton has compromised the U.S. defense arsenal by making war against a regime far less threatening than China, Russia, Cuba or North Korea.'

"It said that Clinton was 'squandering' $5.5 billion and imperiling the 24,000 American troops then in the Persian Gulf. It praised Rep. Ron Paul, R–Texas, for saying on the floor of the House that 'Saddam Hussein is not threatening our national security.'

"It trotted out Ann Coulter, the right-wing TV ranter, to say, 'A president who uses his duties as commander in chief to bomb foreign countries every time he wants to change the subject ought to be removed with alacrity.'"

—Norman Lockman, syndicated column, April 19, 2004.

"[A]n estimated 500,000 Iraqi children under the age of five have died as a result of the sanctions....

"What has remained invisible is any documentation of how and by whom such a death toll has been justified for so long.... a vast number of lengthy holds had been placed on billions of dollars worth of what seemed unobjectionable — and very much needed — imports to Iraq.... all U.N. records that could answer my questions were kept from public scrutiny...I obtained these documents on the condition that my sources remain anonymous.... the United States has fought aggressively throughout the last decade to purposefully minimize the humanitarian goods that enter the country. And it has done so in the face of enormous human suffering, including massive increases in child mortality and widespread epidemics.

"According to Pentagon officials, that was the intention. In a June 23, 1991, *Washington Post* article, Pentagon officials stated that Iraq's electrical grid had been targeted by bombing strikes in order to undermine the civilian economy. 'People say, You didn't recognize that it was going to have an effect on water or sewage,' said one planning officer at the Pentagon. 'Well, what were we trying to do with sanctions — help out the Iraqi people? No. What we were doing with the attacks on infrastructure was to accelerate the effect of the sanctions.'"

— Joy Gordon, article, *Harpers*, November 2002.

George W. Bush and Dick Cheney:
Iraq *Is not* a Threat

"I don't believe [Saddam] is a significant military threat today."

—Vice President Dick Cheney, CNN, March 2001, Anthony Arnove, *Asheville Global Report*, March 23–29, 2006 (Source: *In These Times*).

"Iraq is probably not a nuclear threat at the present time."

—Secretary of defense Donald Rumsfeld, interview with "Fox News" on February 12, 2001.

"Frankly, they have worked. He [Saddam] has not developed any significant capability with respect to weapons of mass destruction. He is unable to project conventional power against his neighbors."

—Colin Powell speaking to Egypt's foreign minister in Cairo in February 2001 about the UN sanctions in force against Iraq, cited by Eric Alterman in his column of August 29, 2004 in *The Nation.*

"We have been able to keep weapons from going into Iraq. We have been able to keep the sanctions in place to the extent that items that might support weapons of mass destruction development have had some controls.

"It's been quite a success for ten years."

—Secretary of State Colin Powell, interview with "Face the Nation" on February 11, 2001.

The US and the UN "have succeeded in containing Saddam Hussein and his ambitions. Iraq's forces are about one third their original size. They don't really possess the capability to attack their neighbors the way they did ten years ago....Iraq is not threatening America.

—Secretary of State Colin Powell, at a meeting with German foreign Minister Joschka Fischer in February of 2001.

Iʀᴀǫ Is ᴀ Tʜʀᴇᴀᴛ

"Simply stated, there is no doubt that Saddam Hussein now has weapons of mass destruction."

—Vice President Dick Cheney, August 26, 2002. Jonathan Schell column, *The Nation,* June 30, 2003.

"Right now, Iraq is expanding and improving facilities that were used for the production of biological weapons."

—George W. Bush, Sept. 12, 2002.

"Intelligence gathered by this and other governments leaves no doubt that the Iraq regime continues to possess and conceal some of the most lethal weapons ever devised."

—George W. Bush, two days before he attacked Iraq.

"The Iraq regime possesses and produces chemical and biological weapons. It is seeking nuclear weapons."

—George W. Bush on Oct. 7, 2002.

"Iraq has a growing fleet of manned and unmanned aerial vehicles that would be used to disperse chemical or biological weapons across broad areas. We're concerned that Iraq is exploring ways of using the UAVs for missions targeting the United States.

—George W. Bush on Oct. 7, 2002.

"Iraq is reconstituting its nuclear weapons program. Hussein has held numerous meetings with Iraq nuclear scientists, a group he calls his 'nuclear mujahideen' — his nuclear holy warriors.

—George W. Bush on Oct. 7, 2002.

"We have sources that tell us that Saddam Hussein recently authorized Iraq field commanders to use chemical weapons — the very weapons the dictator tells us he does not have.

—George W. Bush on Feb. 8, 2003.

"We know that Saddam Hussein is determined to keep his weapons of mass destruction, is determined to make more."

—Colin Powell on Feb. 5, 2003

"We know where they are. They are in the area around Tikrit and Baghdad."

—Donald Rumsfeld on March 30, 2003.

"Most Americans now believe that Saddam Hussein was behind the September 11 attacks and support the war...in the mistaken belief that it is necessary for self-defense. The 9/11 connection is ceaselessly, demagogically promoted by the administration. In his speech warning of imminent invasion if Saddam failed to leave Iraq in forty-eight hours, George W. Bush alluded to this discredited canard seven times."

—Katha Pollitt, column, *The Nation*, April 7, 2003.

"If you tell a lie big enough and keep repeating it, people will eventually come to believe it."

—Josef Goebbels, Minister of Propaganda under Hitler

THE WAR

"As a massive US military buildup intensifies in the Persian Gulf, United Nations (UN) weapons inspectors, in their second month in Iraq, conceded this week that they had found no evidence of the weapons of mass destruction that the White House claims to exist.

"The US has set in motion the final buildup of soldiers and equipment for an invasion of Iraq, which now looks all but certain to happen sometime in February — whatever the UN inspectors inside the country unearth or fail to unearth."

> — Eamon Martin, article, *Asheville Global Report*, January 2–8, 2003.

"Iraqi armored forces consist mainly of aging Soviet-era armor and are about half the strength of 1991, when Iraq boasted the world's fourth largest army.

"The remnants of Saddam's air force — about 90 French Mirages and Soviet MIGs — remain impounded in Iran, where they fled to escape destruction during the first Gulf War. Other Iraqi planes or helicopters can take off only at peril of being shot down."

> —Richard Pyle, AP column, *The Asheville Citizen Times*, March 30, 2003.

"The U. S. defense budget approaches $400 billion, larger than the defense budgets of the next 20 countries combined.... Seventy percent of U.S. government-financed research is for new weaponry. The U.S. Navy is larger than all the navies of the world combined."

> —Harry J. Petrequin, *Asheville Citizens Times*, March 30, 2003.

"Although the assertion that Iraq still had weapons of massive destruction was the official justification for the country's invasion, there has perhaps never been a war in which the inequality of firepower between the combatants has been so great.

"The comparative casualty rates between the Iraqi forces and those of the coalition will be, as in 'Operation Desert Storm,' well over 100 to one."

> —John Berger, article, *The Nation*, May 12, 2003.

• March 19, 2003 — U.S. forces launch missiles and bombs at targets in Iraq, signaling the start of the war.

THE MEDIA

"This will be no war — there will be a fairly brief and ruthless military intervention.... the president will give an order. [The attack] will be rapid, accurate and dazzling.... It will be greeted by the majority of the Iraqi people as emancipation. And I say, bring it on."

> —Christopher Hitchens

"It won't take weeks. You know that, professor. Our military machine will crush Iraq in a matter of days and there's no question that it will."

—Bill O'Reilly, Fox News, Feb. 10, 2003.

"The scuds he swore he didn't have were fired at Kuwait, and Iraq was launching lame denials while the craters still smoked."

—Peter Bronson, *Cincinnati Enquirer*, March 23, 2003.

"In these first 24 hours we had six confirmed scud launches."

—Karl Zinsmeister, *National Review Online*, March 26, 2003.

"Jacques Chirac, Gerhard Schroeder, Nelson Mandela, Kofi Anan and other apologists were shown to be feckless fools."

—Karl Zinsmeister, *National Review Online*, March 26, 2003.

"People in countries with no troops in Iraq have already, as this is written, seen Iraq fighting with weapons Saddam Hussein claimed he did not have."

—Michael Barone, *U.S. News and World Report*, March 31, 2003.

"'Swooping silently out of the Persian Gulf night,' exulted James Dao of the *New York Times*, Navy SEALs claimed 'a bloodless victory in the battle for Iraq's vast oil empire.'"

—Michael T. Klare, article, *The Nation*, May 12, 2003.

"April 9, 2003 — After days of bombing, Baghdad falls into U.S. hands."

—*Public Citizen News*, May/June 2003.

"Major combat operations in Iraq have ended. In the battle of Iraq, the United States and our allies have prevailed."

—George W. Bush, May 1, 2003.

"Well, the hot story of the week is victory....The Tommy Franks/ Don Rumsfeld battle plan, war plan, worked brilliantly.... all the naysayers have been humiliated so far....The final word is hooray."

—Morton Kondracke, Fox News, April 12, 2003.

"The only people who think this wasn't a victory are Upper West-side liberals, and a few people here in Washington."

—Charles Krauthammer, Inside Washington, WUSA–TV, April 19, 2003.

"Some journalists, in my judgment, just can't stand success, especially a few liberal columnists and newspapers and a few Arab reporters."

—Lou Dobbs, CNN, April 14, 2003.

"More than anything else, real vindication for the administration. One, credible evidence of weapons of mass destruction. Two, you know what? There were a lot of terrorists here, really bad guys. I saw them."

—Bob Arnot, MSNBC, April 9, 2003.

"Why don't the damn Democrats give the president his day? He won today. He did well today."

—Chris Matthews, MSNBC, April 9, 2003.

"I'm waiting to hear the words, 'I was wrong,' from some of the world's most elite journalists, politicians and Hollywood types.... Maybe disgraced commentators and politicians alike, like Daschle, Jimmy Carter, Dennis Kucinich and all these others...their wartime predictions were arrogant, they were misguided and they were dead wrong.

—Joe Scarborough, MSNBC, April 10, 2003.

"My friends, here's the news. We are winning in Iraq. We are winning in Iraq. We are winning in Iraq."

—John McCain.

"As in recent U. S. military attacks on Third World countries, the media pretended that this was a 'war' as opposed to a straightforward attack by a distant superpower on a virtually defenseless target state — an unlevel playing field par excellence and a massacre of enemy forces that had been disarmed, bombed, spied on under the guise of inspections, and starved for the prior dozen years. These pretenses were essential to allowing the defeat of Iraq to be a military marvel and matter of pride, rather than a source of embarrassment and shame at beating up yet another hapless and deliberately crippled victim."

—Edward S. Herman, *Z Magazine*, June 2003.

"Incredibly, President George W. Bush told French President Jacques Chirac in early 2003 that Iraq must be invaded to thwart Gog and Magog, the Bible's satanic agents of the Apocalypse.

"Honest. This isn't a joke. The President of the United States, in a top-secret phone call to a major European ally, asked for French troops to join American soldiers in attacking Iraq as a mission from God.

"The Palestinian foreign minister later said the American president told him he was 'on a mission from god' to defeat Iraq. At that time, The White House called this claim 'absurd.'...

"It's awkward to say openly, but now-departed President Bush is a religious crackpot, an ex-drunk of small intellect who 'got saved.' He never should have been entrusted with the power to start wars.

For six years, Americans really haven't known why he launched the unnecessary Iraq attack. Official pretexts turned out to be baseless.... Was the invasion loosed to gain control of Iraq's oil — or to protect Israel — or to complete Bush's father's vendetta against the late dictator Saddam Hussein?

"Now, added to the other suspicions, comes the goofy possibility that abstruse, supernatural, idiotic, laughable Bible prophecies were a factor. This casts an ominous pall over the needless war that has killed more than four thousand young Americans and cost U.S. taxpayers perhaps $1 trillion."

—James A. Haught essay, *free inquiry*, Aug./Sept. 2009.

ANALYSIS

"Word comes now, via the Washington Post and the New York Times, of a small intelligence agency in the State Department — 165 analysts, a tenth of the CIA's complement — that more or less got it right.

"The Bureau of Intelligence and Research at State was critical of the stated reasons for going to war from the very first.

"It challenged as unsubstantiated the views of other intelligence agencies that Saddam was rebuilding his nuclear weapons program.

"Nor would it go along with the theory that Iraq could develop a weapon in the next 10 years, given that it didn't see any movement in that direction at present.

"In addition, it was skeptical of the idea that the conquest of Iraq would help spread democracy across the Arab world.

"The reason this intelligence was given so little weight (none, actually) was that the ruling cabal — Bush, vice President Cheney, Defense Secretary Rumsfeld, Deputy Defense Secretary Wolfowitz — didn't want to hear it.

"Perhaps the saddest aspect of the farce is that not even Secretary of State Colin Powell paid any attention to the analysis of what were, after all, his own people. Instead, he went before the U.N. and made a bogus case for the invasion using bogus evidence."

—Donald Kaul, syndicated column, July 31, 2004.

"Before the war, the Bush administration portrayed Iraq as full of killer poisons with strange names and deadly effects, which terrorists could get hold of and unleash on U.S. cities...

The administration also contended many of the weapons were ready to be used on the battlefield.

"'Our conservative estimate is that Iraq today has a stockpile of between 100 and 500 tons of chemical weapons agent,' Powell said at the United Nations in February.

"In October, U.S. intelligence agencies said that Iraq had begun 'renewed production of chemical warfare agents,' probably including mustard, sarin, cyclosarin and VX.

"Chemical weapons have not been found.

"Powell suggested military units had biological weapons in the field. On May 30, Lt. Gen. James Conway, the top Marine in Iraq, said, ...'We've been to virtually every ammunition supply point between the Kuwaiti border and Baghdad, but they're simply not there.'"

"Powell also had told the United Nations that 'numerous intelligence reports over the past decade from sources inside Iraq' indicated 'a covert force of up to a few dozen scud-variant ballistic missiles.'"

"None has been found.

"U. S. allegations that Iraq was trying to develop a nuclear weapon have also not been verified...No centrifuges have been reported or found.

"In his state of the union address, Bush said that Britain had learned that Saddam 'recently sought significant quantities of uranium from Africa.'"

"The claim rested significantly on a letter or letters between officials in Iraq and Niger...the communications are now accepted as forged."

—John J. Lumpkin, article, *The Associated Press*, June 8, 2003.

THE MEDIA AGAIN

"The evidence he presented to the United Nations — some of it circumstantial, some of it absolutely bone-chilling in its detail — had to prove to anyone that Iraq not only hasn't accounted for its weapons of mass destruction but without doubt still retains them. Only a fool — or possibly a Frenchman — could conclude otherwise."

> —Richard Cohen, *Washington Post*, Feb. 6, 2003, the day after Colin Powell's mendacious speech to the UN Security Council.

"Colin Powell did more than present the world with a convincing and detailed x-ray of Iraq's secret weapons and terrorism programs yesterday. He also exposed the enduring bad faith of several key members of the UN Security Council when it comes to Iraq and its 'web of lies,' in Powell's phrase....To continue to say that the Bush administration has not made its case, you must now believe that Colin Powell lied in the most serious statement he will ever make, or was taken in by manufactured evidence. I don't believe that. Today, neither should you."

—Jim Hoagland, *Washington Post*, Feb. 6, 2003.

"A key British Foreign Office diplomat responsible for dialoguing with UN inspectors said on June 20 that claims the US and UK governments made about Iraq's alleged weapons of mass destruction (WMD) were 'totally implausible.'

"'I'd read the intelligence on WMD for four and a half years, and there's no way that it could sustain the case that the government was presenting. All of my colleagues knew that, too,' said Carne Ross, a member of the British mission to the UN in New York during the run-up to the invasion."

—*Asheville Global Report*, June 23–29, 2005 (source Guardian (UK))

"In 1995, Hussein Kamel, the Iraqi defector in charge of Saddam's WMD program, told the CIA that Saddam had destroyed his chemical and biological weapons and had none left. Yet, on his way to Auschwitz in 2003, George Bush told a Polish television audience, 'We found the weapons of mass destruction.'

"According to Dick Cheney, Iraq has been 'very busy enhancing its capabilities in the field of chemical and biological agents...(and) to pursue the nuclear program they began many years ago....We've gotten this from the firsthand testimony of defectors, including Saddam's own son-in-law,' a reference to Lt. Gen. Hussein Kamel, the former Iraqi weapons chief and Iraq's highest ranking defector.

"Ritter pointed out that Cheney was omitting an inconvenient part of Kamel's story" (see below).

—Steve Rendall, *Extra!* March/April 2006.

"On Iraq's WMD, Scott Ritter, the former top weapons inspector, claimed that when he left in 1998, 90 to 95 percent of Iraq's chemical and biological weapons (CBW) had been destroyed and any remaining anthrax or sarin would be useless sludge. It was recently disclosed (by Cheney and others) that the number one Iraqi expatriate, Hussein Kamel, whose testimony had been repeatedly cited by U.S. officials, had told his interrogators in 1995 that Saddam Hussein had destroyed his chemical and biological weapons and had none left, a point not made public until March 2003 (John Barry, "The Defector's Secret," *Newsweek*, March 3, 2003).

—Edward S. Herman, article, *Z Magazine*, June 2003.

On a trip to Baghdad, Ritter "urged Iraqi officials to allow inspections and warned Americans that attacking Iraq would be a 'historic mistake'.... At CBS Evening News (9/30/02), correspondent Tom Fenton said that Ritter 'is now what some would call a loose cannon.'...

"CNN news executive Eason Jordan told Catherine Calloway: 'Well, Scott Ritter's chameleon-like behavior has really bewildered a lot of people.... U.S. officials no longer give Scott Ritter much credibility.' When Paula Zahn interviewed Ritter (CNN American Morning, 8/13/02), she suggested he was in league with Saddam Hussein: 'People out there are accusing you of drinking Saddam's Kool-Aid.'

"Though the absence of WMDs vindicated his views of the Iraqi threat and the value of inspections, it didn't result in his media rehabilitation. Instead of being sought out and consulted for how he got things right, he became largely invisible."

—Steve Rendall, *Extra!* March/April 2006.

"Hans Blix is a seventy-five-year-old Swedish lawyer and public servant...called out of retirement...to lead the United Nations Monitoring, Verification and Inspection Commission (UNMOVIC)...Blix, before he was vindicated by the postwar search for weapons in Iraq, was systematically treated with contempt by leading members of the Bush administration....

"*The Washington Post* reported that Deputy Secretary of Defense Paul Wolfowitz had requested a CIA investigation of Blix's performance at IAEA and had 'hit the ceiling' when nothing could be found to undermine Blix and the inspection program. According to the *Post*, Wolfowitz allegedly feared that the inspection could torpedo plans for military action against Saddam Hussein....

"Of the people Blix talked to, President Jacques Chirac of France was almost alone in believing that the UN inspections had disarmed Iraq long ago....

"Hans Blix...was spied on, publicly reviled, and called a liar.... Karl Rove....was convinced of the historical duplicity of the Swedes.... War was inevitable... because Saddam Hussein refused to turn over his weapons of mass destruction, an impossible dilemma for the Iraqi despot since he had none to turn over....

"With what seemed great conviction, Powell paraded before the council pictures of alleged installations and sinister vehicles, which we now know to have been a collection of nonexistent smoking guns. He convinced many people, including that most skeptical of journalist, the late Mary McCrory....

"This is the sense of messianic big ideas not properly thought through, a certainty that sometimes even hints at divine rightness, and an undertone of manifest destiny under the guidance of Almighty God."

—Brian Urquhart, book review, *Plan of Attack*, by Bob Woodward, *The New York Review*, June 10, 2004.

"Whenever Bush gets criticized, his palace guard descends upon the person who dares to question his Highness.

"That's the way it was when Paul O'Neill, Bush's former Treasury Secretary, said Bush wanted to go to war against Iraq way before 9/11. Within hours, the Bush goons were threatening O'Neill with prosecution for allegedly publicizing classified information.

"That's the way it was when former ambassador Joseph Wilson went public with his account of how the Bush Administration played up the false story of uranium in Niger. Within days, the White House was outing Wilson's wife, Valerie Plame, as a CIA officer, with Karl Rove reportedly saying, 'His wife's now fair game.'"

—Comment, *The Progressive*, May 2004.

"Paul Wolfowitz: 'Well, I just don't understand why we are beginning by talking about this one man, bin Laden.'

"[Richard A.] Clarke: We are talking about a network of terrorist organizations called al Qaeda, that happens to be led by bin Laden, and we are talking about that network because it and it alone poses an immediate and serious threat to the United States.'

"Wolfowitz:" Well, there are others that do as well, at least as much. Iraqi terrorism, for example.... You give bin Laden too much credit.'" ...

"'At first, I was incredulous that we were talking about something other than getting al Quaeda. Then I realized with almost a sharp physical pain that Rumsfeld and Wolfowitz were going to try to take advantage of this national tragedy to promote their agenda about Iraq.

"Clarke said he told Powell that this was foolish. 'Having been attacked by al Quaeda, for us now to go bombing Iraq in response would be like invading Mexico after the Japanese attacked Pearl Harbor....

"'All along, it seemed inevitable that we would invade,' he writes. 'Iraq was portrayed as the most dangerous thing in national security. It was an *idée fixe*, a rigid belief, received wisdom, a decision already made and one that no fact or event could derail.' In the lead up to the war, the Bush Administration repeatedly tried to lump September 11 and Iraq together. Writes Clarke: 'What a horrible thing it was to give such a false impression to our people and our troops.'"

—Comment, *The Progressive*, May 2004.

"Last week, Murray Waas reported on the *National Journal* Web site that ten days after September 11, 2001, 'Bush was told in a highly classified briefing that the U.S. intelligence community had no evidence linking the Iraqi regime of Saddam Hussein to the attacks and that there was scant credible evidence that Iraq had any significant collaborative ties with al Quaeda.' This information too, was not shared with Congress before the war, and was likewise kept from the commissions and senatorial committees that have since investigated the run up to it."

> —Hendrik Hertzberg, The Talk of the Town column, *The New Yorker*, December 5, 2005.

"The independent commission investigating the Sept. 11 attacks said Wednesday that no evidence exists that al-Qaida had strong ties to Saddam Hussein — a central justification the Bush administration had for toppling the former Iraqi regime. Bush also argued that Saddam had weapons of mass destruction, which have not been found."

> —The Associated Press, June 18, 2004.

"President Bush on Thursday disputed the Sept.11 Commission's finding that there was no 'collaborative relationship' between Saddam Hussein and the al-Qaida terrorist network responsible for the attacks.

"'There was a relationship between Iraq and al-Qaida,' Bush insisted following a meeting with his Cabinet at the White House."

> —*Asheville Citizen–Times,* June 18, 2004.

"As recently as Monday, Cheney said Saddam 'had long-established ties with al-Qaida,' and Bush defended the vice-president's assertion.

"The commission investigating the Sept. 11 attacks bluntly contradicted the White House. It said there was no evidence Iraq and al-Qaida had a collaborative relationship.'

> —*Asheville Citizen–Times,* June 17, 2004.

"After hundreds of American soldiers have died and billions of U.S. dollars have been spent, a Senate panel is saying the justification for the war in Iraq was wrong.

> —Ken Guggenheim, report, *The Associated Press,* July 10, 2004.

"Colin Powell, the former US Secretary of state, harshly criticized the Bush administration on Sept. 9 for its failures in Iraq, calling the country a mess and voicing concerns that it may slide into civil war.

"Powell who left the administration in January also said that his speech in February 2003 to the UN, making the case for war, was a painful blot on his record....

"Turning to his pre-war address to the UN Security Council, when he forcefully made the case for invasion and offered proof that Iraq had weapons of mass destruction, Powell said that he felt terrible about the claims he made. Asked whether the speech would tarnish his reputation, he replied, 'Of course it will. It's a blot. I'm the one who presented it on behalf of the United States to the world, and [it] will always be part of my record. It was painful. It's painful now....

"Powell, 68, did not blame George Tenet, the CIA's director at the time, for the misleading information.... Instead, he blamed lower-level intelligence analysts for not speaking out during the five days he pored over reports at the CIA as he prepared his speech....

"Powell said that he had "never seen evidence to suggest" a connection between the attacks of Sept. 11, 2001, and the regime of Saddam Hussein, unlike Dick Cheney, the vice-president, who has made such a claim."

—*Asheville Global Report*, Sept 15–21, 2005 (Source: Times (UK)

"The only part that kind of annoys me is 'Well, did you lie? Or were you misleading?' No, I didn't lie, and I wasn't misleading. If I was lying and knew what the truth was, which has to be the basis of a lie — you know the truth — we wouldn't have sent 1,400 people wandering around Iraq looking for the stuff. They didn't find it. So the intelligence was wrong. And that's all you can really say about it."

—Colin Powell, Interview, AARP Magazine, July/August, 2006.

"Bush, Cheney, Donald Rumsfeld, Condoleezza Rice, and Colin Powell issued 237 statements that were 'misleading at the time they were made,' according to "Iraq on the Record," a report by Representative Henry Waxman of California and the democratic staff of the House Committee on Government Reform."

—Comment, *The Progressive*, April 2006.

"I would say...that would clearly be a more serious issue than even Watergate. It would be a graver charge" and "fit into the definition of high crimes and misdemeanors, which we in Britain used to have as a basis for impeachment, and which, of course, you still have as a basis of impeachment."

—Labor MP Malcolm Savage in a CNBC interview about allegations that legislators and citizens were lied to and led into war by the Bushites, *The Nation*, June 23, 2003.

"On October 2, David Kay gave an interim report of his findings before House and Senate intelligence committees. Although he had directed a team of 1,200 people who had searched Iraq for three months, they had not managed to find any biological, chemical, or nuclear weapons."

—Ed Regis, essay, *Harper's Magazine*/ July 2004.

"Four months after Charles A. Duelfer, who led the weapons hunt in 2004, submitted an interim report to Congress that contradicted nearly every prewar assertion about Iraq made by top Bush administration officials, a senior intelligence official says the findings will stand as the ISG's final conclusions and will be published this spring....

"The ISG has interviewed every person it could find connected to programs that ended more than 10 years ago, and every suspected site within Iraq has been fully searched, or stripped bare."

—Dafna Linzer, report, *The Washington Post National Weekly Edition,* January 23, 2005.

"Colonel Sam Gardner came around to a conclusion that horrified him: The Bush administration had turned psychological operations against Americans. No longer were just foreign enemies being targeted for coercion and deception. Now the target was the U.S. public.

"'It was not bad intelligence. It was much more. It was an organized effort. It began before the war, and continues as post-conflict distortions,' wrote Gardner in a fifty-six-page self-published report....

"The American public became the focus of a high-intensity domestic psy-ops program. The lies coming out of the Bush administration picked up in frequency and audacity. False claims about the presence of nonexistent weapons of mass destruction were but one thread in this elaborate tapestry of deceit. 'Disloyal' allies such as France and Germany were targeted and smeared. The lies took many forms. Sometimes it was an outright official fabrication. At other times, government officials would deliberately not correct a lie gaining currency in the street. There were unofficial leaks and stories planted on background. Finally, there were black operations, where false documents may have been forged in elaborate schemes to smear and deceive. "In total," Gardner asserts, "There were over fifty stories manufactured or at least engineered, that distorted the picture of Gulf [War] II for the American and British people." ...

"The themes of the invasion propaganda were twofold. The war on terror is a fight between good and evil (and it didn't hurt to invoke images of a Christian crusade against Islam). And Iraq was responsible for the 9/11 attacks — 'What propaganda theorists would call the 'big lie,' says Gardner."

—Amy Goodman, *The Exception to the Rulers.*

"In a 2003 interview, Gen. Tommy Franks ran the martial law flag up the pole, stating that a major terrorist attack might mean discarding the Constitution in favor of a military government. You can check out this option in an article called 'When the war Hits Home:

U.S. Plans for Martial Law, Tele-Governance and the Suspension of Elections by Wayne Madsen and John Stanton."

—Bruce Mulkey, local column, *Asheville Citizen–Times*, May 2004.

"Sandra Day O'Connor, a Republican-appointed judge who retired last month after 24 years on the Supreme Court, has said the U.S. is in danger of edging towards dictatorship if the party's right wingers continue to attack the judiciary."

—Julian Borger, *Asheville Global Report*, Mar. 16–22, 2006. Source: *Guardian (UK)*.

"The Bush administration has been able to convey the impression of having been (along with Congress and the rest of us) the innocent victim of a CIA misinformation campaign — much easier since the committee postponed its examination of the Administrations' pre-war hype until after the election. But this misimpression is also a product of the selective amnesia of much of the media that covered the release of the report."

—Eric Alterman, column, *The Nation*, August 2/9, 2004.

"Bush and "his henchmen made their case for the invasion of Iraq and sold it to the American people (if not the United Nations), then proceeded to go through with it....

"They're trying to lie their way out of it, of course, but their efforts to show that Saddam Hussein was an imminent threat to us or that he participated in any substantial way in the Sept. 11 attacks are pathetic. Mainly what they and their defenders are arguing is the fall-back position: that they were victimized by the 'bad intelligence.'..."

—Donald Kaul, syndicated column, July 31, 2004.

"The 9/11 Commission reported that Clarke, the CIA, and others had warned the administration as many as forty times of the threat posed by Osama bin Laden, but that is not what the administration wanted to hear, and it did not hear it....

"What brings any student of intelligence to a kind of shocked halt is the fact that CIA analysts did not get anything right — every claim about Saddam's WMD was wrong — completely wrong, flatly wrong, wrong by a country mile....

"But the President did nothing....

"[C]hemical and biological weapons were not found... because they did not exist....It is unlikely that the United States had ever been more comprehensively and significantly wrong about anything ever, than it was in identifying the reasons for going to war in Iraq....

"[T]hey all knew the case was weak but surrendered to pressure from above and hoped to be saved by a miracle — they convinced themselves that *something* would turn up when the troops got to Baghdad....

"[D]efining our opponents as terrorists disguises the more important fact that most of them, probably in excess of 90 percent, are Iraqis angry with Americans.... Americans have invaded their country, have killed anywhere between 10,000 and 100,000 civilians, plus an unknown number of combatants....

"But if our reason for war was to counter a threat posed by terrorists with weapons of mass destruction, a threat proved since illusory, while the actual resistance we meet in Iraq is angry and nationalist in an uncomplicated way, then it is hard to escape the conclusion that we are fighting an unnecessary war."

> —Thomas Powers, essay, *The New York Review*, December 16, 2004.

"George Bush has made the christian faith an obscenity. To rationalize what he's doing in Iraq because God told him to do it or to make Jesus some kind of warmonger is another immorality. And for people in America to buy that?

"We need to just get... out of Iraq.... so we have to get George Bush out of office. We have to get our troops home. A Mission Accomplished would be for the Iraqi people to rebuild their government and have whatever system of government they want. Because — you know what? — It's their country....

"We've made a horrible mess of that country. The people there want peace, they want their electricity back, they want their water back, and they want their jobs. They want America out....

"Just because I'm against the policies of the Israeli government toward Palestine does not mean I'm anti-Israeli or anti-Semitic. Just because I'm against George Bush and his policies doesn't mean I'm anti-American. I just believe that we have to force our leaders to work for peace and not for killing....

"You can't be successful in Iraq. The generals on the ground have said that. There is not a military solution.... It's insane. Are we fighting terrorism or are we creating terrorism? Obviously, we're creating terrorism and an insurgency by our military presence there."

> —Cindy Sheehan, interview with David Barsamian, *The Progressive*, March 2006.

"We all have lost a loved one in war. I say *lost*, but I don't like that euphemism because Casey wasn't lost; he was killed by George Bush's murderous policies in the Middle East.

> —Cindy Sheehan, interview with David Barsamian, *The Progressive*, March 2006.

"Iraq is only the beginning. The *Boston Globe* (9/10/02) reports: 'As the Bush administration debates going to war against Iraq, its most hawkish members are pushing a sweeping vision for the Middle East that sees the overthrow of President Saddam Hussein of Iraq as merely a first step in the region's transformation.... After an ouster of Hussein,' they say, 'the United States will have leverage to act against Syria and Iran, will be in a better position to resolve the Israeli–Palestinian conflict, and will be able to rely less on Saudi oil.'

"There is open discussion within Israel and the U.S. ruling circles of massive "transfer"— the ethnic cleansing of historic Palestine. (Defense Secretary Rumsfeld has called Jewish settlements in the West Bank and Gaza legitimate Israeli spoils of war; Dick Armey, the Republican Majority Leader in the House, has spoken in favor of expelling Palestinians to Jordan.)

"The Rand Corporation's Pentagon briefing echoed this theme: It called Iraq the "strategic pivot" and Egypt "the prize." In their view, the entire region should be reconfigured to U. S. specifications."

    —Larry Everest and Leonard Innes, article, *Z Magazine*, December 2002.

"Now, in October of 2009, the Shiite government of Iraq, put in power by the George W. Bush administration, has announced that "only" 86,000 Iraqis died in George W Bush's eight-year war against Iraq. Compare this figure to the figure of 158,000 civilian Iraqis killed in the first Bush's earlier six-weeks long war. That estimate was prepared by the U.S. Census Bureau to the displeasure of H. W. Bush who tried to suppress it. Now, we have an astonishingly low figure for the second war: the bizarre claim that twice as many Iraqis were killed in the very brief, six weeks long, first Iraq war as were killed in the much more intensive seven-year plus and geographically more extensive second attack against Iraq. Can anyone believe it? Take a long look at the below estimates provided by Lancet early in the second war. As always, the media is accepting the lower figures from the Bush administration without any question or disagreement.

"Over a year ago an international team of epidemiologists, headed by Les Roberts of Johns Hopkins School of Public Health, completed a 'cluster sample survey' of civilian casualties in Iraq. Its findings... estimated that at least 98,000 Iraqi civilians had died in the previous 18 months as a direct result of the invasion and occupation of their country.... Their most significant finding was that the vast majority of violent deaths were caused by 'coalition' forces using 'helicopter gunships, rockets or other forms of aerial weaponry,' and that almost half (48 percent) of these were children, with a median age of 8.

"The team's findings were published in the *Lancet*, the official journal of the British Medical Association....

"Soon after the study was published, U.S. and British officials launched a concerted campaign to discredit its authors and marginalize their findings without seriously addressing the validity of their methods or presenting any evidence to challenge their conclusions....

"Michael O'Toole, the director of the Center for International Health in Australia, says: 'I just don't see any evidence of significant exaggeration.... If anything, the deaths may have been higher because what they are unable to do is survey families where everyone has died....

"By dismissing the study's findings out of hand, U.S. and British officials created the illusion that the authors were suspect or politically motivated and discouraged the media from taking them seriously. This worked disturbingly well. Even opponents of the war continue to cite much lower figures for civilian casualties and innocently attribute the bulk of them to Iraqi resistance forces or 'terrorists.'

> —Nicholas J.S. Davies, investigative report, *Z Magazine*, February 2006.

"'The United States,' he writes, 'is becoming not just a militarized state but a military society: a country where armed power is the measure of national greatness, and war, or planning for war, is the exemplary (and only) common project.'

"Why does the US Department of Defense currently maintain 725 official military bases outside the country and 969 at home (not to mention numerous secret bases)? Why does the US spend more on 'defense' than all the rest of the world put together? .... This country is obsessed with war: rumors of war, images of war, 'preventive war,' 'surgical' war, 'prophylactic' war, 'permanent' war. As President Bush explained at a news conference on April 13, 2004, 'This country must go on the offense and stay on the offense.'"

> —Tony Judt, review of *The New American Militarism: How Americans are Seduced by War* by Andrew J. Bacevich, *The New York Review*, June 14, 2005.

"Every ten years or so, the United States needs to pick up some crappy little country and throw it against the wall, just to show the world we mean business."

> —Michael Ledeen (Iran–Contra operative, consultant to Secretary of State Alexander Haig, and now resident scholar in the Freedom Chair at the American Enterprise Institute) — cited by Lewis H. Lapham, Notebook, *Harper's Magazine*, June 2003.

"'Afghanistan and other troubled lands today cry out for the sort of enlightened foreign administration once provided by self-confident Englishmen in jodhpurs and pith helmets,' wrote Max Boot in the *Weekly Standard*. Michael Ledeen in the *American Enterprise* urged the United States to 'wage revolutionary war against the terrorist regimes, and gradually replace them.' Such a course, he argued, would win firm support from the oppressed people of these countries."

—Matthew Lyons, *Z Magazine*, article, January 2003.

Charles J. Dunlap: People don't fully appreciate what the military is. By design, it is authoritarian, socialistic, undemocratic. Those qualities help the armed forces to serve their very unique purpose in our society: namely, external defense against foreign enemies....

Charles J. Dunlap: Americans today have an incredible trust in the military.... In other words, the armed forces are much more trusted than the civilian institutions that are supposed to control them.

A.J. Bacevich: The question that arises is whether, in fact, we're not already experiencing what is in essence a creeping coup d'état. But it's not people in uniform who are seizing power. It's militarized civilians.... The ideology of national security has become ever more woven into our politics....

Bill Wasik: Everyone seems to agree that the armed forces fight on the Republican side. And this is borne out in polls: self-described Republicans outnumber Democrats in the military by more than four to one, and only 7 percent of soldiers describe themselves as liberal....

Charles J. Dunlap: The military is an inherently conservative organization, and this is true of all militaries around the world....

Robert H. Kohn: Well, at this point the military has a long tradition of getting what it wants. If we ever attempted to truly demobilize — i.e., if the military were suddenly, radically cut back — it could lead if not to a coup then to very severe civil–military tension.

—From a forum, *American coup d'état*, in January 2006 in Arlington, Virginia, sponsored by *Harper's Magazine* and published in that magazine in its April 2006 issue.

"In 1983, during the formative years of spin, 241 Marines were blown up by one terrorist blast in Beirut. Two days later, on October 25, Reagan landed 1,200 marines in Grenada, which is 3,000 miles away from Beirut. By the time the invasion force grew to 7,000 marines, the campaign was over....After this instant victory over a ragtag foe, Reagan was stimulated enough to accept his supporters' claim that America had now put an end to our shame in Vietnam. Reagan understood what Americans wanted, and that was spin. It was more important to be told you were healthy than to be healthy....

"The sorriest thing to be said about the US, as we sidle up to fascism (which can become our fate if we plunge into a major depression, or suffer a set of dirty-bomb catastrophes), is that we expect disasters. We await them. We have become a guilty nation. Somewhere in the moil of the national conscience is the knowledge that we are caught in the little contradiction of loving Jesus on Sunday, while lusting the rest of the week for mega-money....For Bush and Rove, 9/11 was the jackpot.

—Norman Mailer, letter, *The New York Review*, November 4, 2004.

"The common view that internal freedom makes for humane and moral international behavior is supported neither by historical evidence nor by reason....

"The value of being allowed to protest relatively unmolested is certainly real, but... established institutions, with overwhelmingly dominant power, tend to line up in goose-step fashion in support of any state foreign venture, no matter how immoral....In 1975, the Tri-lateral Commission...published a study entitled *The Crisis of Democracy*, which interprets public participation in decision making as a threat to democracy, one that must be contained if elite domination is to persist unhindered by popular demands. The population must be reduced to apathy and conformism if democracy... is to be kept workable and allowed to survive....

"[S]ystematic policies toward Third World countries make it evident that the alleged commitment to democracy and human rights is mere rhetoric, directly contrary to actual policy.... Economic freedom has often required political servitude....Since a favorable investment climate and stability quite often require repression, the United States has supplied the tools and training for interrogation and torture and is thoroughly implicated in the vast expansion of torture during the past decade....

"Among the symbols used to frighten and manipulate the populace of the democratic states, few have been more important than 'terror' and 'terrorism.' These terms have generally been confined to the use of violence by individuals and marginal groups. Official violence, which is far more extensive in both scale and destructiveness, is placed in a different category altogether....The numbers tormented and killed by official violence — wholesale as opposed to retail terror — during recent decades have exceeded those of unofficial terrorists by a factor running into the thousands."

—Noam Chomsky and Edward Herman, a 1979 essay reprinted by *Z Magazine* in its April 2006 issue.

Chapter 20. Barbarism: Torture

Torture is not exactly an ism but it is certainly an act of terrorism whether used by a state or a private gang. Short of murder and perhaps rape (a form of terrorism), it is the most extreme cruelty human beings can resort to. In fact, it quite often results in death and always results in degradation and debilitation. Tortured people never recover. Those who perform acts of torture, order it, or defend it are guilty of a criminal atrocity. They are also deeply corrupted by their own brutality. The groups and countries to which they belong are permanently stained by their viciousness. There is no defense for such behavior. People who torture are evil. Aside from its immorality, torture cannot work. Indeed, it is certain to multiply resistance and resentment in its victims and in their families, friends, countrymen, and fellow religionists. Anyone who tortures opens the gate for maximum barbarism and assures that it will spread and boomerang.

The Fox show "24" is based on the "ticking bomb" scenario. In every episode, the hero, Jack Bauer, tortures a suspect, the suspect confesses, and Bauer saves some imagined victim. A study by the Parents Television Council tallied 102 television scenes from 1996 to 2001. The torturers in almost all cases were nazis or drug lords. A study covering such torture scenes from 2002 to 2005 showed 624 torture scenes, almost all carried out by a "hero." Military interrogators along with the dean of the U.S. Military Academy at West point came away from visiting the studio worried about the "toxic" effect on soldiers. The West Point educator said, "Jack Bauer is a criminal.

In real life, he would be prosecuted." FBI interrogator Joe Navarro said, in a *New Yorker* article, "only a psychopath can torture and be unaffected. You don't want people like that in your organization. They are untrustworthy, and tend to have grotesque other problems."

At a meeting with FBI interrogators, Bob Cochran, creator of "24," asked them "what they would do if they faced the imminent threat of nuclear blast in New York City and had custody of a suspect who knew how to stop it." This "ticking bomb scenario" is often used to justify torture. Sometimes the question is changed around to ask how far an interrogator should go to save the life of a child, sometimes how far a father should go to save his son's or daughter's life (the premise of several movies). Bob Cochran admitted, "Most terrorism experts will tell you that the ticking time bomb situation never occurs in real life, or very rarely. But on our show it happens every week."

As to whether or not torture works, there are certain logical and practical problems with the ticking bomb scenario. It assumes all kinds of arrangements and circumstances that are extremely unlikely, perhaps impossible. Arguing from a made-up television or movie scenario to a real life situation cannot be accurately representative or instructive. Fictional scenarios are reverse engineered; they are constructed of assumptions and made up events and sequences that rarely ever occur as imagined. Thus, the real torturers are reduced to inventing things, guessing, taking wild stabs in the dark, assuming things about the minds and motives of their victims as well as about their unknown accomplices. Torturers cannot read the minds of their victims and cannot know what remains hidden. Responding to a supposed truthful confession might well cause enormous harm by distorting the emotions of the interrogators themselves, even by sending them off into wild attacks against innocents and bystanders.

There are a number of uncertainties in this. First of all, how can the interrogators possibly know that they face the imminent threat of a nuclear blast? They haven't tortured their captive yet. Did he give up this information without being tortured? Did they torture someone else? Did the information come from a rumor, an overheard conversation, or was it just a hunch? Torture may cause the captive to clam up altogether or to invent something malignant or useless. Of necessity, torturers always resort to guesswork and projections. For example, how can the torturers know in advance that this particular captive knows how to disarm the bomb? Indeed, all of the torturers assumptions and suppositions are the products of their imaginations, not known facts. Torturers know how tentative their extractions are and it leaves them uncertain about the information they have forced out of the victim's mouth. They cannot know with any certainty what to do next. The whole process of torturing to force actionable information out of a captive is built on quicksand. Anyway, why should anyone trust torturers to do the right thing? They may deliberately do the wrong thing. They may have an agenda of their own. They are not rational or worthy people as proven by their cowardly willingness to harm helpless people to protect their careers or please their overlords.

Torturers ask questions that are based on gross assumptions. They are usually looking for, demanding a specific piece of information or they may be just fishing blindly. In either case, they are putting ideas in the mind of their victim, words in his mouth. They literally cause false confessions, guide their victims to tell them what they want to hear. The victim will certainly lie, either for malign reasons or to stop the pain. If he does confess to something, the torturers cannot know if it is the truth. If the captive really is a man willing, even eager, to die for his belief, would he break under pressure and tell the truth? Could such a man be believed? Isn't it more likely that he will say something that will lead his enemies to take some self-destructive, dangerous, or irrational action? If he actually knew there really was a ticking bomb, wouldn't he give his torturers a false time or situation that would kill those trying to disarm it? Wouldn't the torturers themselves know that? Would they want to go rushing in?

Cheney insists that the people he and his cronies were torturing were the "worst of the worst." If that were true, wouldn't they all be suicidists? Why would fanatical people eager to die for their god cave in to torture? Of course, we know that Cheney was lying again. Perhaps he needs to be tortured to get *him* to tell the truth. He and Bush were torturing and abusing people indiscriminately and at random. Nearly all of their captives were Iraqis. Indeed, during their entire time in power, they captured very few actual terrorists, very few al Qaeda members. Except in a few rare cases, they didn't know the difference between terrorists and mere patriots defending their country against an unjust assault and an illegal occupation, nor did they care. In fact, they deliberately broadened their war to include people and countries that clearly were not terrorist. They did this to increase their own power and to prolong their time in office. Their attacks and tortures were as dishonest and incompetent as they were counterproductive; and they are certain to cause blowback for a long time to come.

Lately, out of office, Dick Cheney has been visiting his friends in the right-wing media where he is defending and justifying his torture program and attacking Barack Obama for canceling his and Bush's policies of abuse and torture. He claims that his program saved "thousands of lives" and prevented "dozens of attacks" against the US here at home. His media collaborators aren't asking him any critical questions at all. There are plenty of questions to ask.

Mr. Cheney, what are the specific details? Exactly which plots that saved thousands of lives can you name and describe? What specific events can you set forth and exactly who saved those lives? Where and when did you arrest the plotters? What were their names? Who specifically arrested them and at what times and locations? Name some of the people whose lives you saved? Can you name even one? You've supplied no facts, no times, no places, no names of the plotters, no names of those almost victims. Can you supply a list of witnesses, even one witness? If torture works so well, can you put any of your victims on television or radio so they can tell us what you claim they told you? Can you even repeat the specific words and facts that came out of the mouths of any of your victims?

You say you "only" waterboarded three people and that they gave you "actionable" information that saved thousands of lives. (You left out all the thousands of others who were abused, raped, tortured, rendered, and killed in other ways and by other "techniques.") You waterboarded one of these three eighty three times, another 183 three times. Obviously, torture didn't work the first eighty-two and the first 182 times in these cases. In light of these failures, how can you make such big claims about the effectiveness of torture in these and other cases? Would you have tortured these of your victims thousands of times more if needed; would you have tortured them to death? Do you love and trust torture so much?

Even you must know, Mr. Cheney, that you and Bush have made literally hundreds of millions of new enemies for this country by your extreme actions, especially by the abuse, rape, torture, and mass slaughter you have fathered and especially among the five million people you have driven out of their homes in Iraq, two and a half million out of the country altogether. You have made enemies of all of these victims and of their family members, their friends, their countrymen, their fellow religionists, and their sympathizers.

How have you made this country or its citizens safer? Don't you know that all countries, all terrorists, all insurgents, and all other current and future enemies now have a justification to do to Americans just what you have done to so many Iraqis, Afghanis, and others?

How did it make sense for you to attack the innocent people of Iraq as a way of punishing terrorists from another country? Why did you and Bush torture and kill those innocents, people who were on our side and against Osama bin Laden? When you attack a whole people, when you torture and kill members of their families and their friends, you turn them into enemies. You turn them all into supporters of Osama bin Laden, evil though he may seem to them. Not only do you make enemies of them for today but for all time. You can't torture people unjustly and not arouse their hatred. Torturing somebody, invading their country, killing them is not a sane way to punish terrorists from another country, indeed a country, Saudi Arabia, that you and Bush love dearly. Democracy does not come from the brutality of torturers like you and Bush nor does security come from an unjust invasion and cruel occupation.

You have even corrupted your own family, tainted them with your own deep and poisonous perversion of character. You have sent your own daughter out into the media to justify your evil behavior, to invent absurd arguments in defense of your indefensible actions. Have you no shame, no regret, no conscience? Are you free of nightmares or doubts? Do you ever look behind you? Are you ashamed to face your neighbors, the huge mass of people you have disgusted and outraged? What kind of a monster are you?

If it's all right for the CIA and the military to torture people, then where does it stop? Why can't all of our policemen torture our own people when they think it might save a life or prevent a crime? We see them doing it all of the time on television and in the movies, don't we (except when they are being thwarted by "liberal" judges.") Why can't citizens do it to one another when they have a grievance or think they are stopping someone from doing something they don't approve of? Why not just give Bush and Cheney and all of their followers the right to torture all citizens any time they feel like it? Why have a Bill of Rights? Why have any rules or laws at all?

The torture and abuse carried out by Bush–Cheney was random and indiscriminate. It was used against uncounted hundreds, indeed thousands of captives who were completely helpless as naked and chained victims languishing in one of the numerous gulags set up by Bush–Cheney. To one degree or another, all of those people were abused and tortured. None of them received lawful treatment under American or international standards. Most of them were picked up in sweeps in Iraq or, to a lesser extent, in Afghanistan. The military itself estimated that 70 to 90 percent of the captives were jailed by mistake. Most of them were not even insurgents. Very, very few were al Qaeda members. According to the military, none of the abused and tortured prisoners at Abu Ghraib were foreigners. In other words, not a single one was a terrorist or an al Qaeda member.

Something like a thousand people were held captive for months and years in the torture prison at Guantanamo Bay, Cuba. In the last months of the Bush presidency, five hundred or more of them were suddenly and arbitrarily released. A little more than two hundred and fifty were retained. Cheney, after having released these captives, then claimed that they had returned to their old terrorist pursuits. Why did Cheney release them, then? If the released captives were innocent all along and became terrorists after release, was it because they were tortured? Were Bush and Cheney manufacturing terrorists with their torture program? Of the hundreds of millions of Arab and muslim peoples around the world, how many of them have been turned into terrorists and enemies of the United States by the Bush–Cheney torture program? As always, Republicans like Bush and Cheney think that the way to make friends is by torturing people, even by killing them and their families. Does anyone sane believe this?

What was evil about the September 11th al Qaeda attack against the United States was that it was an indiscriminate attack against innocent people. Then, in pretended response, Bush and Cheney launched a senseless and indiscriminate attack against twenty-five million completely innocent Iraqis. The invading Americans treated everyone there in Iraq as enemies because Bush and Cheney told them that the Iraqis were responsible for the September 11th attack. They routinely broke into homes arbitrarily, abused the families, and swept up all of the males, frequently including old men and children. Many frightened and peaceful people were injured or killed. Millions of families were divided and destroyed. Nearly five million were driven out of their homes completely; of these, two and one half million were driven out of their country entirely. Many were shipped to the gulags. The entire war was indiscriminate and all of the victims were innocent of ever having made or ever having threatened to make any attack against the United States or against any of its people.

The scale and extremity of what Bush and Cheney did to the people of Iraq far exceeded anything Saddam Hussein ever did to them. Furthermore, his attacks, however brutal, were not indiscriminate. The violence in Iraq was entirely created by Bush and Cheney. The numbers killed and exiled do not even include the millions more who were wounded, degraded, broken, persecuted, and embittered. The attack against Iraq was one of the greatest atrocities in modern history. It was mass murder. It was genocide. It was a holocaust.

It is quite clear that the torture scenarios invented to justify the Bush–Cheney assault against much of the world were the products of sick minds. More than half of our population now believes that torture is a justified and legitimate part of American policy. What a sad day! Evidently Barack Obama believes it too. He is refusing to investigate or punish anyone at all for the tortures already known to have been committed. It seems he believes torture is sometimes necessary and that the torturers should not be punished or even named and exposed, that is, if they are Americans. What an odd and brutal form of American exceptionalism.

Set forth below is a portion of a syndicated column of May 29, 2009 by Paul Craig Roberts:

> A despairing country elected a president who promised change....
>
> The change that we are witnessing is in Obama, not in policies. Obama is morphing into Dick Cheney....
>
> Obama said he would close the torture prison at Guantanamo and abolish the kangaroo courts known as military tribunals.... now he say he is going to...continue the process,...
>
> The policy of kidnapping people (usually on the basis of disinformation supplied by their enemies) and whisking them off to Third World prisons to be interrogated is to be continued....
>
> Rendition, Obama says, has been reformed and will no longer involve torture.
>
> How would anyone know? Is Obama going to assign a U.S. government agent to watch over the treatment given to disappeared people....
>
> Obama has defended the Bush–Cheney warrantless wiretapping program... and broadened the government's legal argument that "sovereign immunity" protects government officials from prosecution and civil suits when they violate U.S. law and constitutional protections of citizens....

Obama, in other words, is committed to covering up the Bush regime's crimes and to ensuring that his own regime can continue to operate in the same illegal and unconstitutional ways.

Obama is fighting the release of the last batch of horrific torture photos that have come to light. Obama claims that release of the photos would anger insurgents and cause them to kill our troops. That, of course, is nonsense.

In August 2009 came word that Obama and his attorney general had appointed a prosecutor to investigate *some* of the crimes of the Bush administration. However, only "unauthorized" and "improvised" practices will be prosecuted. This means that Obama recognizes Bush as an absolute dictator subject to no law of any kind. Nothing Bush and Cheney ordered can be considered wrong or unlawful, according to Obama, and only those who went *beyond or outside of* their orders can be considered criminals.

Even though Obama himself has withdrawn memos justifying and ordering abuse and torture and has called them illegitimate, he now tells us that they were fully justified despite the existence of a huge body of American and international law and precedent saying the opposite. Thus, Obama has approved the idea that he himself and all future presidents can issue orders that will allow any level of barbarism, cruelty, abuse, torture, and slaughter that he and his successors desire to inflict on the world. The lawlessness of this argument puts an end to every principle of decency, democracy, and justice for this country. The United States is now an outlaw nation worse than any other on earth. The word is that anything goes just as long as there was a prefabricated excuse. Our criminals were just following orders.

Quoted below are selected parts of an essay by Dick Cole in the October 8, 2009 issue of *The New York Review.*

On Monday, August 24... (the) administration released a previously classified 2004 report by the CIA's inspector general that strongly criticized the techniques employed to interrogate "high-value" al-Qaeda suspects at the CIA's secret prisons. The report revealed that CIA agents and contractors, in addition to such "authorized" and previously reported tactics as waterboarding, wall-slamming, forced nudity, stress positions, and extended sleep deprivation, also employed a variety of "unauthorized, improvised, inhumane and undocumented methods."

These included threatening suspects with a revolver and a power drill; repeatedly applying pressure to a detainee's carotid artery until he began to pass out; staging a mock execution; threatening to sexually abuse a suspect's mother; and warning a detainee that if another attack occurred in the United States, "We're going to kill your children.".

The inspector general also reported...CIA officials often lacked any objective basis for concluding that detainees were withholding information and therefore should be subjected to the "enhanced" techniques. The inspector general further found no evidence that any imminent terrorist attacks had been averted by virtue of information obtained from the CIA's detainees. In other words, there were no "ticking time bombs"...

The same day, Attorney General Eric Holder...simultaneously announced that he would not prosecute "anyone who acted in good faith within the scope of the legal guidance given by the Office of Legal Counsel regarding the interrogation of detainees.

At the United Nations Review Conference on Racism, a representative of Kenya, Amina Mohamed, said, "Madam President, it is not a crime against humanity just for today, nor just for tomorrow, but for always and for all time. Nuremberg made it clear that crimes against humanity are not time bound." That was on September 9, 2001.

> Now true and false must change their names,
> Old law and justice be reversed,
> If new authority put first
> The wrongful right this murderer claims,
> This act shall now to every man
> Commend the easy path of crime....
> For fear, enforcing goodness,
> Must somewhere reign enthroned,
> And watch men's ways, and teach them,
> Through self-inflicted sorrow,
> That sin is not condoned.
> What man, no longer nursing
> Fear in his heart — what city,
> Once fear is cast away,
> Will bow the knee to Justice
> As in an earlier day?

—The chorus from *The Furies* by Aeschylus, *addressed now to Barack Obama.*